Garfield
thinks big

BY JIM DAVIS

Ballantine Books ● **New York**

2016 Ballantine Books Trade Paperback Edition

Published in the United States by Ballantine Books, an imprint of Random House,
a division of Penguin Random House LLC, New York.

BALLANTINE and the HOUSE colophon are registered trademarks of Penguin Random House LLC.

Originally published in slightly different form in the United States by Ballantine Books,
an imprint of Random House, a division of Penguin Random House LLC, in 1997.

ISBN 978-0-425-28516-9
ebook ISBN 978-0-425-28551-0

Printed in the United States of America on acid-free paper

randomhousebooks.com

9 8 7 6 5 4 3 2 1

First Colorized Edition

THINGS WE NEED MORE OF...

marathon naps
all-night smorgasbords
bacon
wrestling on TV
jelly donuts
back scratchers
scary movies
dog muzzles
fuzzy slippers
Elvis impersonators
cheese
roller coasters
teddy bears
weekends
pizza

THINGS WE CAN DO WITHOUT...

dogs
aerobics
brussels sprouts
decaf coffee
polka
spiders
bagpipes
fruitcakes
houseguests
lawyers
disco
tattoos
diets
Mondays
dog breath

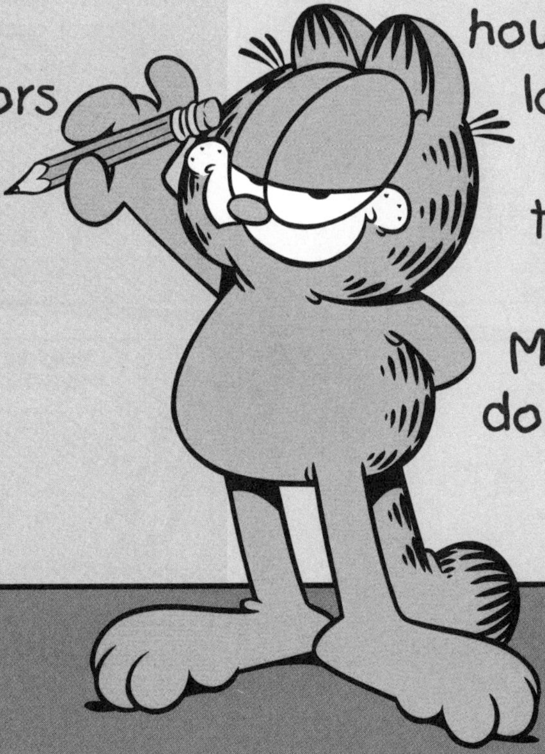

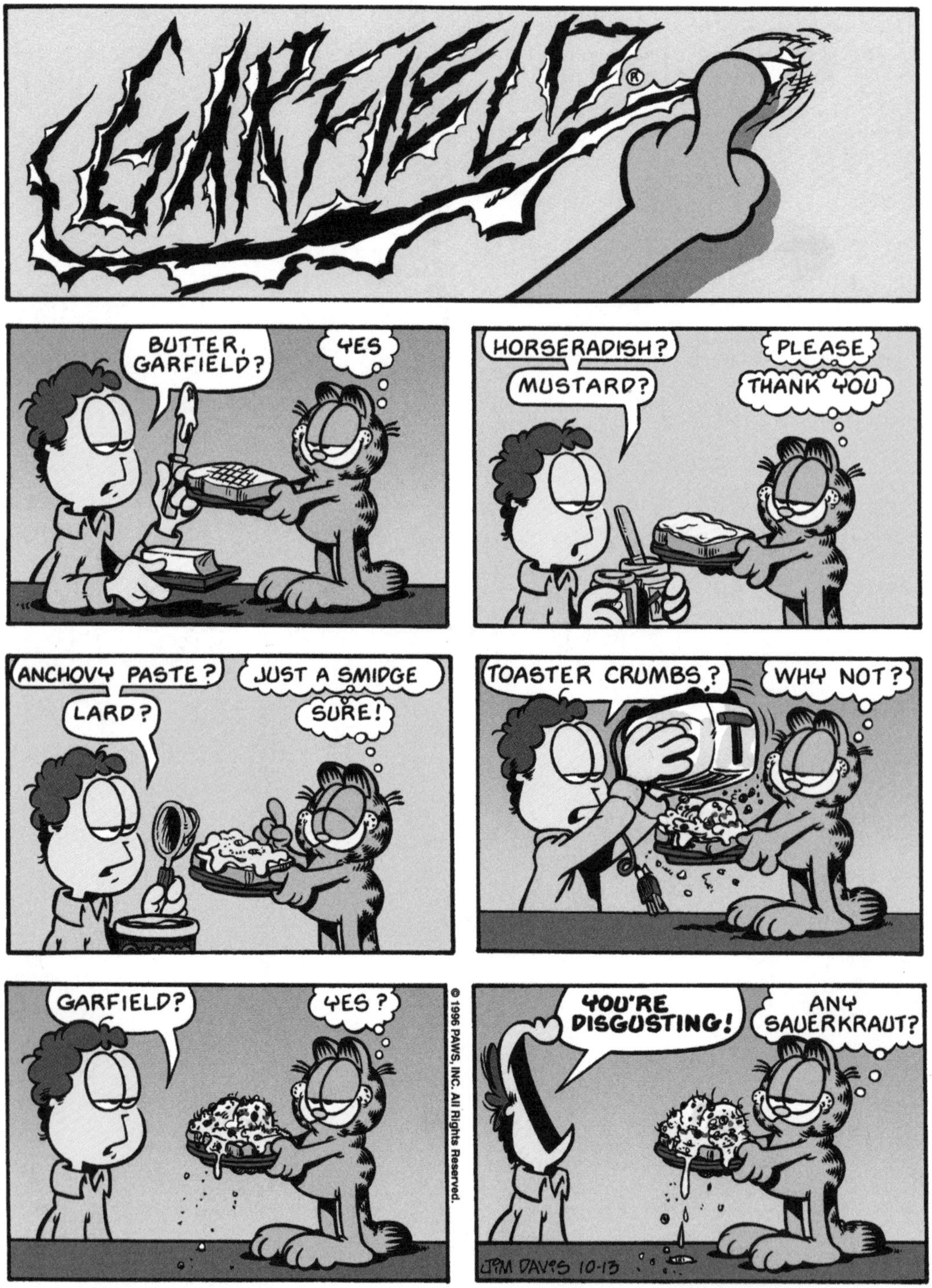
GARFIELD®
BUTTER, GARFIELD?
YES
HORSERADISH?
PLEASE
MUSTARD?
THANK YOU
ANCHOVY PASTE?
JUST A SMIDGE
LARD?
SURE!
TOASTER CRUMBS?
WHY NOT?
GARFIELD?
YES?
YOU'RE DISGUSTING!
ANY SAUERKRAUT?
JIM DAVIS 10-13
© 1996 PAWS, INC. All Rights Reserved.

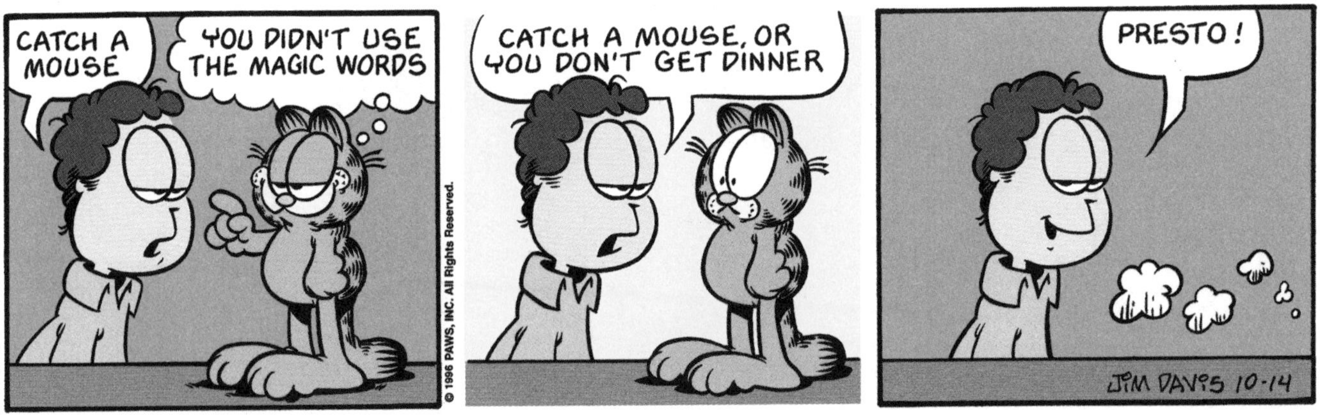
CATCH A MOUSE
YOU DIDN'T USE THE MAGIC WORDS
CATCH A MOUSE, OR YOU DON'T GET DINNER
PRESTO!
JIM DAVIS 10-14

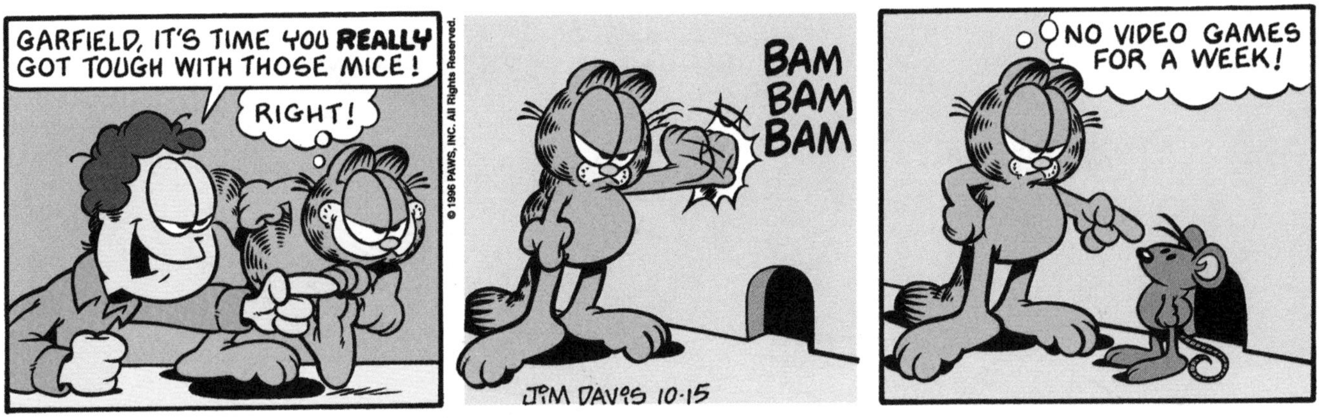
GARFIELD, IT'S TIME YOU **REALLY** GOT TOUGH WITH THOSE MICE!
RIGHT!
BAM BAM BAM
NO VIDEO GAMES FOR A WEEK!
JIM DAVIS 10-15

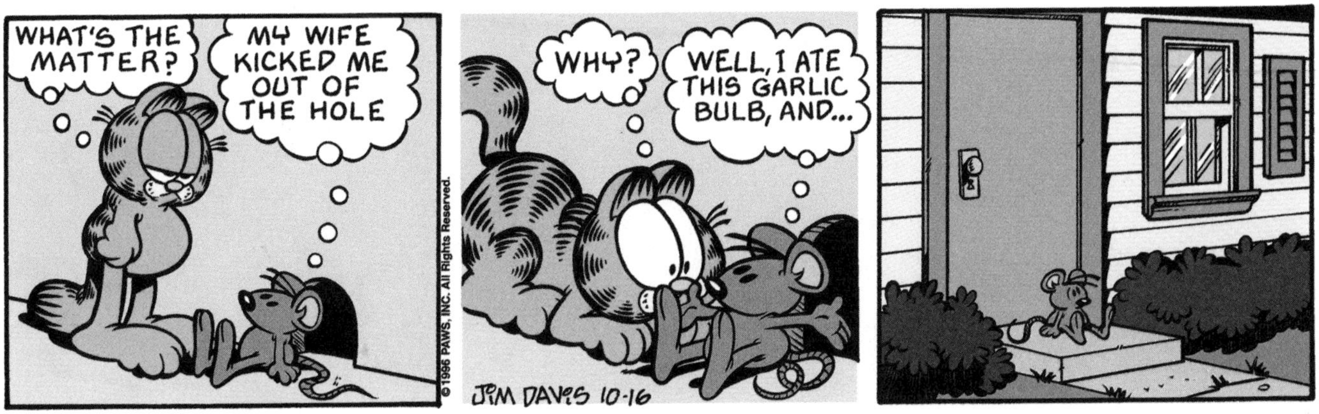
WHAT'S THE MATTER?
MY WIFE KICKED ME OUT OF THE HOLE
WHY?
WELL, I ATE THIS GARLIC BULB, AND...
JIM DAVIS 10-16

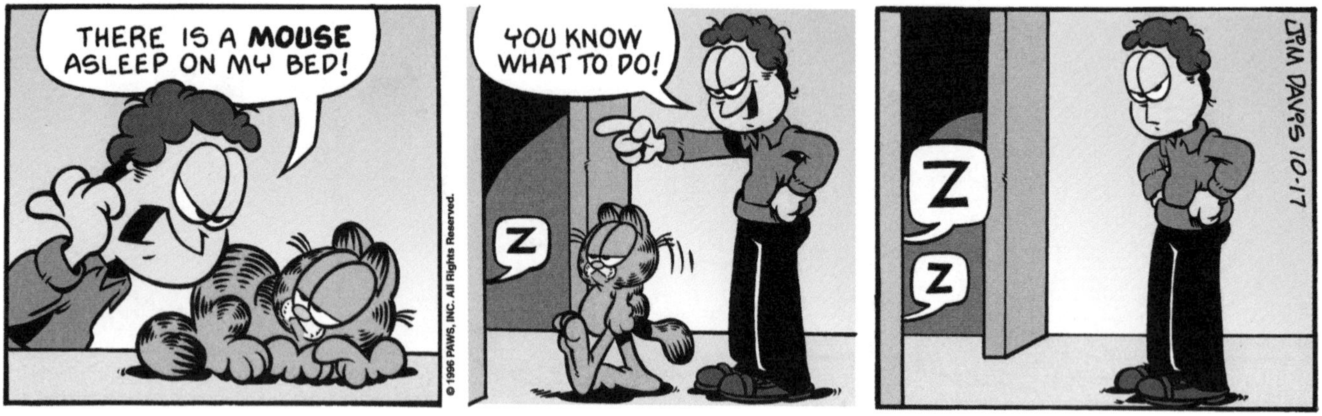
THERE IS A **MOUSE** ASLEEP ON MY BED!
YOU KNOW WHAT TO DO!
Z
Z
Z
JIM DAVIS 10-17

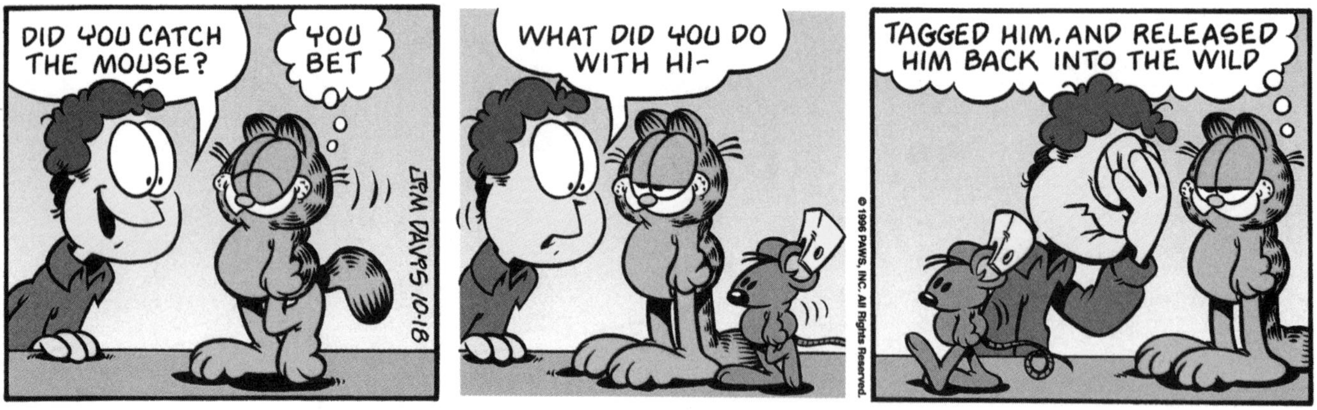
DID YOU CATCH THE MOUSE?
YOU BET
JIM DAVIS 10-18
WHAT DID YOU DO WITH HI-
TAGGED HIM, AND RELEASED HIM BACK INTO THE WILD

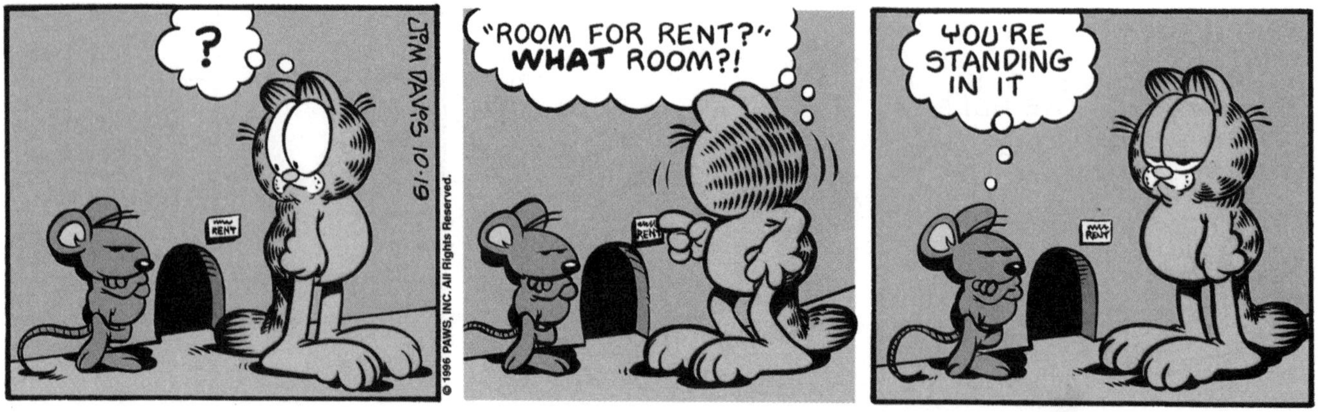
?
JIM DAVIS 10-19
RENT
"ROOM FOR RENT?" **WHAT** ROOM?!
YOU'RE STANDING IN IT

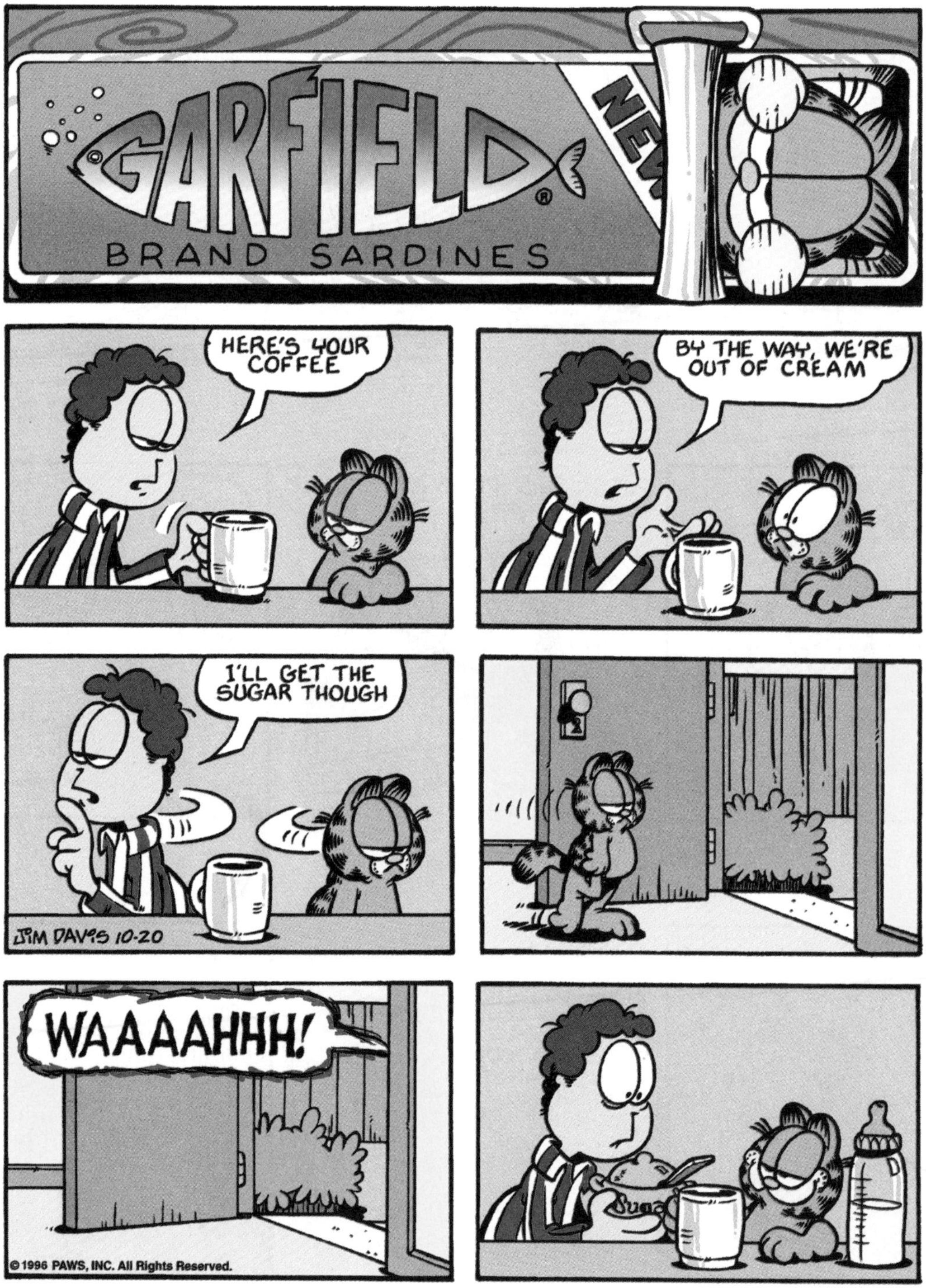
GARFIELD®
BRAND SARDINES
NEW
HERE'S YOUR COFFEE
BY THE WAY, WE'RE OUT OF CREAM
I'LL GET THE SUGAR THOUGH
JIM DAVIS 10-20
WAAAAHHH!

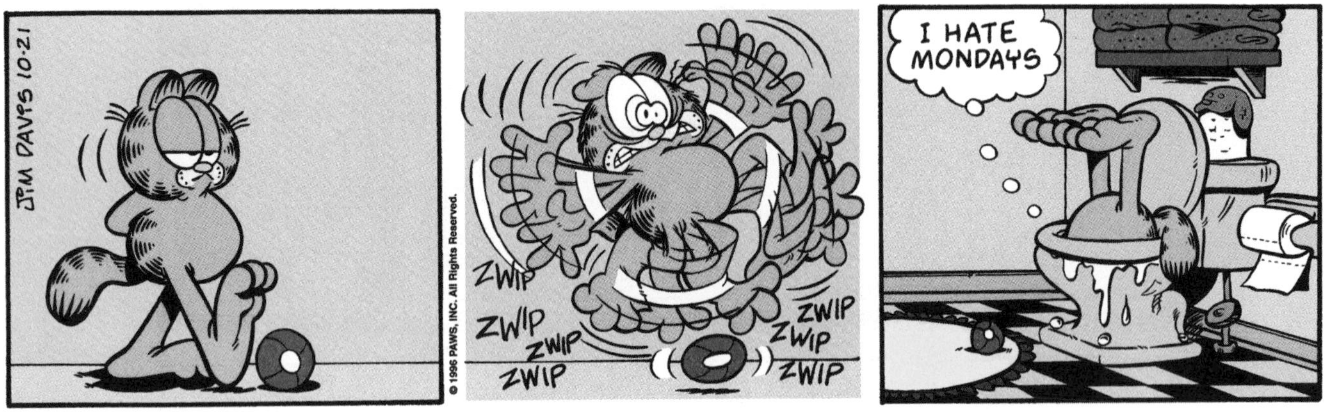
JIM DAVIS 10-21
© 1996 PAWS, INC. All Rights Reserved.
ZWIP
ZWIP
ZWIP
ZWIP
ZWIP
ZWIP
ZWIP
I HATE MONDAYS

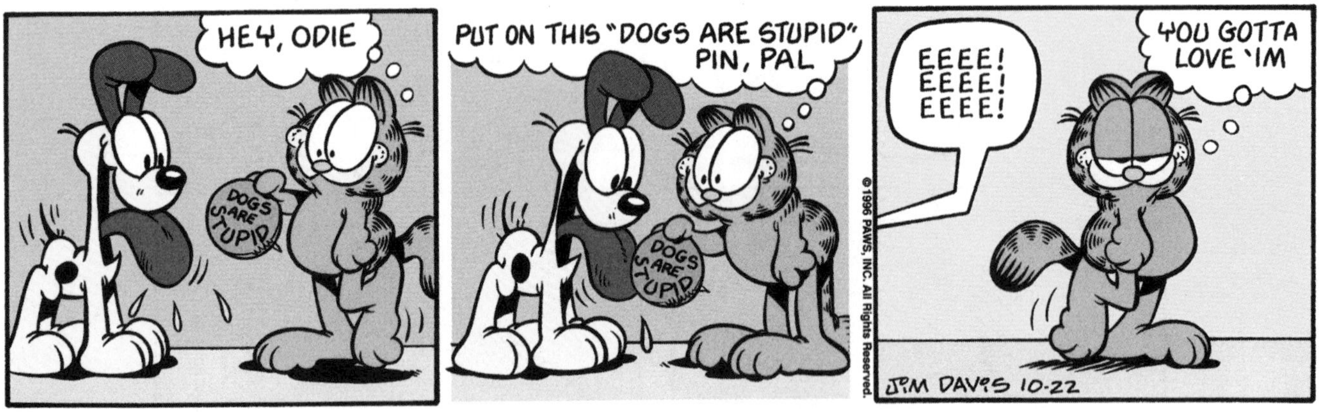
HEY, ODIE
DOGS ARE STUPID
PUT ON THIS "DOGS ARE STUPID" PIN, PAL
DOGS ARE STUPID
© 1996 PAWS, INC. All Rights Reserved.
EEEE! EEEE! EEEE!
YOU GOTTA LOVE 'IM
JIM DAVIS 10-22

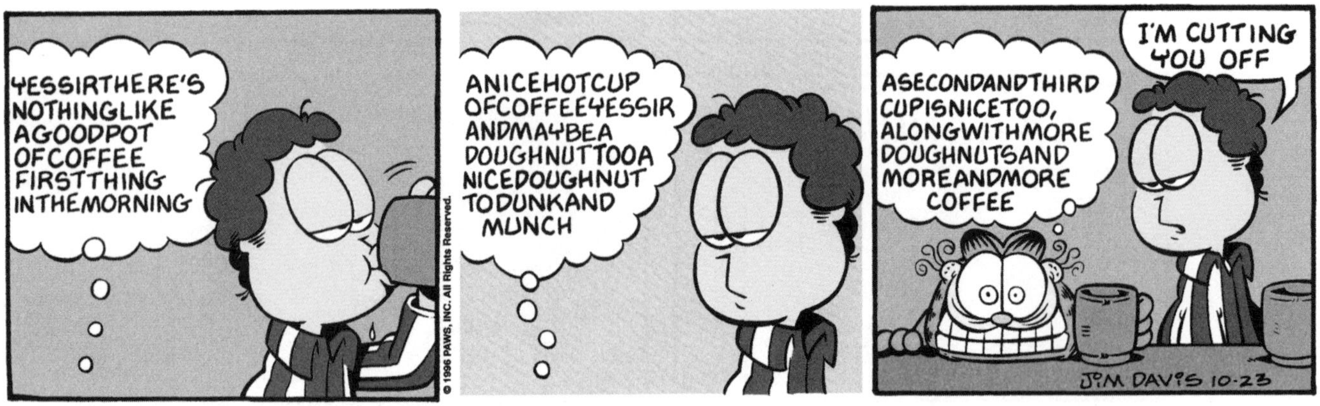
YESSIRTHERE'S NOTHINGLIKE AGOODPOT OFCOFFEE FIRSTTHING INTHEMORNING
© 1996 PAWS, INC. All Rights Reserved.
ANICEHOTCUP OFCOFFEEYESSIR ANDMAYBEA DOUGHNUTTOOA NICEDOUGHNUT TODUNKAND MUNCH
ASECONDANDTHIRD CUPISNICETOO, ALONGWITHMORE DOUGHNUTSAND MOREANDMORE COFFEE
I'M CUTTING YOU OFF
JIM DAVIS 10-23

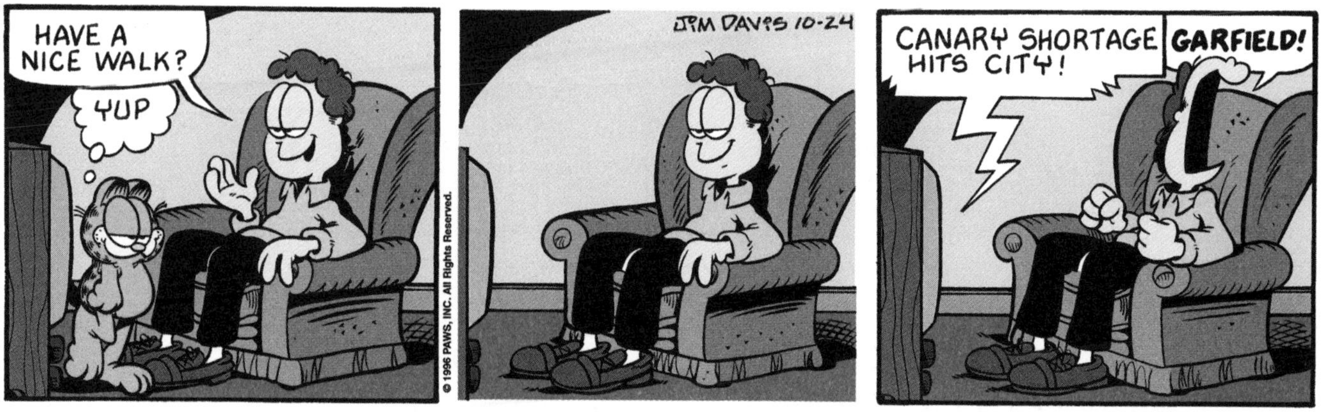
HAVE A NICE WALK?
YUP
© 1996 PAWS, INC. All Rights Reserved.
JIM DAVIS 10-24
CANARY SHORTAGE HITS CITY!
GARFIELD!

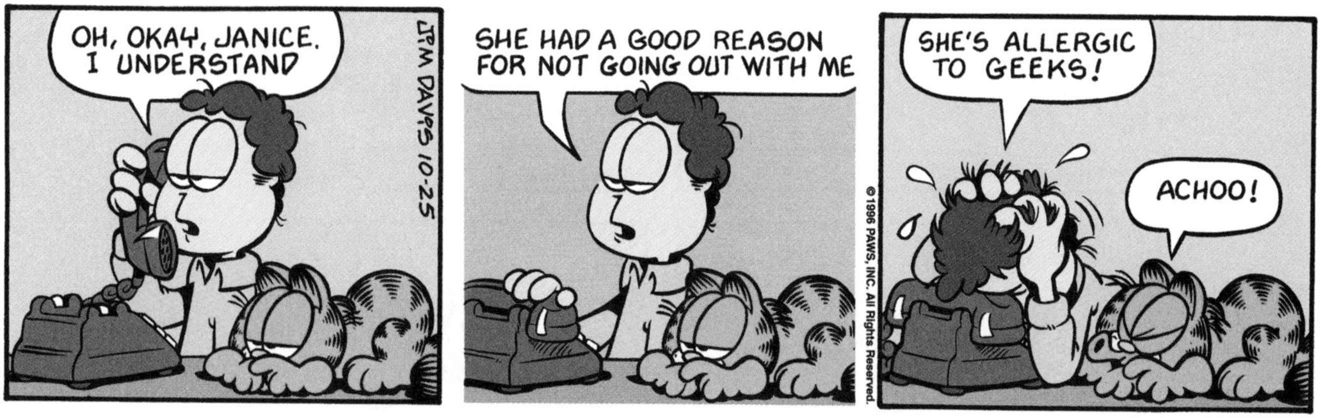
OH, OKAY, JANICE. I UNDERSTAND
JIM DAVIS 10-25
SHE HAD A GOOD REASON FOR NOT GOING OUT WITH ME
© 1996 PAWS, INC. All Rights Reserved.
SHE'S ALLERGIC TO GEEKS!
ACHOO!

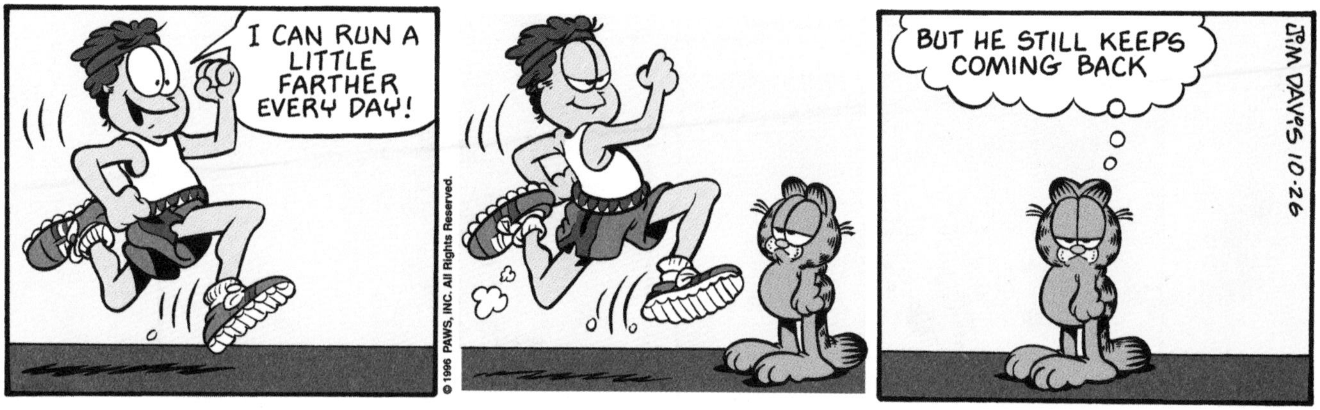
I CAN RUN A LITTLE FARTHER EVERY DAY!
© 1996 PAWS, INC. All Rights Reserved.
BUT HE STILL KEEPS COMING BACK
JIM DAVIS 10-26

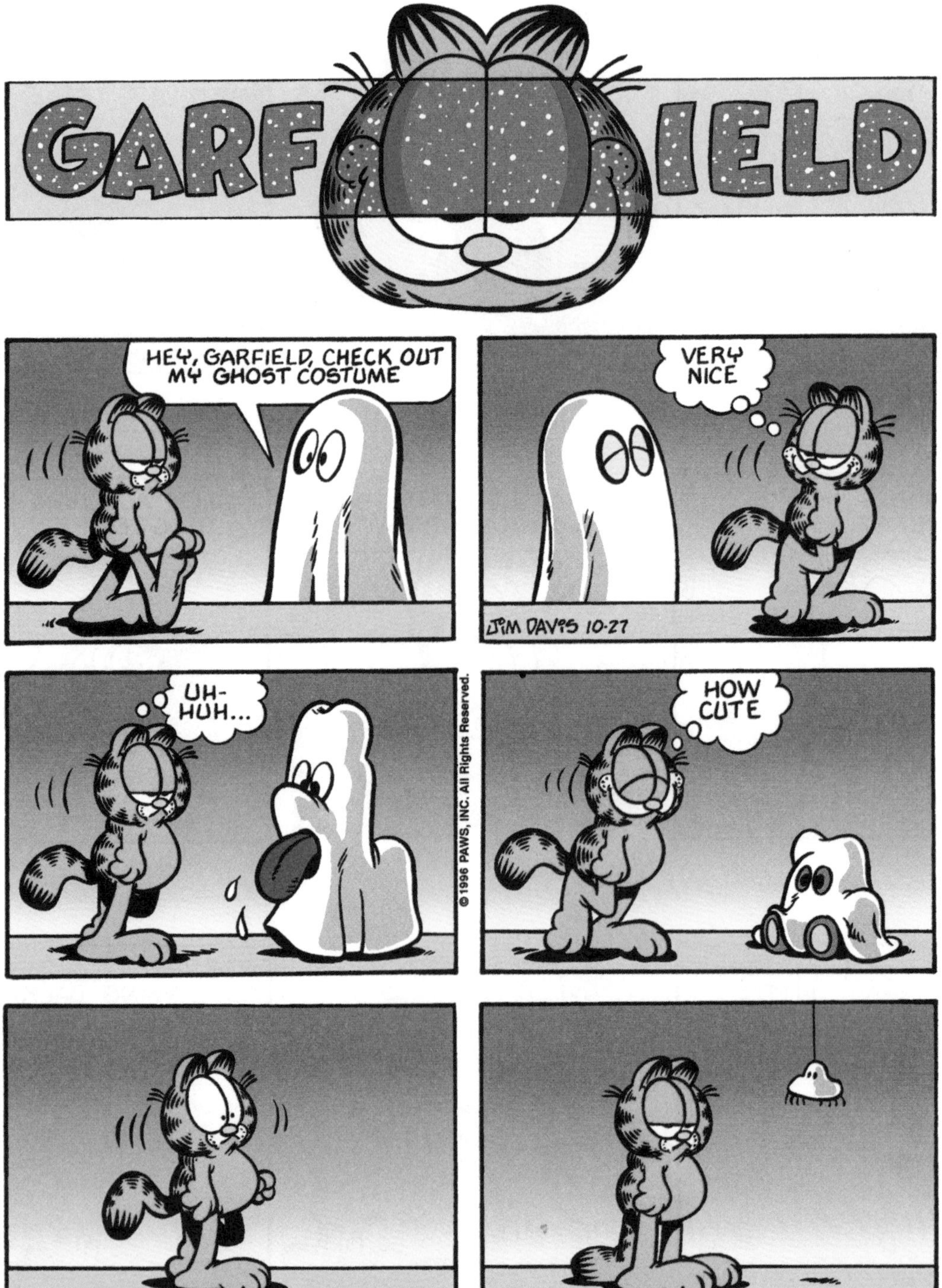
GARFIELD
HEY, GARFIELD, CHECK OUT MY GHOST COSTUME
VERY NICE
JIM DAVIS 10-27
© 1996 PAWS, INC. All Rights Reserved.
UH-HUH...
HOW CUTE

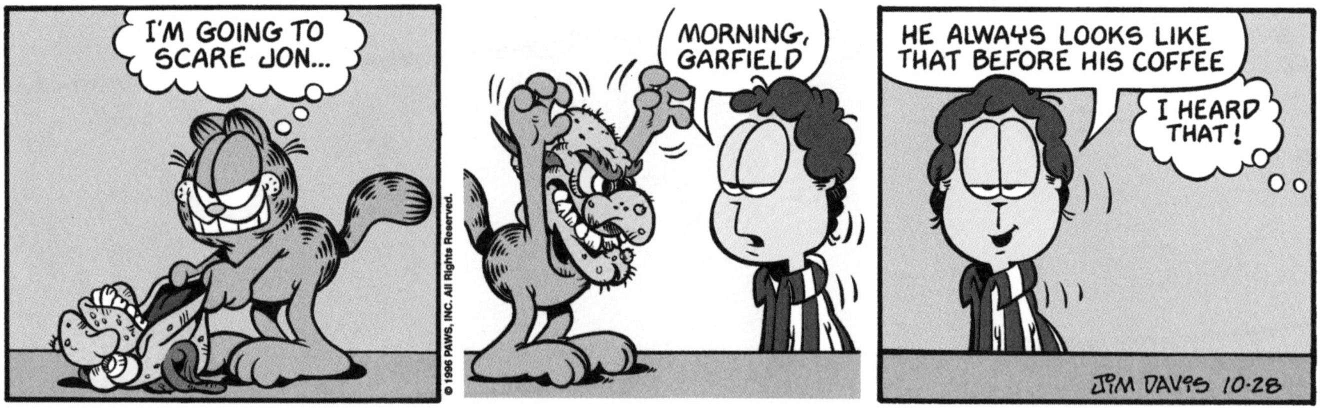
I'M GOING TO SCARE JON...
MORNING, GARFIELD
HE ALWAYS LOOKS LIKE THAT BEFORE HIS COFFEE
I HEARD THAT!
JIM DAVIS 10-28

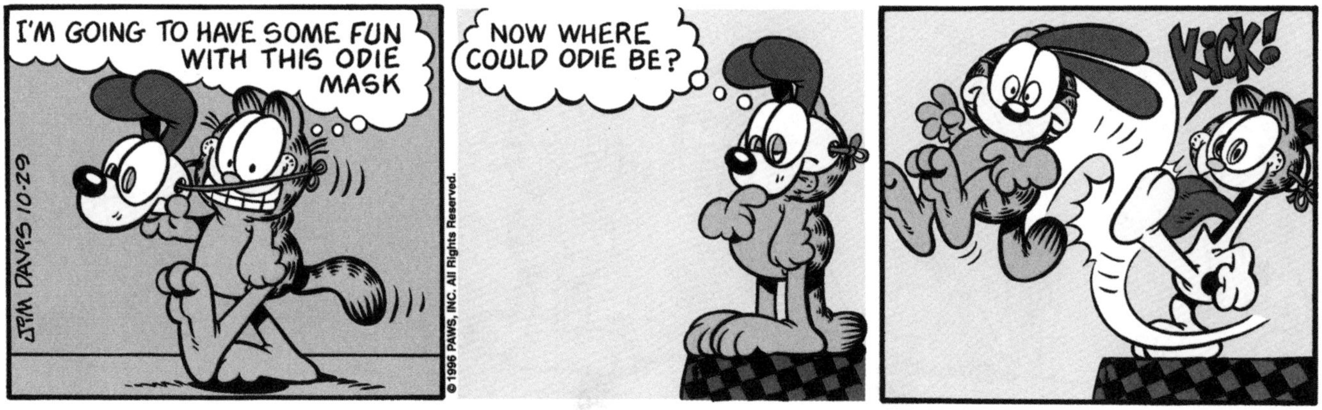
I'M GOING TO HAVE SOME FUN WITH THIS ODIE MASK
JIM DAVIS 10-29
NOW WHERE COULD ODIE BE?
KICK!

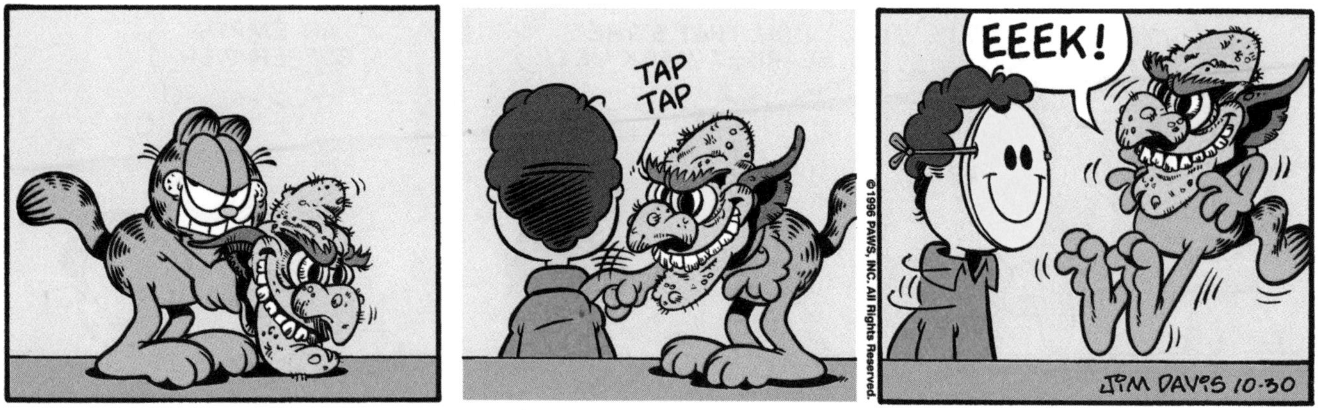
TAP TAP
EEEK!
JIM DAVIS 10-30

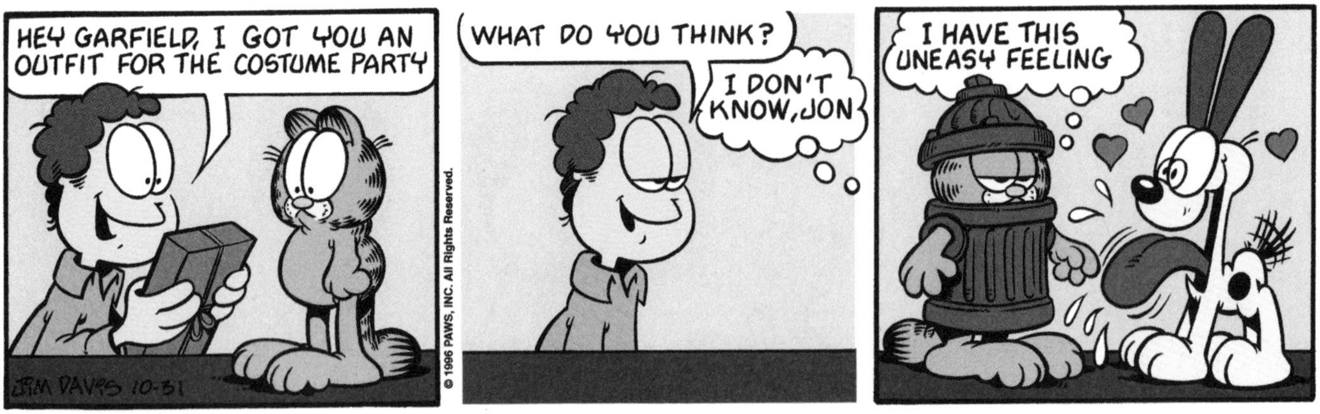
HEY GARFIELD, I GOT YOU AN OUTFIT FOR THE COSTUME PARTY
JIM DAVIS 10-31
© 1996 PAWS, INC. All Rights Reserved.
WHAT DO YOU THINK?
I DON'T KNOW, JON
I HAVE THIS UNEASY FEELING

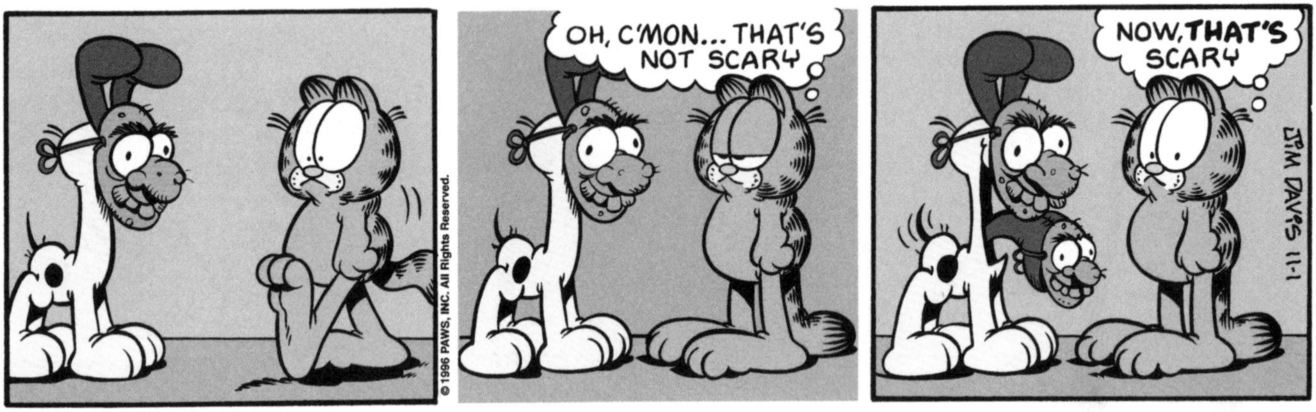
© 1996 PAWS, INC. All Rights Reserved.
OH, C'MON... THAT'S NOT SCARY
NOW, **THAT'S** SCARY
JIM DAVIS 11-1

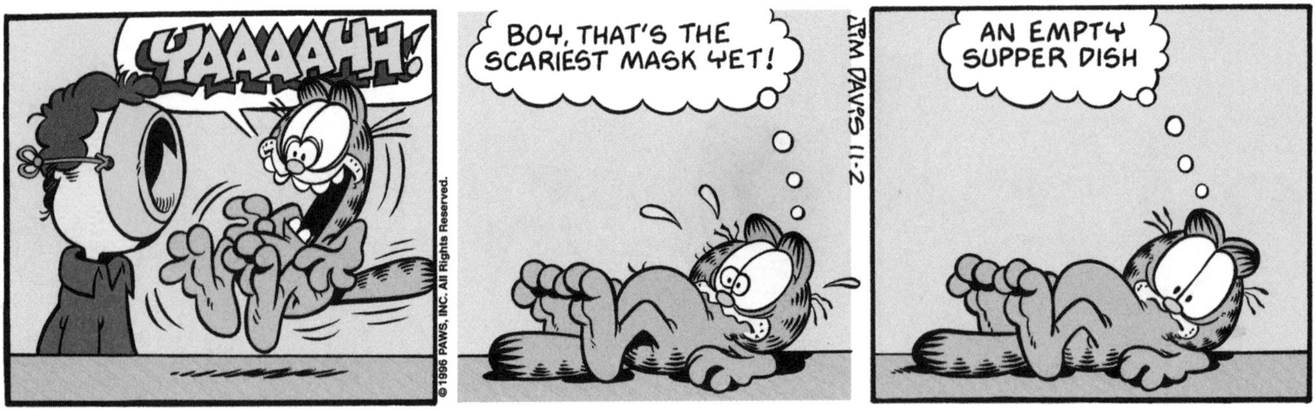
YAAAAHH!
© 1996 PAWS, INC. All Rights Reserved.
BOY, THAT'S THE SCARIEST MASK YET!
JIM DAVIS 11-2
AN EMPTY SUPPER DISH

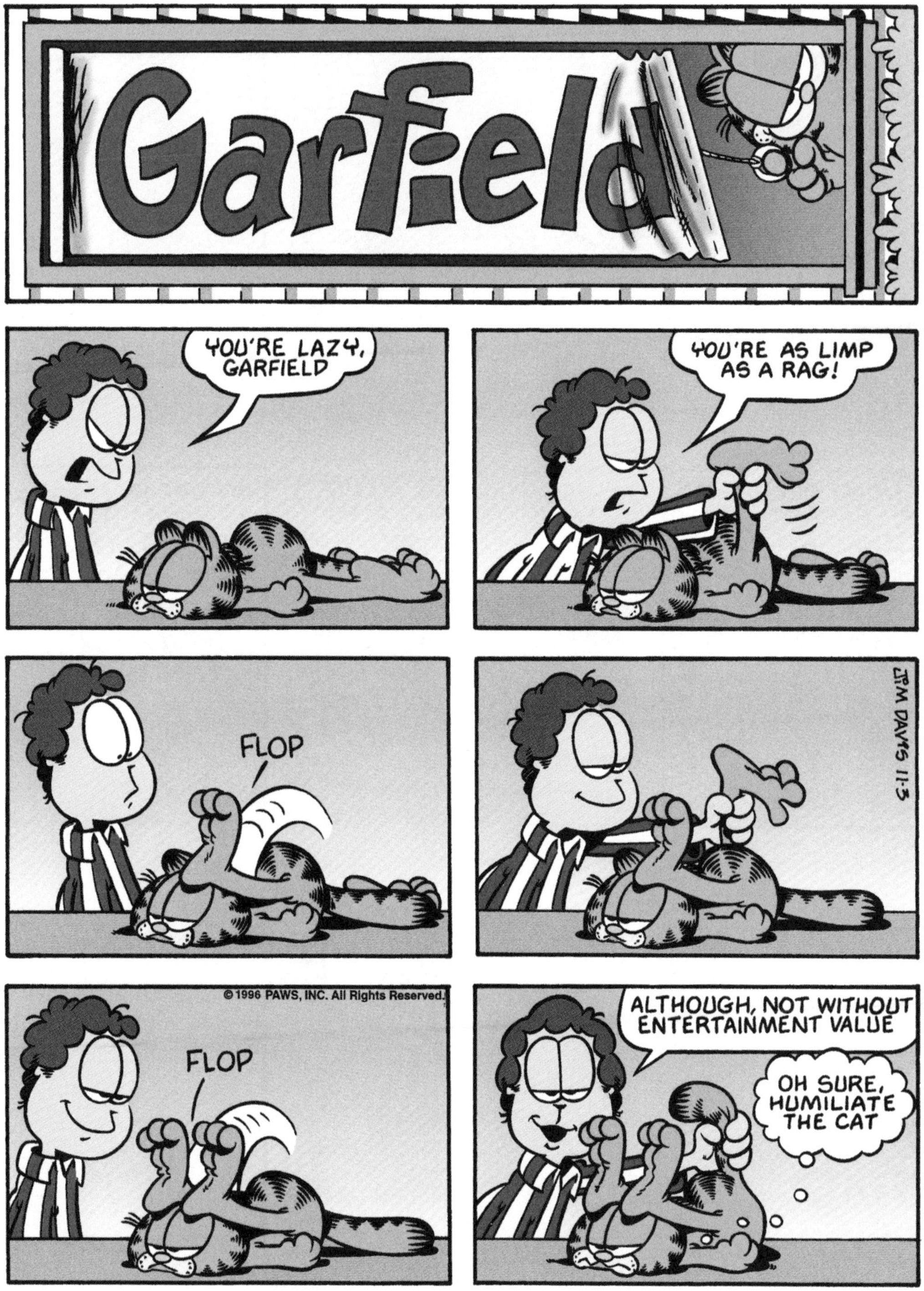
Garfield
YOU'RE LAZY, GARFIELD
YOU'RE AS LIMP AS A RAG!
FLOP
JPM DAVIS 11-3
© 1996 PAWS, INC. All Rights Reserved.
FLOP
ALTHOUGH, NOT WITHOUT ENTERTAINMENT VALUE
OH SURE, HUMILIATE THE CAT

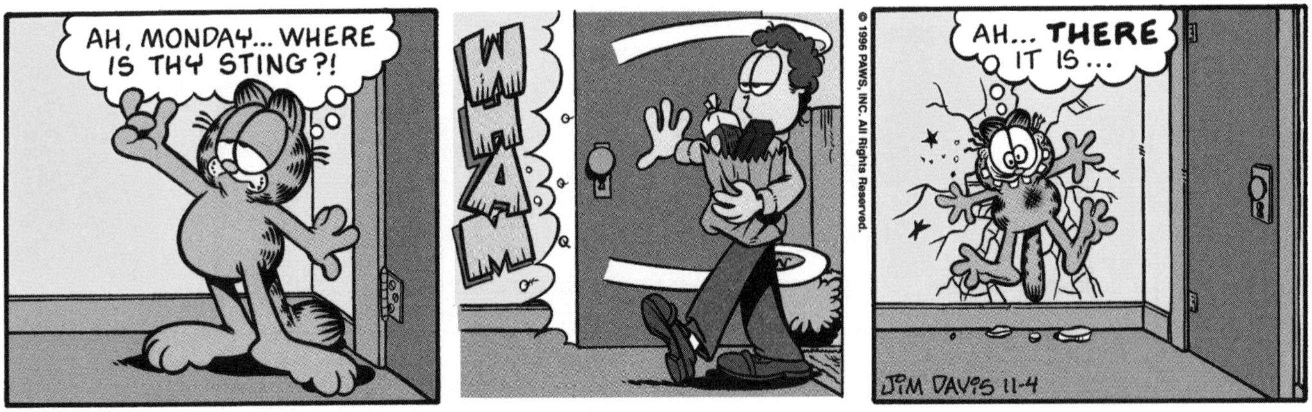
AH, MONDAY... WHERE IS THY STING?!
WHAM
© 1996 PAWS, INC. All Rights Reserved.
AH... **THERE** IT IS...
JIM DAVIS 11-4

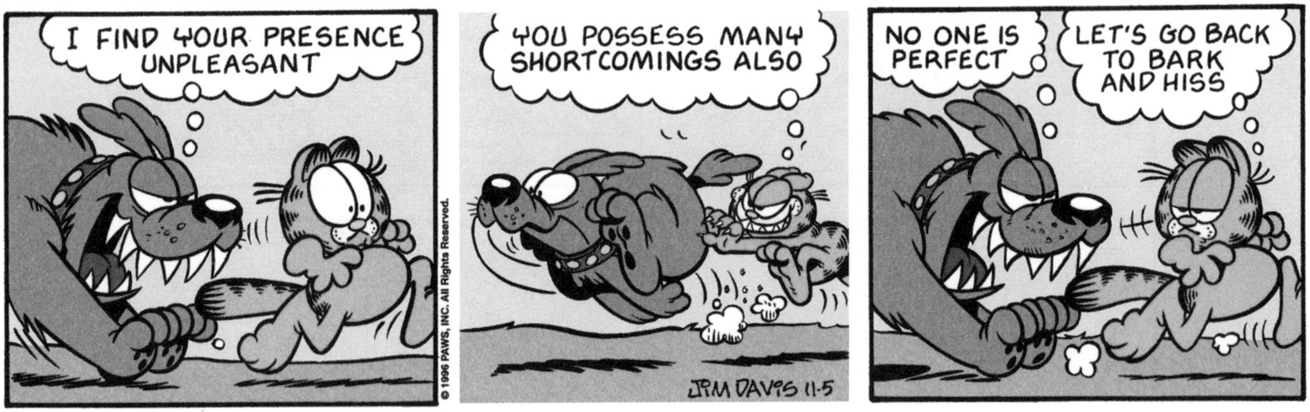
I FIND YOUR PRESENCE UNPLEASANT
© 1996 PAWS, INC. All Rights Reserved.
YOU POSSESS MANY SHORTCOMINGS ALSO
JIM DAVIS 11-5
NO ONE IS PERFECT
LET'S GO BACK TO BARK AND HISS

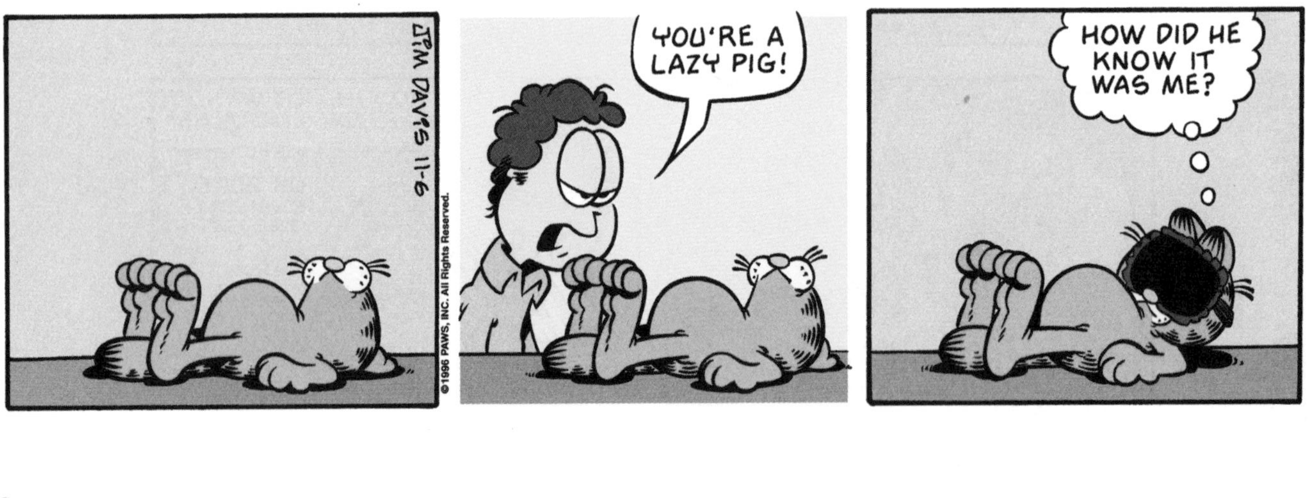
JIM DAVIS 11-6
© 1996 PAWS, INC. All Rights Reserved.
YOU'RE A LAZY PIG!
HOW DID HE KNOW IT WAS ME?

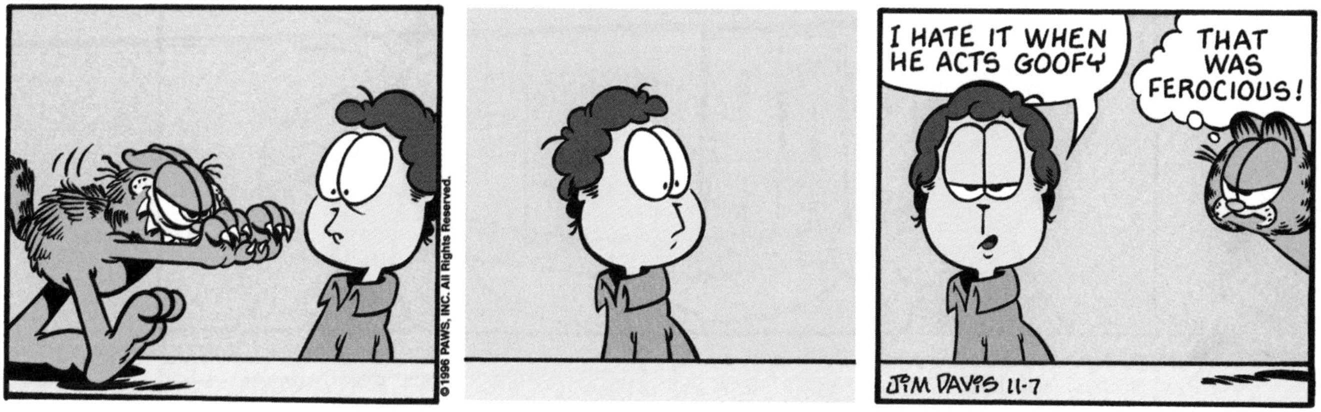
I HATE IT WHEN HE ACTS GOOFY
THAT WAS FEROCIOUS!
JIM DAVIS 11-7
© 1996 PAWS, INC. All Rights Reserved.

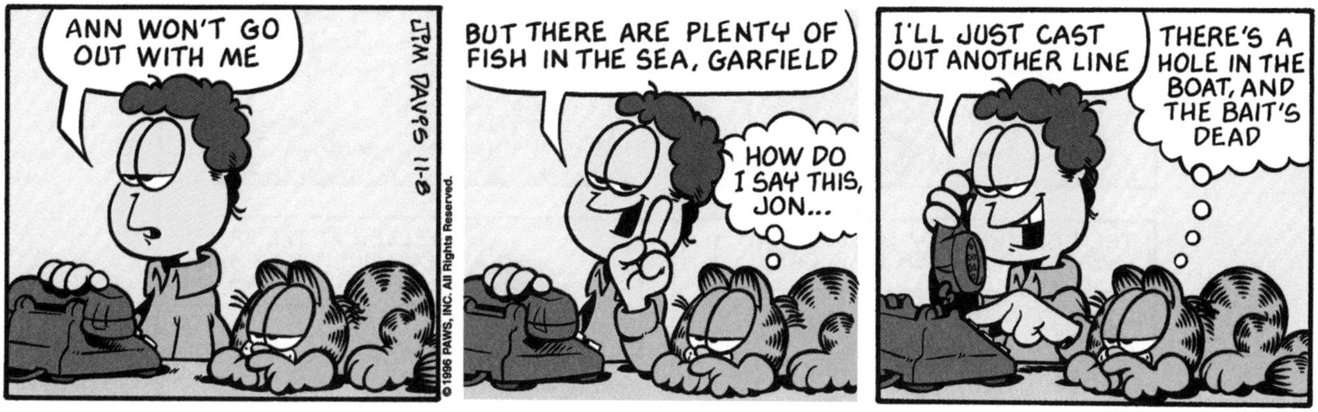
ANN WON'T GO OUT WITH ME
BUT THERE ARE PLENTY OF FISH IN THE SEA, GARFIELD
HOW DO I SAY THIS, JON...
I'LL JUST CAST OUT ANOTHER LINE
THERE'S A HOLE IN THE BOAT, AND THE BAIT'S DEAD
JIM DAVIS 11-8
© 1996 PAWS, INC. All Rights Reserved.

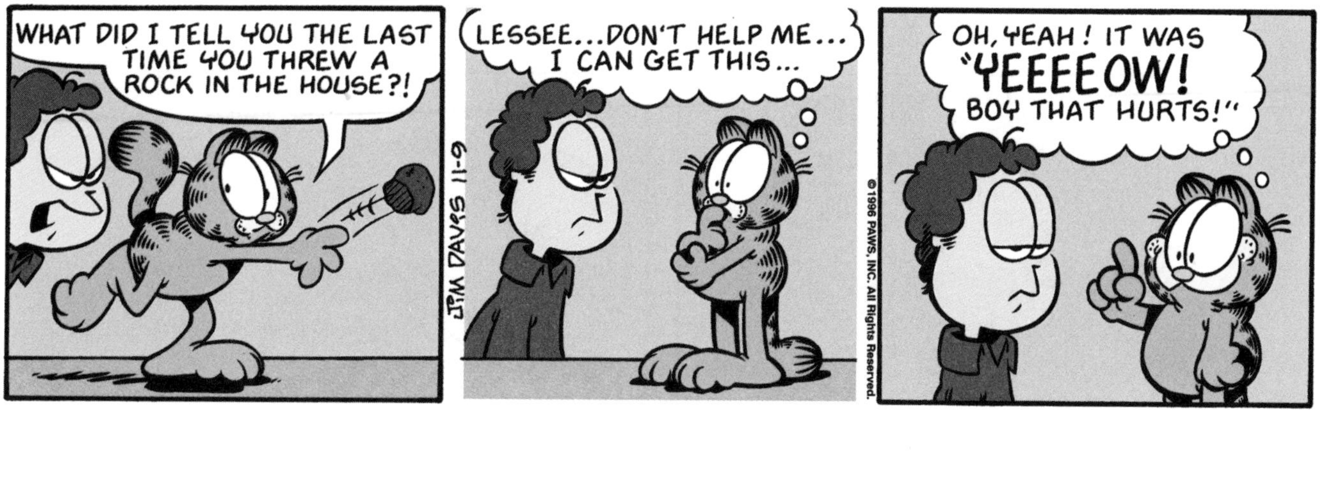
WHAT DID I TELL YOU THE LAST TIME YOU THREW A ROCK IN THE HOUSE?!
LESSEE...DON'T HELP ME... I CAN GET THIS...
OH, YEAH! IT WAS "YEEEEOW! BOY THAT HURTS!"
JIM DAVIS 11-9
© 1996 PAWS, INC. All Rights Reserved.

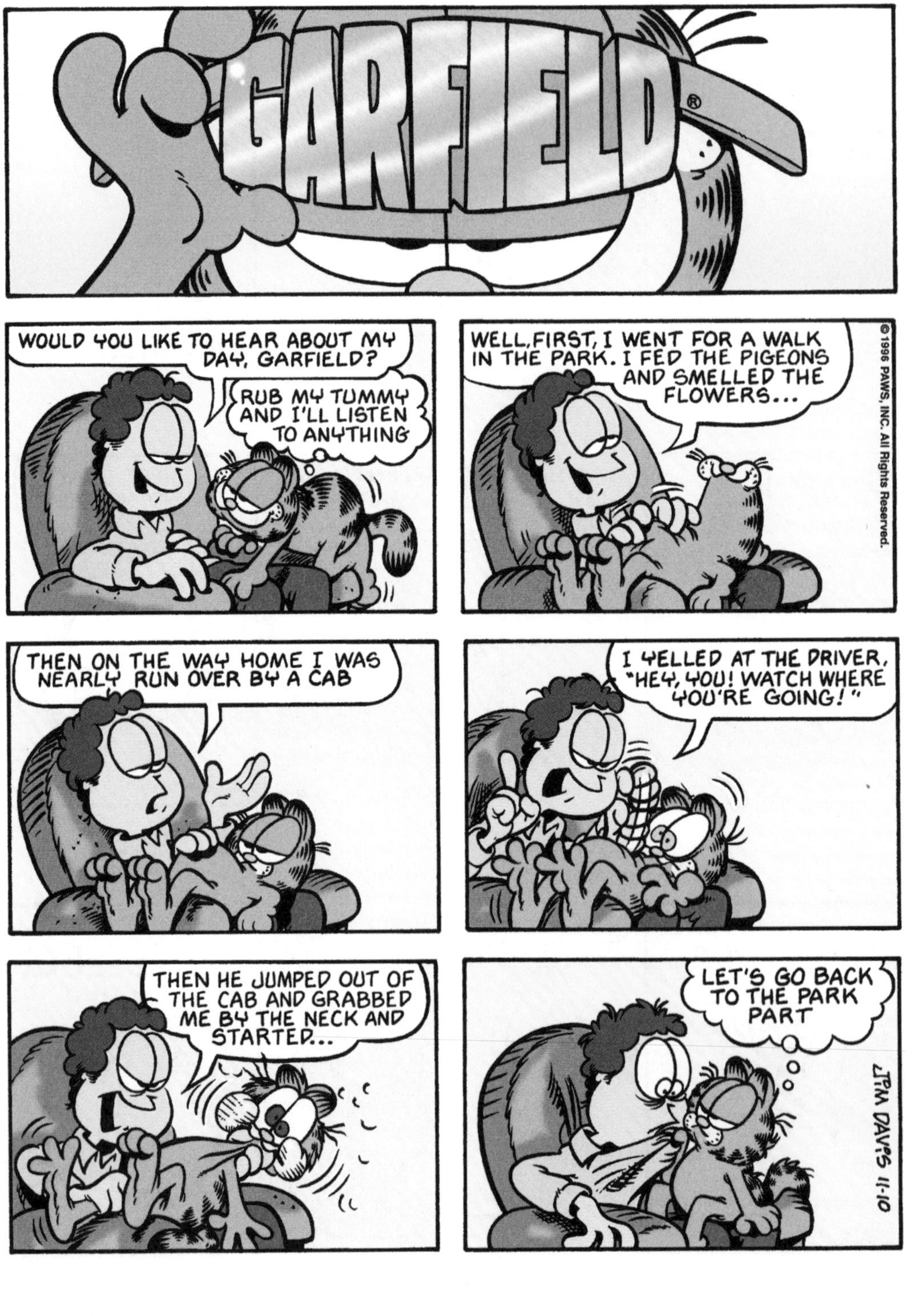
GARFIELD®
WOULD YOU LIKE TO HEAR ABOUT MY DAY, GARFIELD?
RUB MY TUMMY AND I'LL LISTEN TO ANYTHING
WELL, FIRST, I WENT FOR A WALK IN THE PARK. I FED THE PIGEONS AND SMELLED THE FLOWERS...
© 1996 PAWS, INC. All Rights Reserved.
THEN ON THE WAY HOME I WAS NEARLY RUN OVER BY A CAB
I YELLED AT THE DRIVER, "HEY, YOU! WATCH WHERE YOU'RE GOING!"
THEN HE JUMPED OUT OF THE CAB AND GRABBED ME BY THE NECK AND STARTED...
LET'S GO BACK TO THE PARK PART
JIM DAVIS 11-10

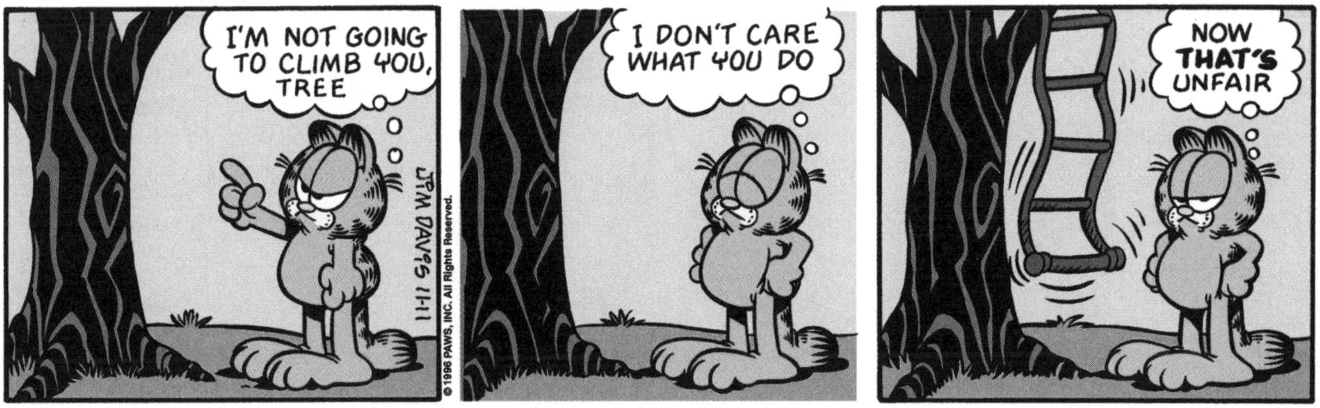
I'M NOT GOING TO CLIMB YOU, TREE
JIM DAVIS 11-11
© 1996 PAWS, INC. All Rights Reserved.
I DON'T CARE WHAT YOU DO
NOW THAT'S UNFAIR

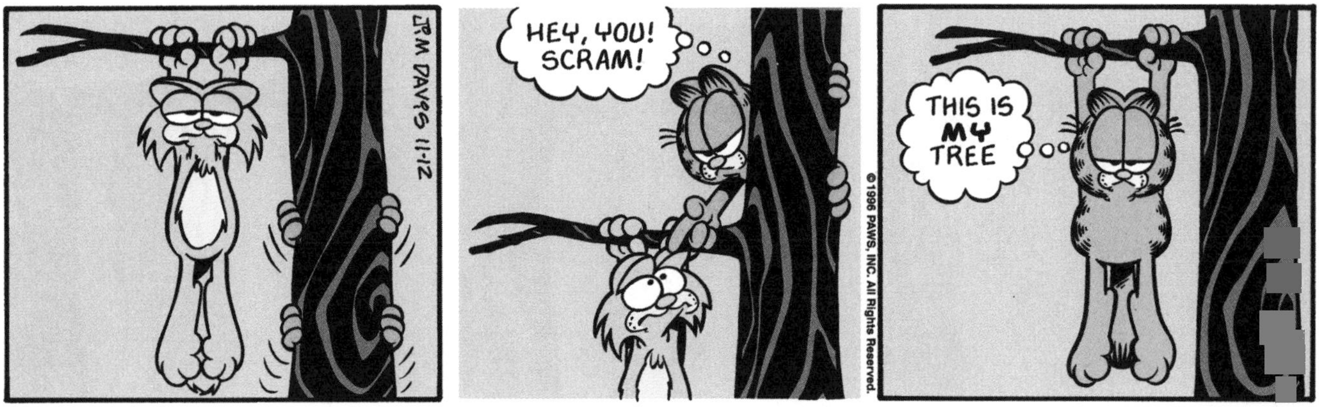
JIM DAVIS 11-12
HEY, YOU! SCRAM!
© 1996 PAWS, INC. All Rights Reserved.
THIS IS MY TREE

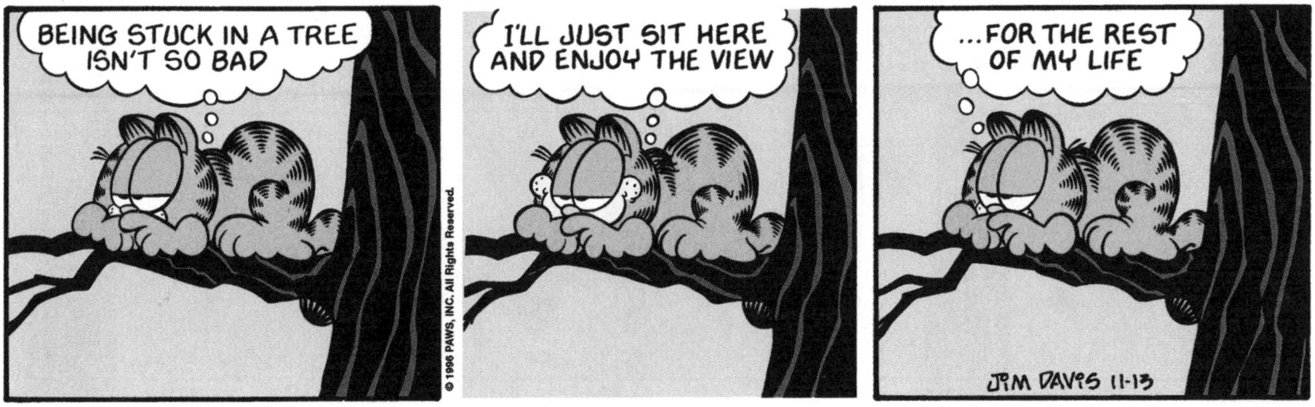
BEING STUCK IN A TREE ISN'T SO BAD
© 1996 PAWS, INC. All Rights Reserved.
I'LL JUST SIT HERE AND ENJOY THE VIEW
...FOR THE REST OF MY LIFE
JIM DAVIS 11-13

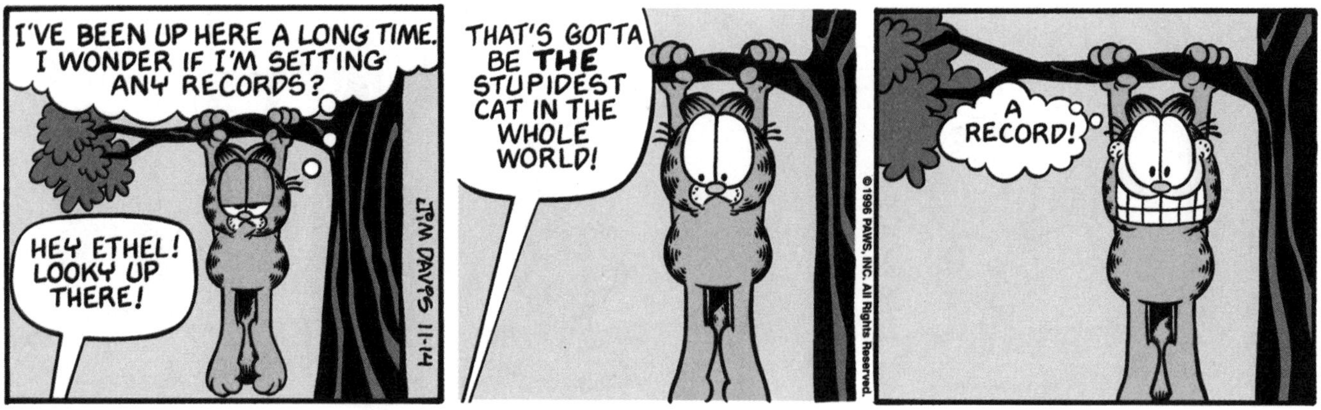
I'VE BEEN UP HERE A LONG TIME. I WONDER IF I'M SETTING ANY RECORDS?
HEY ETHEL! LOOKY UP THERE!
JIM DAVIS 11-14
THAT'S GOTTA BE **THE** STUPIDEST CAT IN THE WHOLE WORLD!
© 1996 PAWS, INC. All Rights Reserved.
A RECORD!

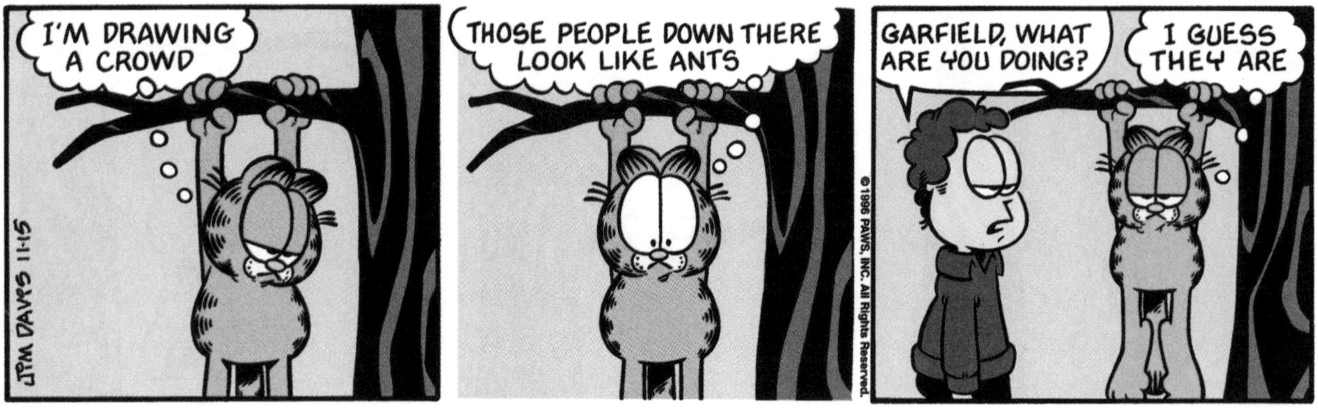
I'M DRAWING A CROWD
JIM DAVIS 11-15
THOSE PEOPLE DOWN THERE LOOK LIKE ANTS
© 1996 PAWS, INC. All Rights Reserved.
GARFIELD, WHAT ARE YOU DOING?
I GUESS THEY ARE

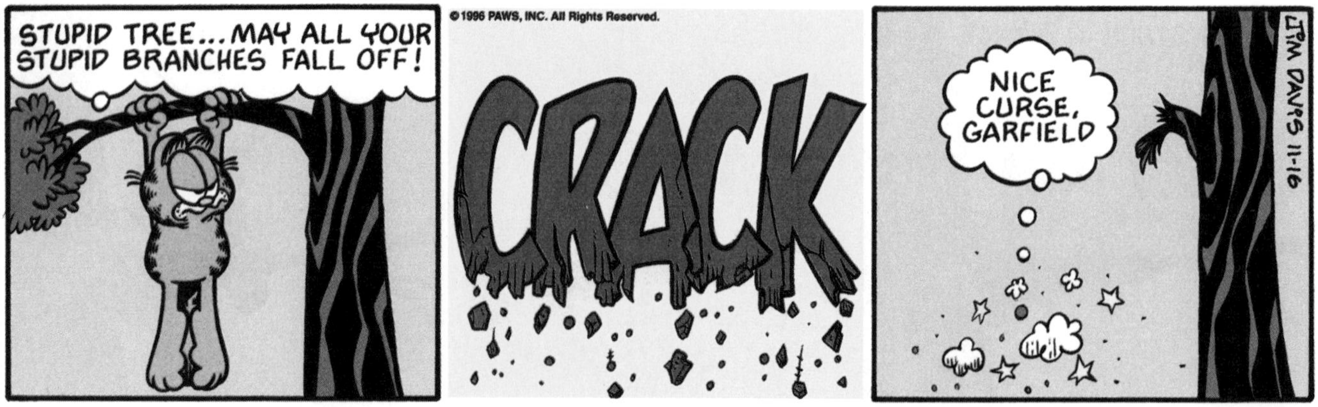
STUPID TREE... MAY ALL YOUR STUPID BRANCHES FALL OFF!
© 1996 PAWS, INC. All Rights Reserved.
CRACK
NICE CURSE, GARFIELD
JIM DAVIS 11-16

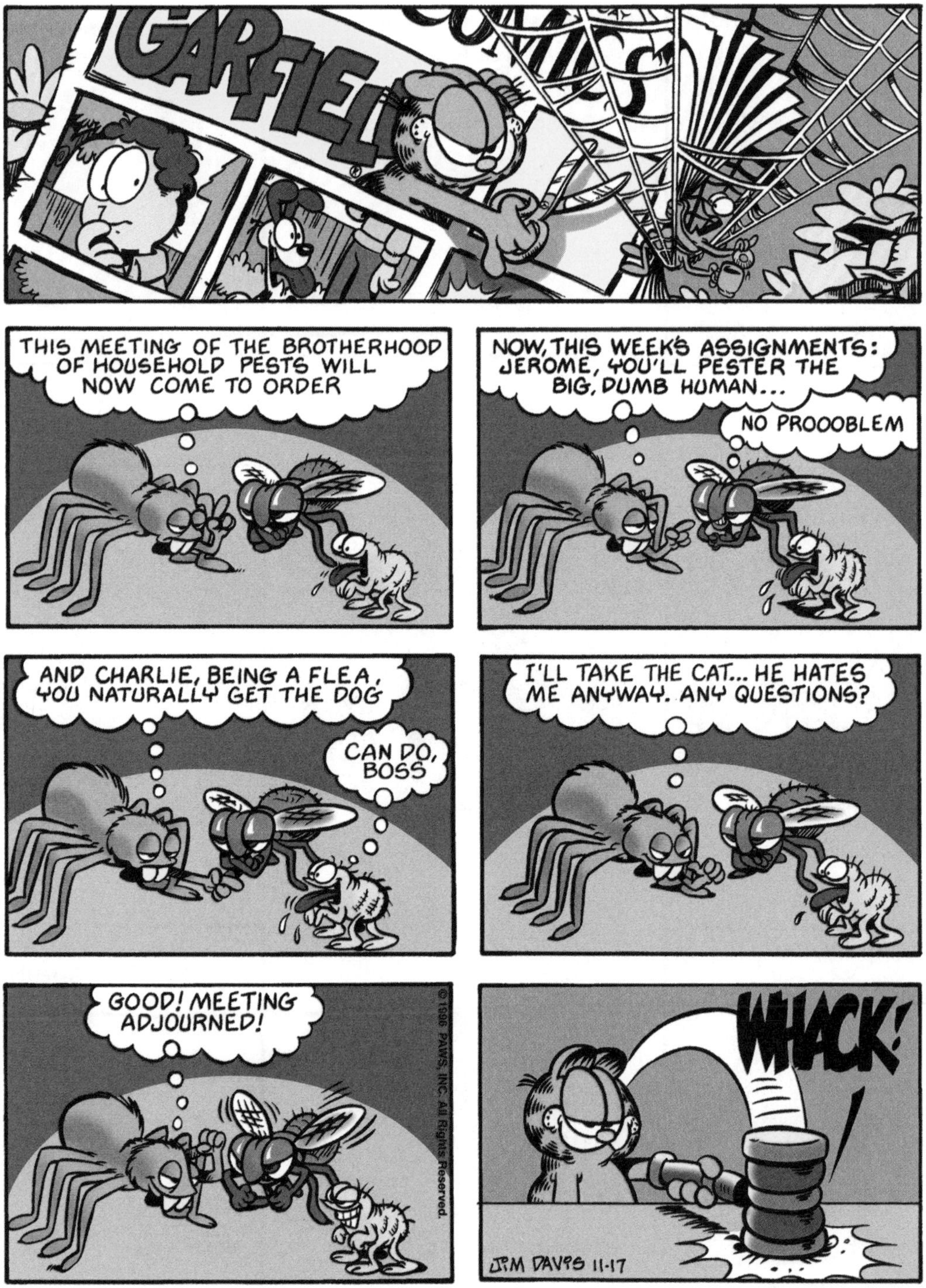
GARFIELD
COMICS
THIS MEETING OF THE BROTHERHOOD OF HOUSEHOLD PESTS WILL NOW COME TO ORDER
NOW, THIS WEEK'S ASSIGNMENTS: JEROME, YOU'LL PESTER THE BIG, DUMB HUMAN...
NO PROOOBLEM
AND CHARLIE, BEING A FLEA, YOU NATURALLY GET THE DOG
CAN DO, BOSS
I'LL TAKE THE CAT... HE HATES ME ANYWAY. ANY QUESTIONS?
GOOD! MEETING ADJOURNED!
© 1986 PAWS, INC. All Rights Reserved.
WHACK!
JIM DAVIS 11-17

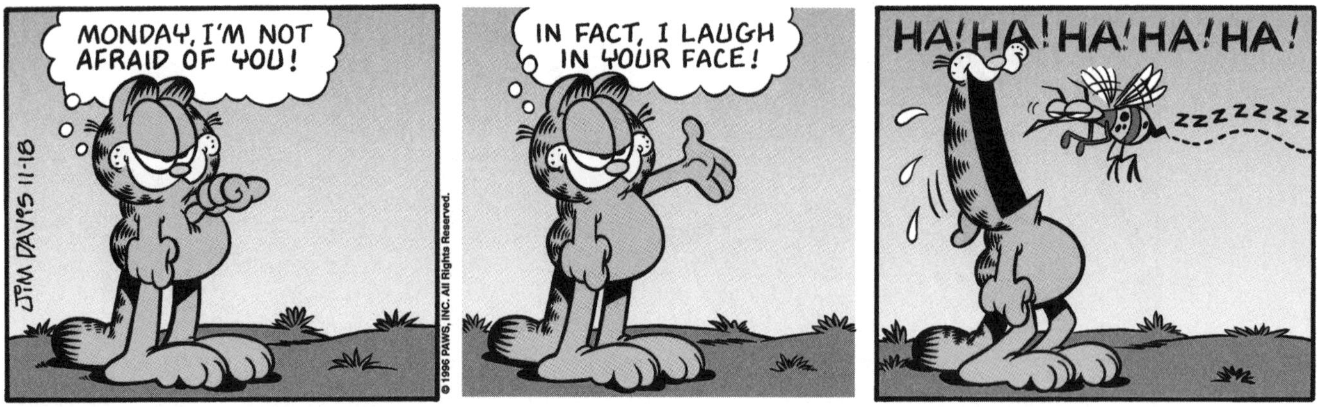
MONDAY, I'M NOT AFRAID OF YOU!
JIM DAVIS 11-18
IN FACT, I LAUGH IN YOUR FACE!
© 1996 PAWS, INC. All Rights Reserved.
HA! HA! HA! HA! HA!
ZZZZZZZ

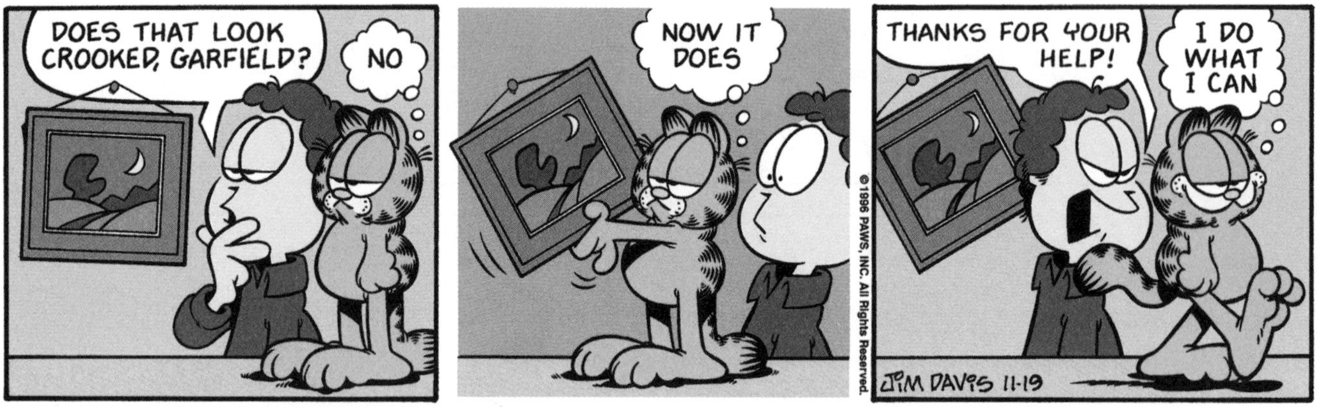
DOES THAT LOOK CROOKED, GARFIELD?
NO
NOW IT DOES
© 1996 PAWS, INC. All Rights Reserved.
THANKS FOR YOUR HELP!
I DO WHAT I CAN
JIM DAVIS 11-19

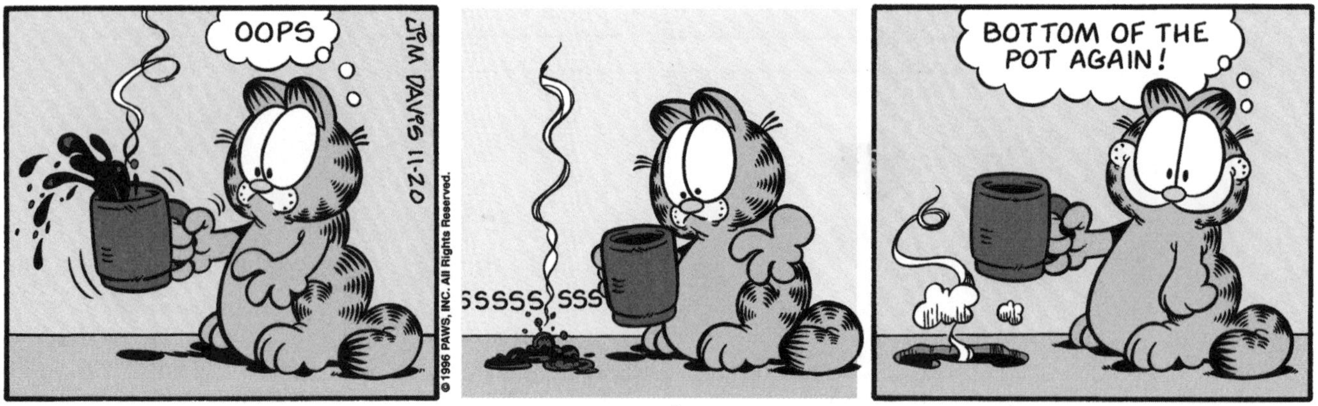
OOPS
JIM DAVIS 11-20
© 1996 PAWS, INC. All Rights Reserved.
SSSSS SSS
BOTTOM OF THE POT AGAIN!

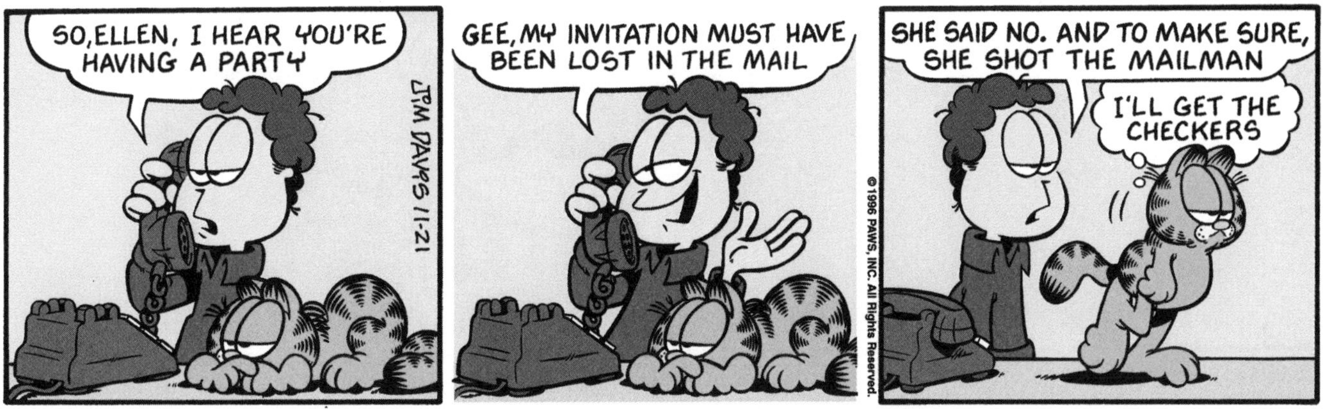
SO, ELLEN, I HEAR YOU'RE HAVING A PARTY
JIM DAVIS 11-21
GEE, MY INVITATION MUST HAVE BEEN LOST IN THE MAIL
© 1996 PAWS, INC. All Rights Reserved.
SHE SAID NO. AND TO MAKE SURE, SHE SHOT THE MAILMAN
I'LL GET THE CHECKERS

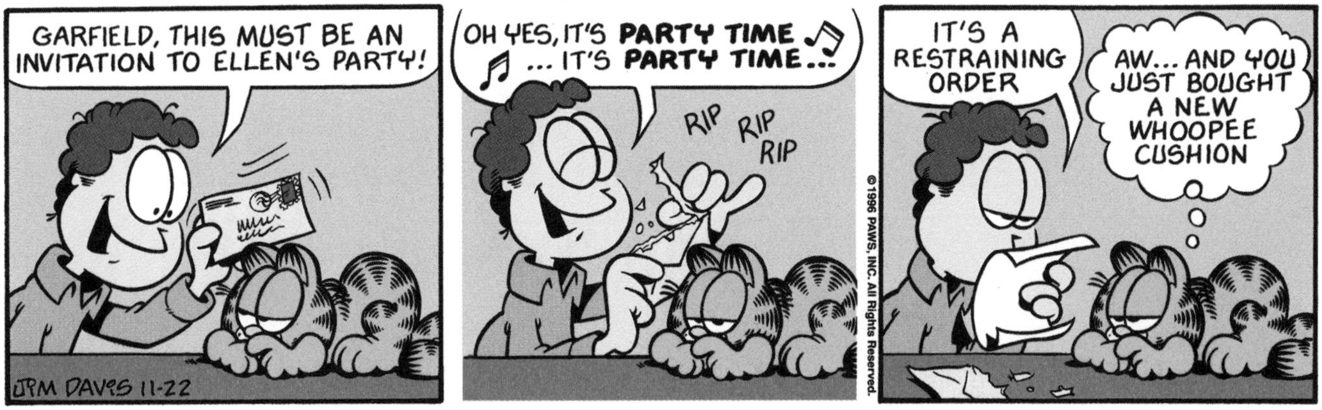
GARFIELD, THIS MUST BE AN INVITATION TO ELLEN'S PARTY!
JIM DAVIS 11-22
OH YES, IT'S **PARTY TIME** ... IT'S **PARTY TIME**...
RIP RIP RIP
© 1996 PAWS, INC. All Rights Reserved.
IT'S A RESTRAINING ORDER
AW... AND YOU JUST BOUGHT A NEW WHOOPEE CUSHION

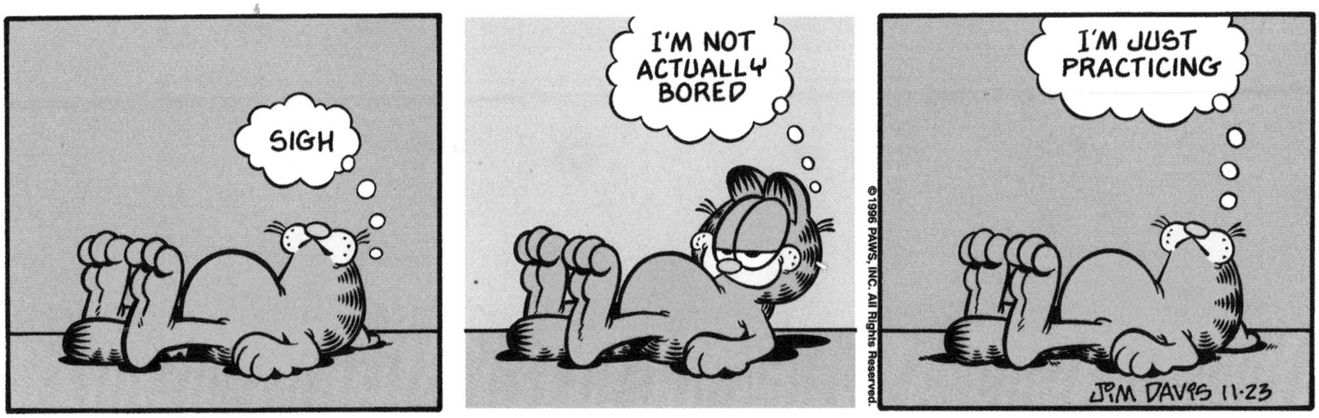
SIGH
I'M NOT ACTUALLY BORED
© 1996 PAWS, INC. All Rights Reserved.
I'M JUST PRACTICING
JIM DAVIS 11-23

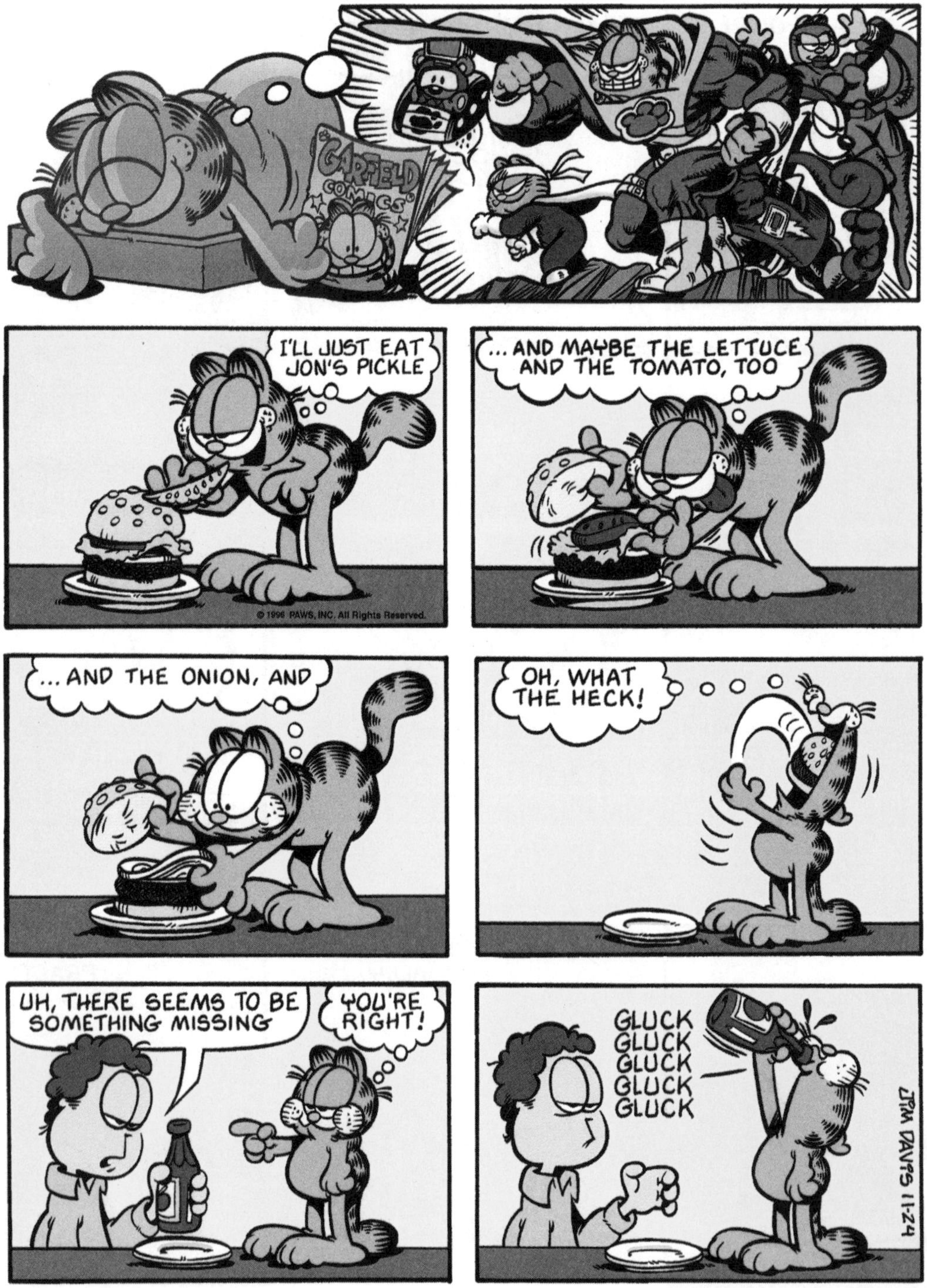
GARFIELD COMICS
I'LL JUST EAT JON'S PICKLE
© 1996 PAWS, INC. All Rights Reserved.
...AND MAYBE THE LETTUCE AND THE TOMATO, TOO
...AND THE ONION, AND
OH, WHAT THE HECK!
UH, THERE SEEMS TO BE SOMETHING MISSING
YOU'RE RIGHT!
GLUCK GLUCK GLUCK GLUCK GLUCK
JIM DAVIS 11-24

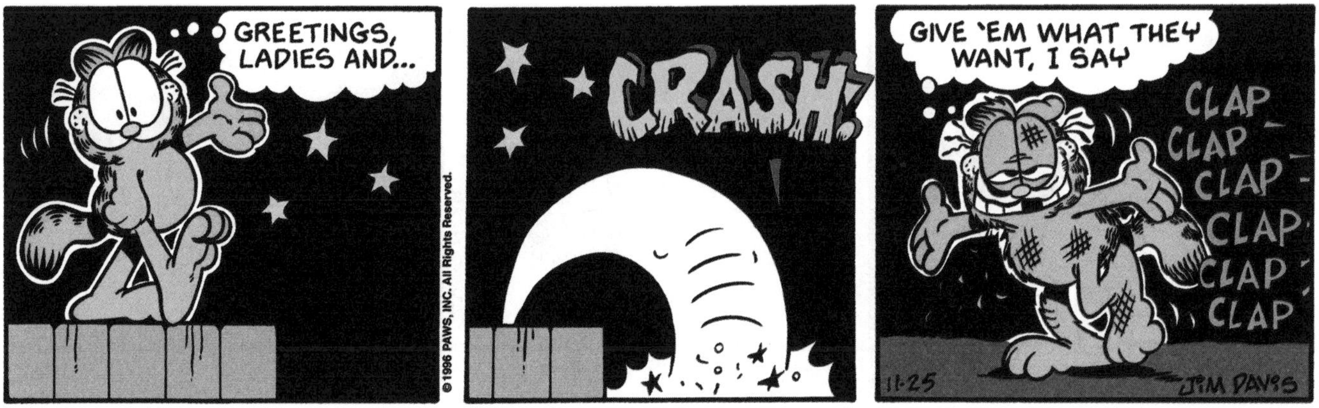
GREETINGS, LADIES AND...
© 1996 PAWS, INC. All Rights Reserved.
CRASH!
GIVE 'EM WHAT THEY WANT, I SAY
CLAP
CLAP
CLAP
CLAP
CLAP
CLAP
11-25
JIM DAVIS

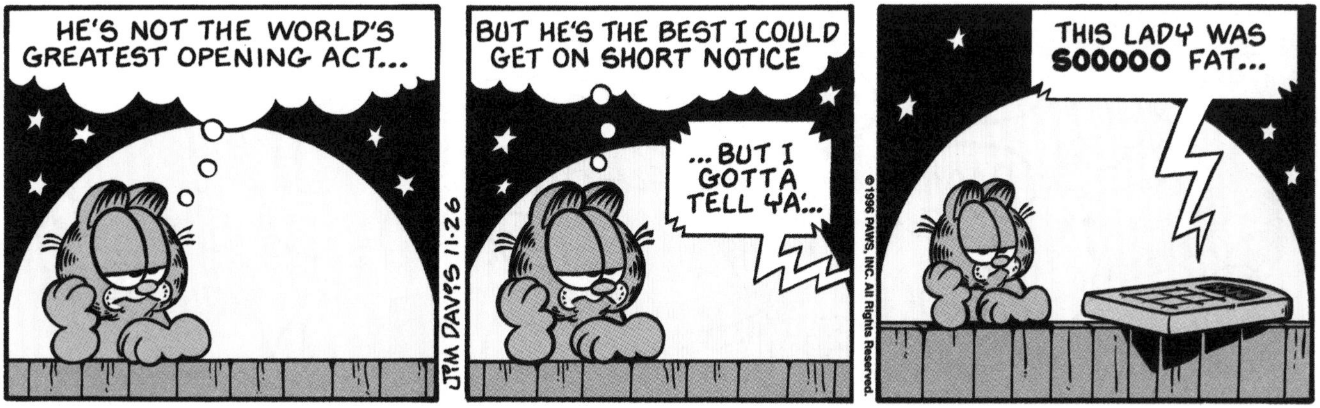
HE'S NOT THE WORLD'S GREATEST OPENING ACT...
JIM DAVIS 11-26
BUT HE'S THE BEST I COULD GET ON SHORT NOTICE
...BUT I GOTTA TELL YA'...
© 1996 PAWS, INC. All Rights Reserved.
THIS LADY WAS SOOOOO FAT...

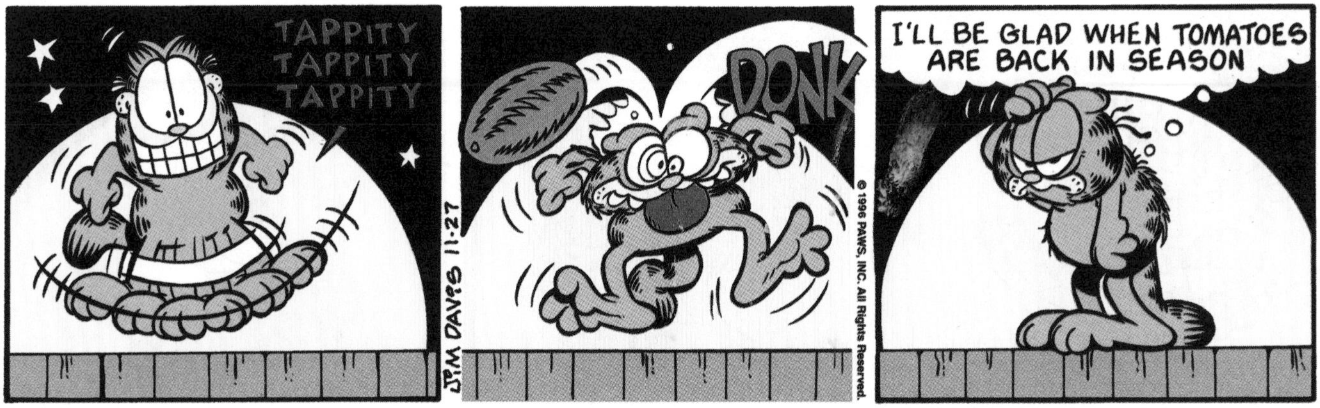
TAPPITY
TAPPITY
TAPPITY
JIM DAVIS 11-27
DONK
© 1996 PAWS, INC. All Rights Reserved.
I'LL BE GLAD WHEN TOMATOES ARE BACK IN SEASON

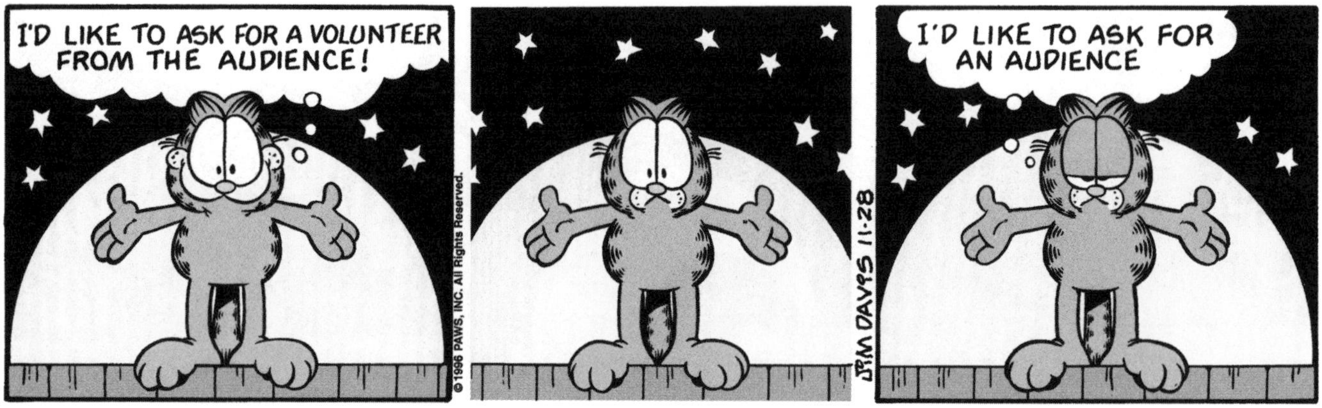
I'D LIKE TO ASK FOR A VOLUNTEER FROM THE AUDIENCE!
© 1996 PAWS, INC. All Rights Reserved.
JIM DAVIS 11-28
I'D LIKE TO ASK FOR AN AUDIENCE

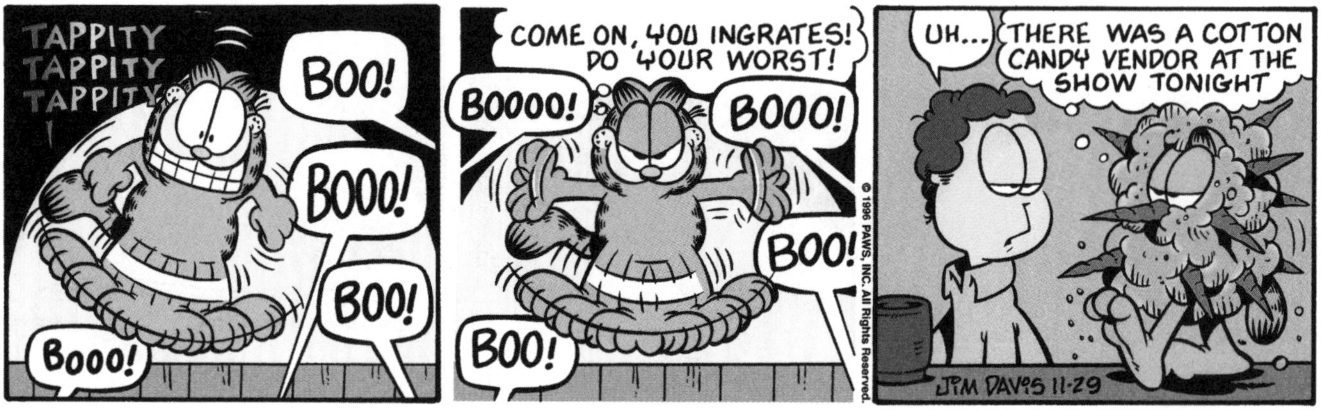
TAPPITY
TAPPITY
TAPPITY
BOO!
BOOO!
BOO!
Booo!
COME ON, YOU INGRATES! DO YOUR WORST!
BOOOO!
BOOO!
BOO!
BOO!
© 1996 PAWS, INC. All Rights Reserved.
UH...
THERE WAS A COTTON CANDY VENDOR AT THE SHOW TONIGHT
JIM DAVIS 11-29

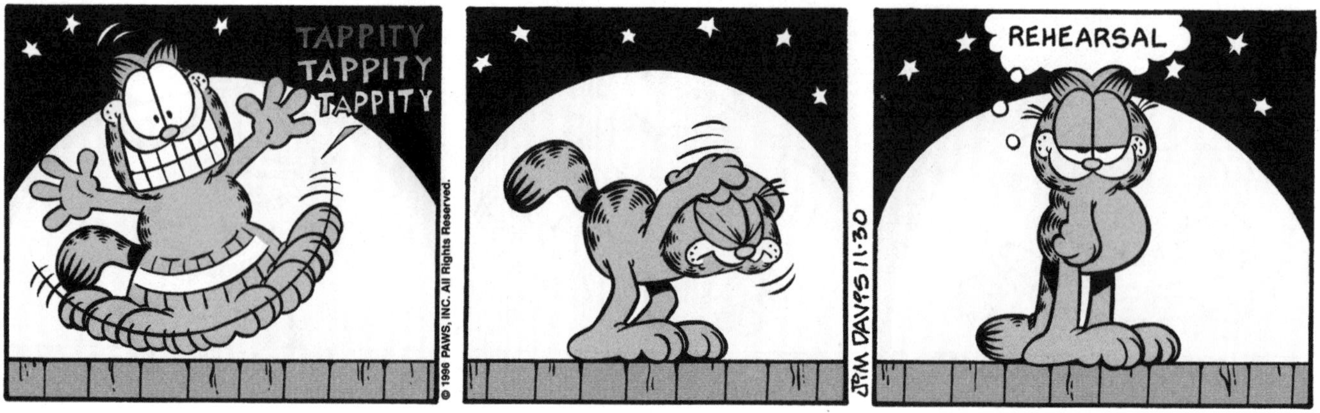
TAPPITY
TAPPITY
TAPPITY
© 1996 PAWS, INC. All Rights Reserved.
JIM DAVIS 11-30
REHEARSAL

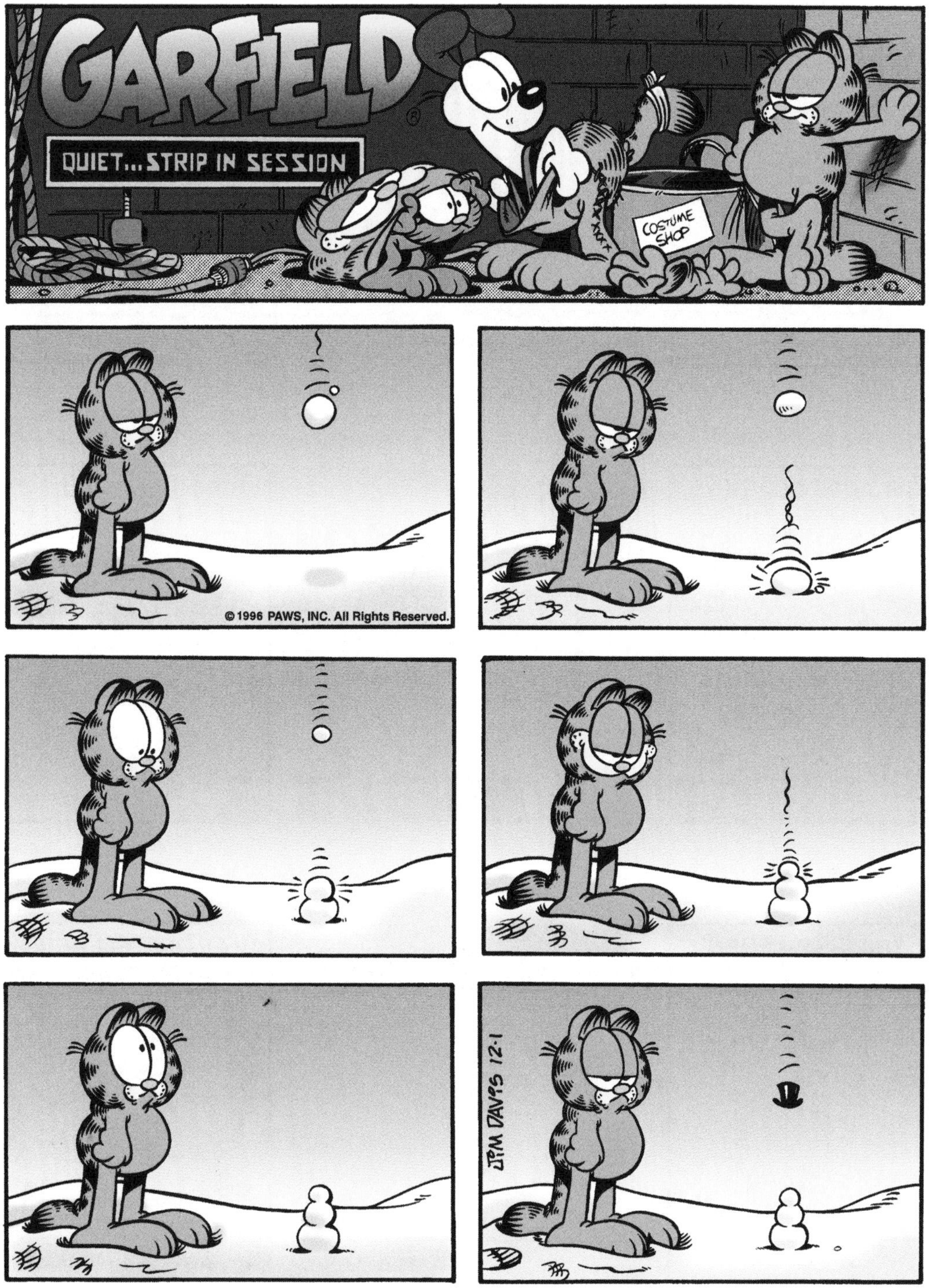
GARFIELD
QUIET... STRIP IN SESSION
COSTUME SHOP
©1996 PAWS, INC. All Rights Reserved.
JIM DAVIS 12·1

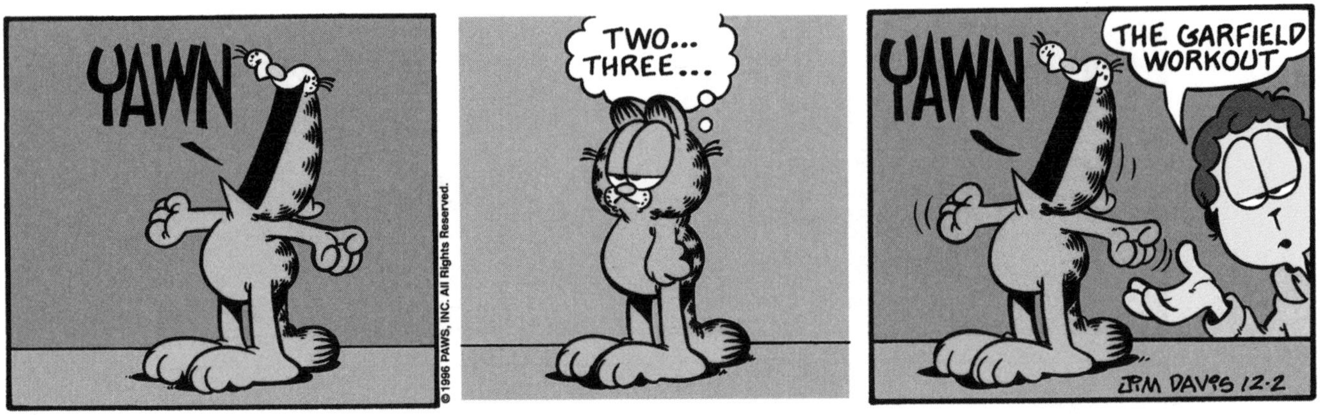
YAWN
© 1996 PAWS, INC. All Rights Reserved.
TWO... THREE...
YAWN
THE GARFIELD WORKOUT
JIM DAVIS 12-2

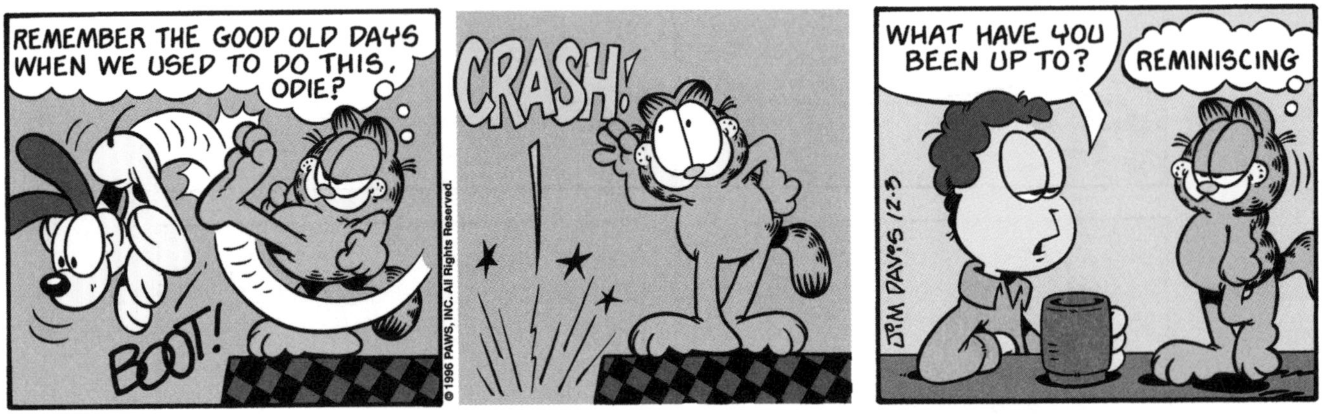
REMEMBER THE GOOD OLD DAYS WHEN WE USED TO DO THIS, ODIE?
BOOT!
© 1996 PAWS, INC. All Rights Reserved.
CRASH!
WHAT HAVE YOU BEEN UP TO?
REMINISCING
JIM DAVIS 12-3

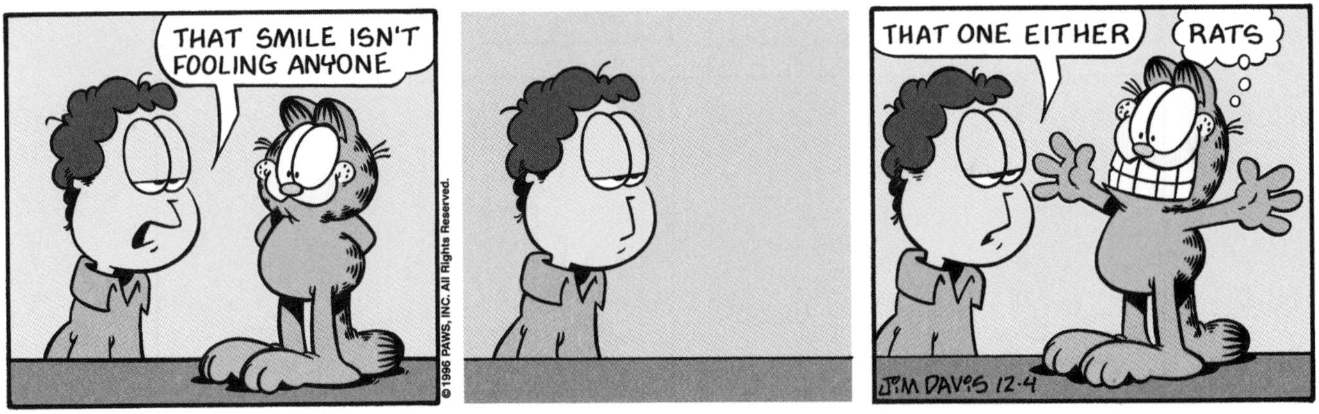
THAT SMILE ISN'T FOOLING ANYONE
© 1996 PAWS, INC. All Rights Reserved.
THAT ONE EITHER
RATS
JIM DAVIS 12-4

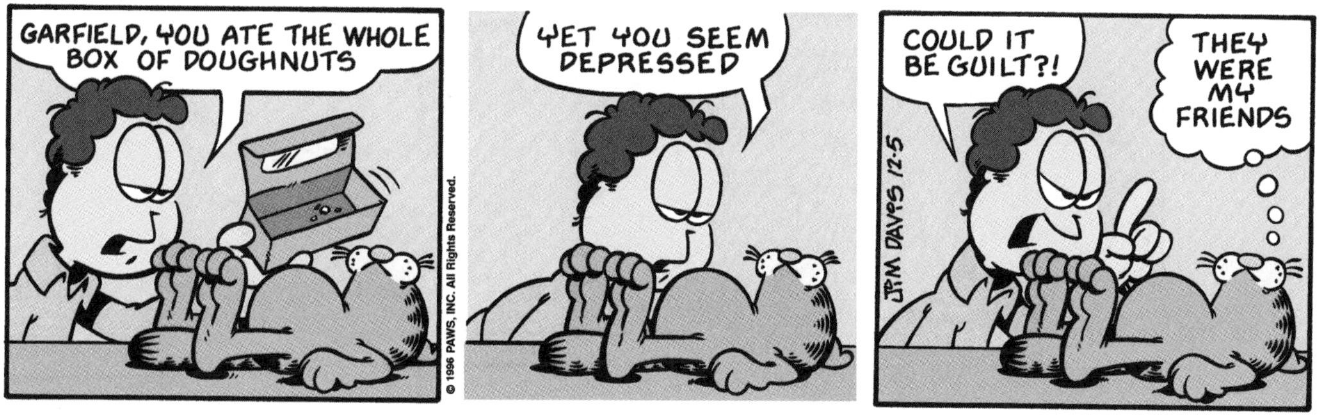
GARFIELD, YOU ATE THE WHOLE BOX OF DOUGHNUTS
© 1996 PAWS, INC. All Rights Reserved.
YET YOU SEEM DEPRESSED
COULD IT BE GUILT?!
THEY WERE MY FRIENDS
JIM DAVIS 12-5

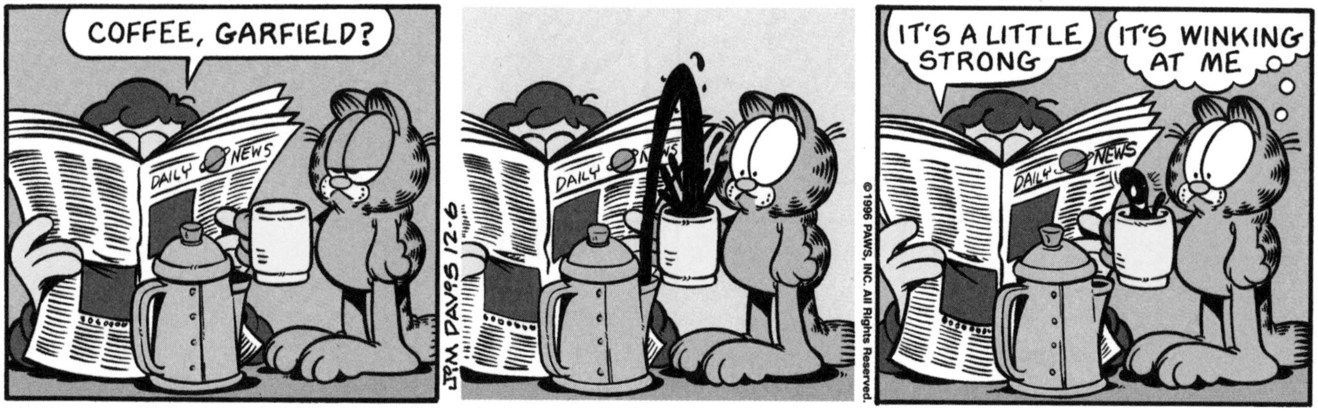
COFFEE, GARFIELD?
DAILY NEWS
JIM DAVIS 12-6
IT'S A LITTLE STRONG
IT'S WINKING AT ME
© 1996 PAWS, INC. All Rights Reserved.

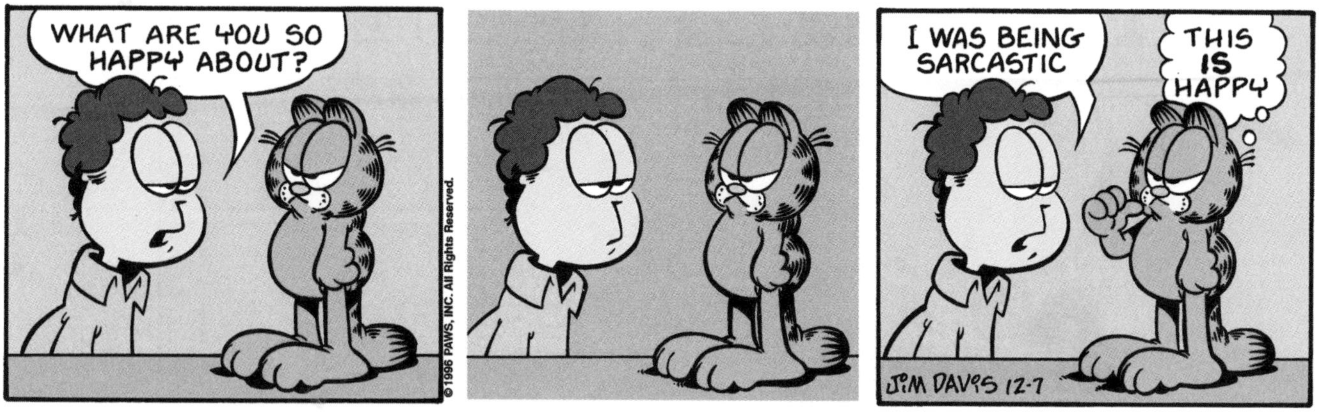
WHAT ARE YOU SO HAPPY ABOUT?
© 1996 PAWS, INC. All Rights Reserved.
I WAS BEING SARCASTIC
THIS **IS** HAPPY
JIM DAVIS 12-7

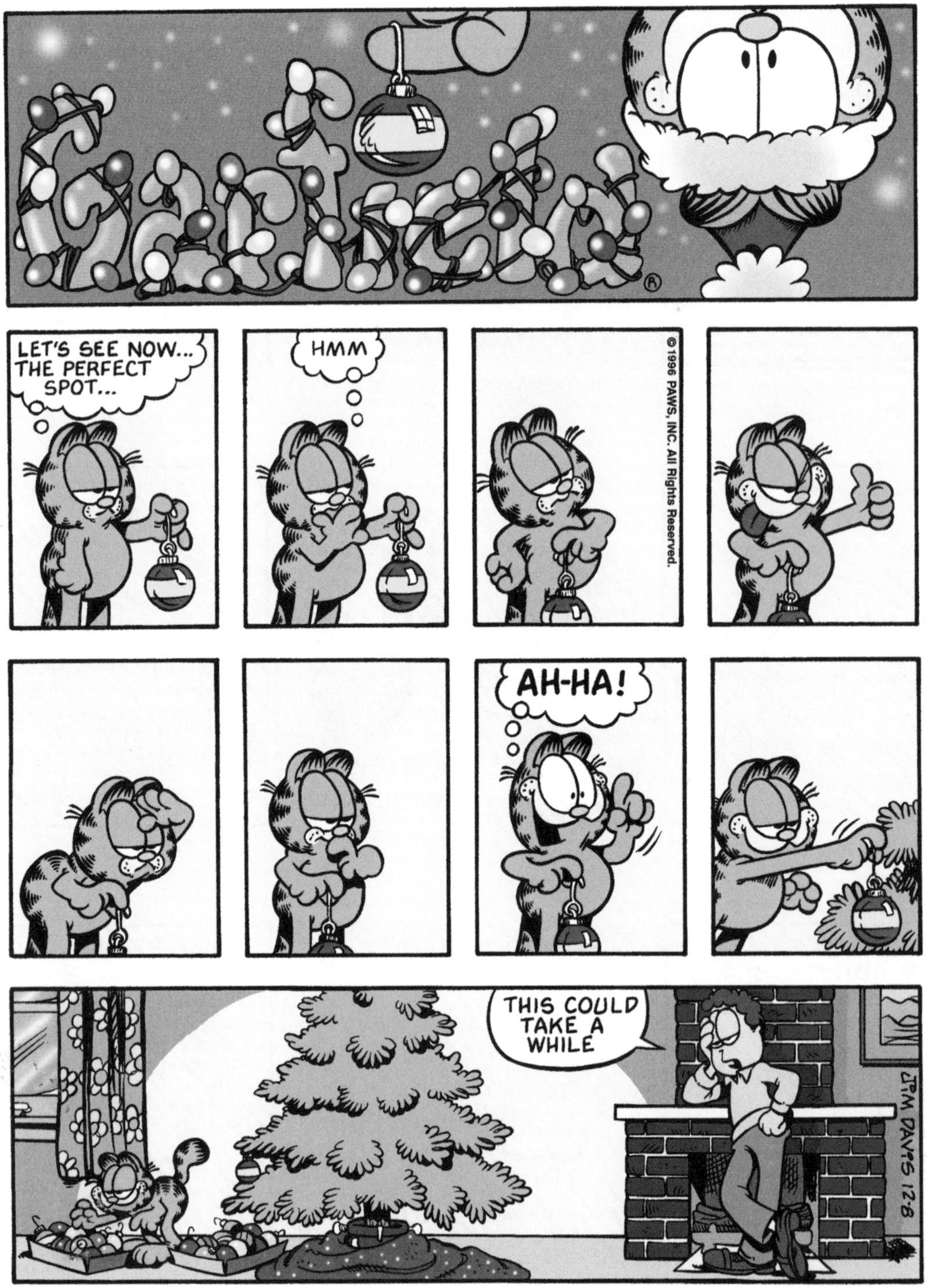

GARFIELD
LET'S SEE NOW... THE PERFECT SPOT...
HMM
© 1996 PAWS, INC. All Rights Reserved.
AH-HA!
THIS COULD TAKE A WHILE
JPM DAVIS 12-8

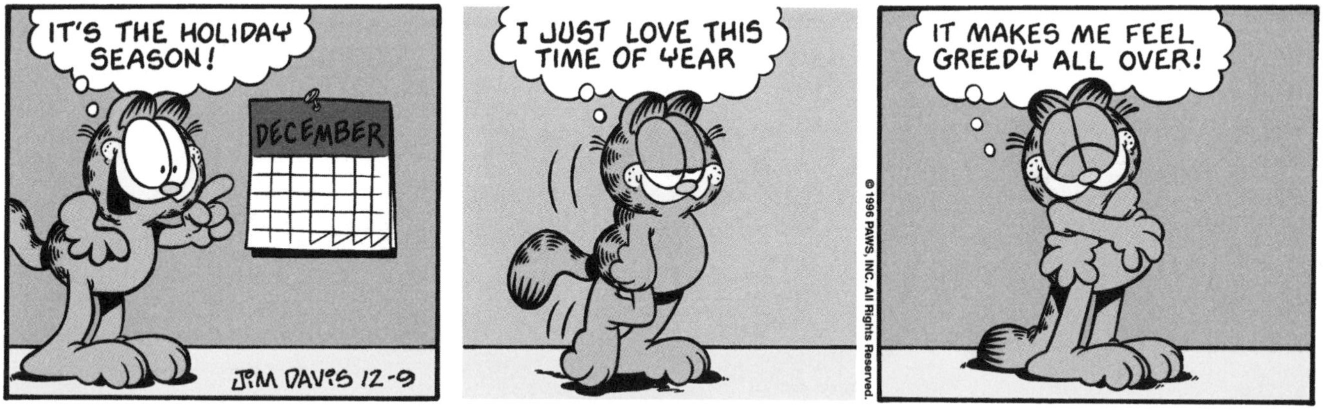
IT'S THE HOLIDAY SEASON!
DECEMBER
JIM DAVIS 12-9
I JUST LOVE THIS TIME OF YEAR
© 1996 PAWS, INC. All Rights Reserved.
IT MAKES ME FEEL GREEDY ALL OVER!

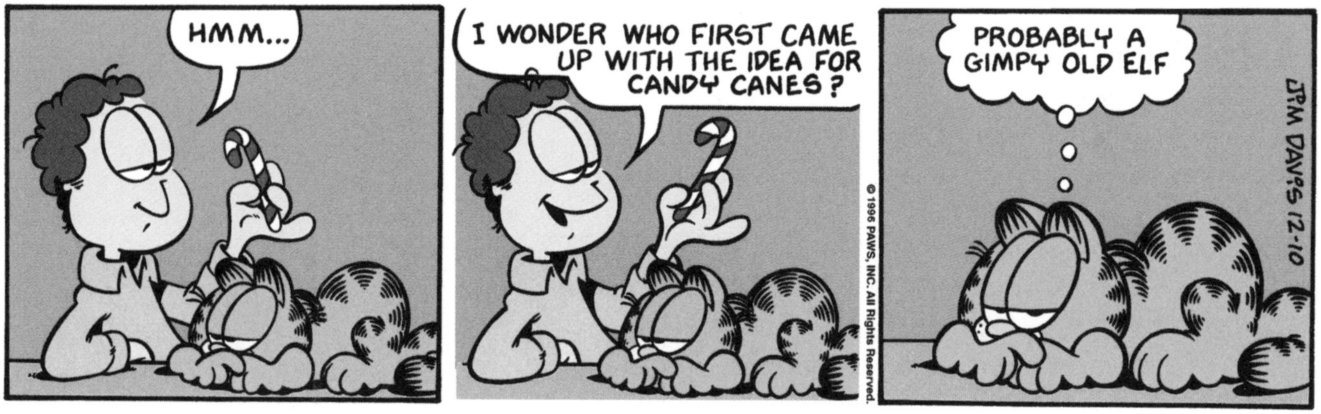
HMM...
I WONDER WHO FIRST CAME UP WITH THE IDEA FOR CANDY CANES?
© 1996 PAWS, INC. All Rights Reserved.
PROBABLY A GIMPY OLD ELF
JIM DAVIS 12-10

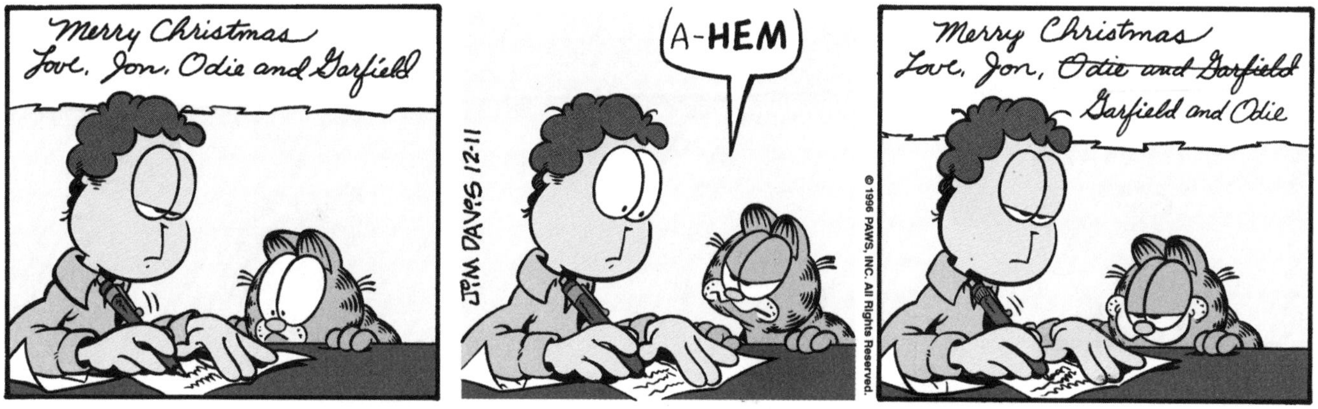
Merry Christmas
Love, Jon, Odie and Garfield
JIM DAVIS 12-11
A-HEM
© 1996 PAWS, INC. All Rights Reserved.
Merry Christmas
Love, Jon, ~~Odie and Garfield~~
Garfield and Odie

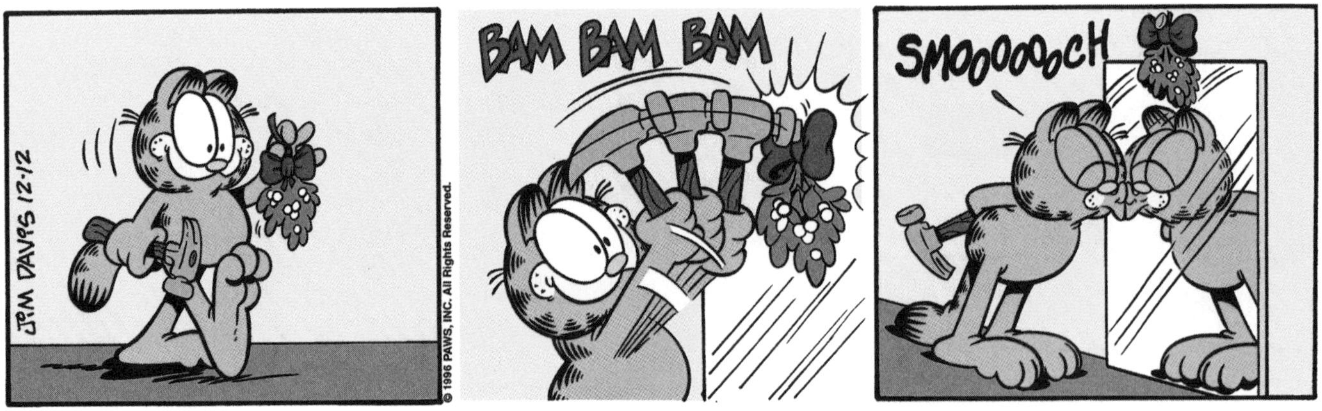
JIM DAVIS 12-12
© 1996 PAWS, INC. All Rights Reserved.
BAM BAM BAM
SMOOOOOOCH

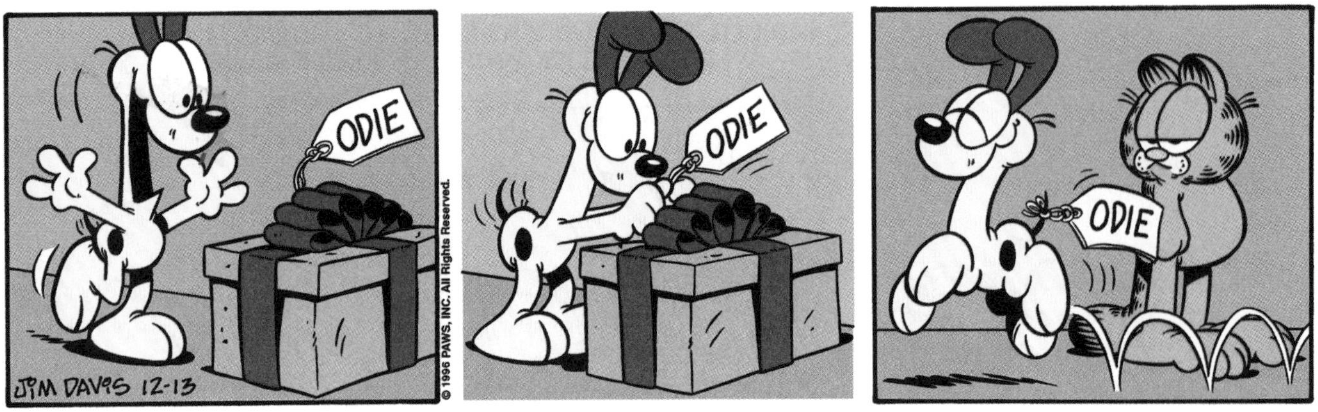
JIM DAVIS 12-13
ODIE
© 1996 PAWS, INC. All Rights Reserved.
ODIE
ODIE

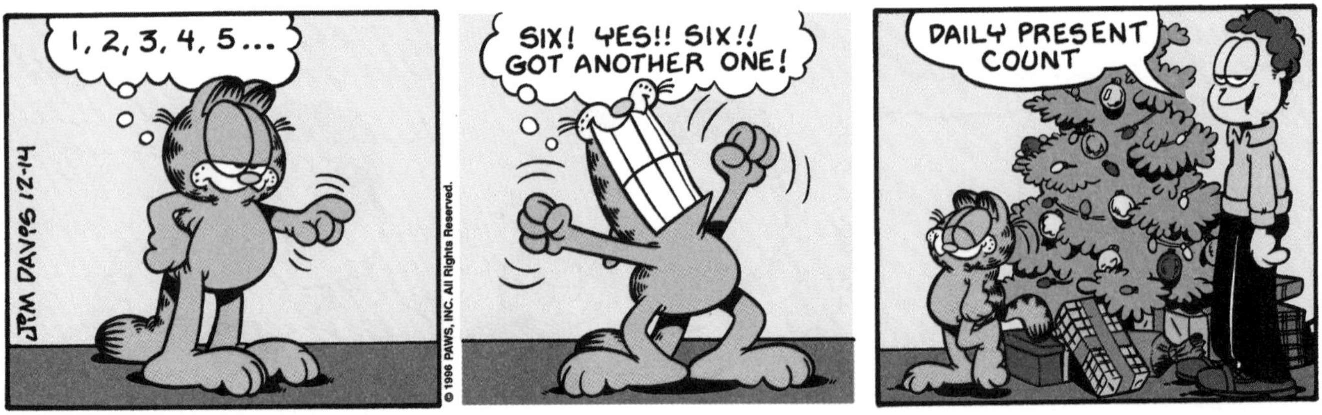
JIM DAVIS 12-14
1, 2, 3, 4, 5...
© 1996 PAWS, INC. All Rights Reserved.
SIX! YES!! SIX!!
GOT ANOTHER ONE!
DAILY PRESENT
COUNT

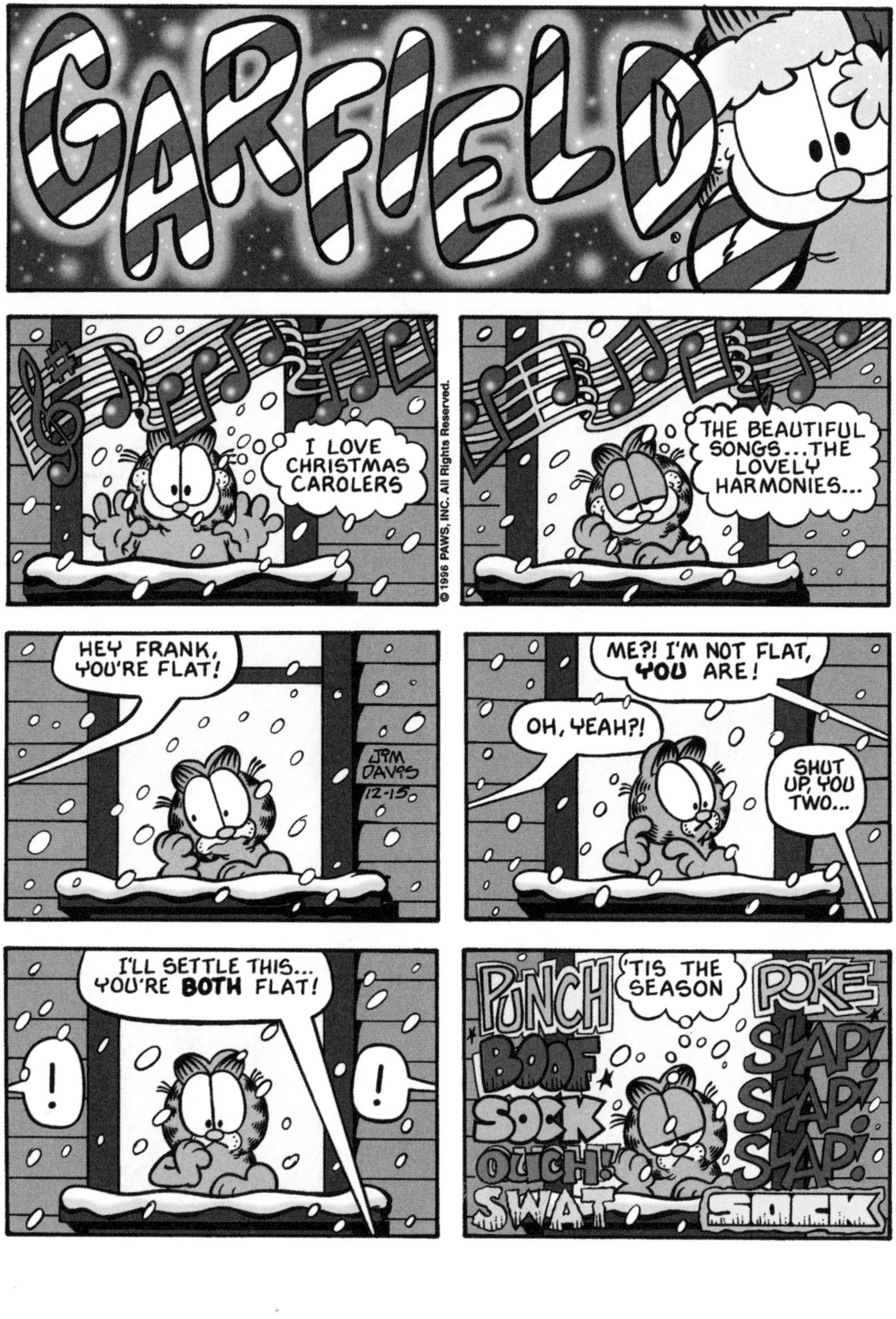
GARFIELD
I LOVE CHRISTMAS CAROLERS
THE BEAUTIFUL SONGS...THE LOVELY HARMONIES...
HEY FRANK, YOU'RE FLAT!
JIM DAVIS 12-15
ME?! I'M NOT FLAT, YOU ARE!
OH, YEAH?!
SHUT UP, YOU TWO...
I'LL SETTLE THIS... YOU'RE BOTH FLAT!
!
!
PUNCH
'TIS THE SEASON
POKE
BOOF
SLAP!
SOCK
SLAP!
OUCH!
SLAP!
SWAT
SOCK

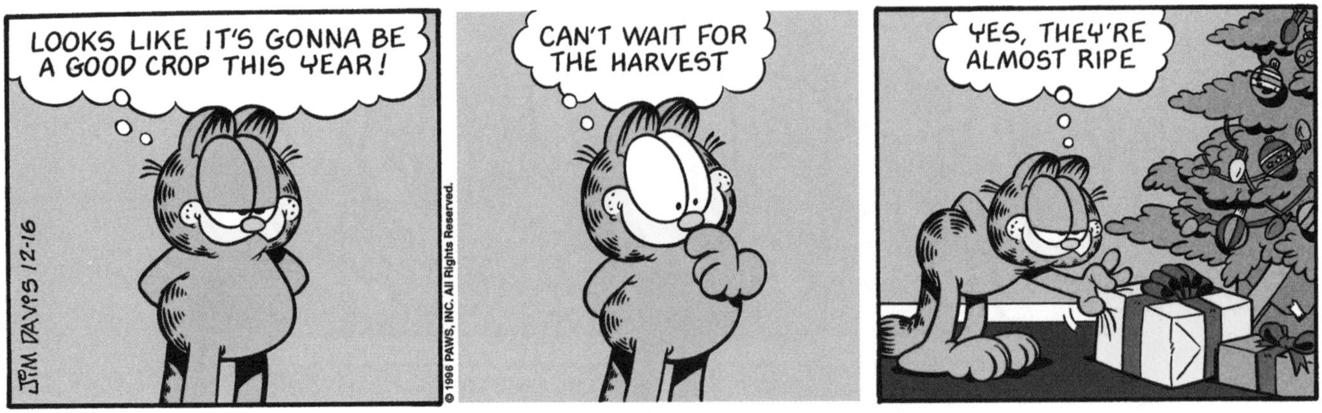
LOOKS LIKE IT'S GONNA BE A GOOD CROP THIS YEAR!
JIM DAVIS 12-16
© 1996 PAWS, INC. All Rights Reserved.
CAN'T WAIT FOR THE HARVEST
YES, THEY'RE ALMOST RIPE

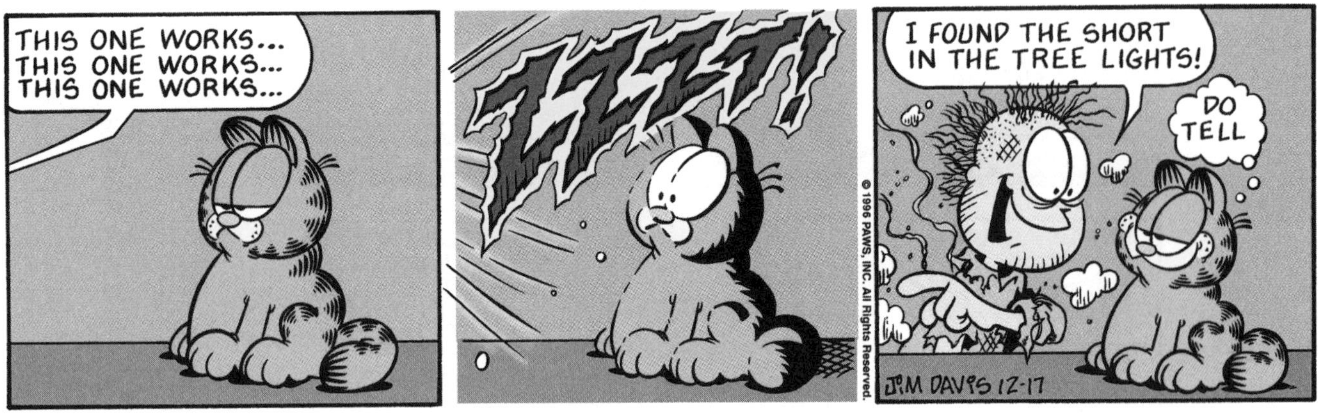
THIS ONE WORKS... THIS ONE WORKS... THIS ONE WORKS...
ZZZZT!
© 1996 PAWS, INC. All Rights Reserved.
I FOUND THE SHORT IN THE TREE LIGHTS!
DO TELL
JIM DAVIS 12-17

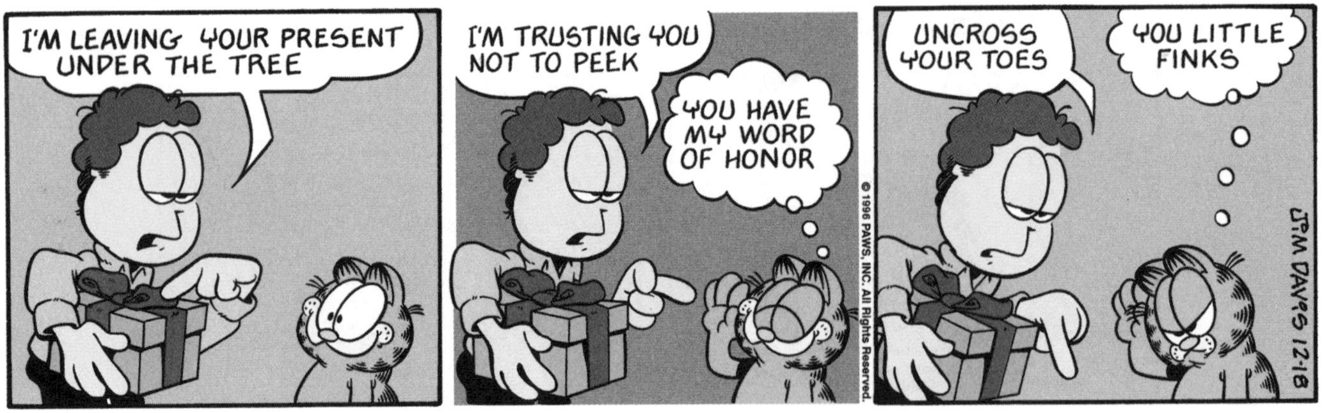
I'M LEAVING YOUR PRESENT UNDER THE TREE
I'M TRUSTING YOU NOT TO PEEK
YOU HAVE MY WORD OF HONOR
© 1996 PAWS, INC. All Rights Reserved.
UNCROSS YOUR TOES
YOU LITTLE FINKS
JIM DAVIS 12-18

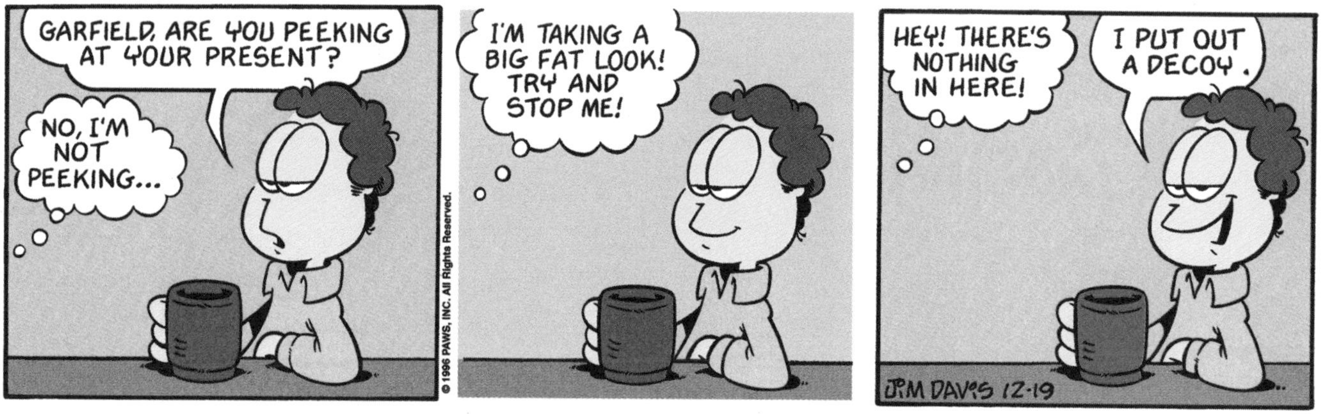
GARFIELD, ARE YOU PEEKING AT YOUR PRESENT?
NO, I'M NOT PEEKING...
I'M TAKING A BIG FAT LOOK! TRY AND STOP ME!
HEY! THERE'S NOTHING IN HERE!
I PUT OUT A DECOY.
© 1996 PAWS, INC. All Rights Reserved.
JIM DAVIS 12-19

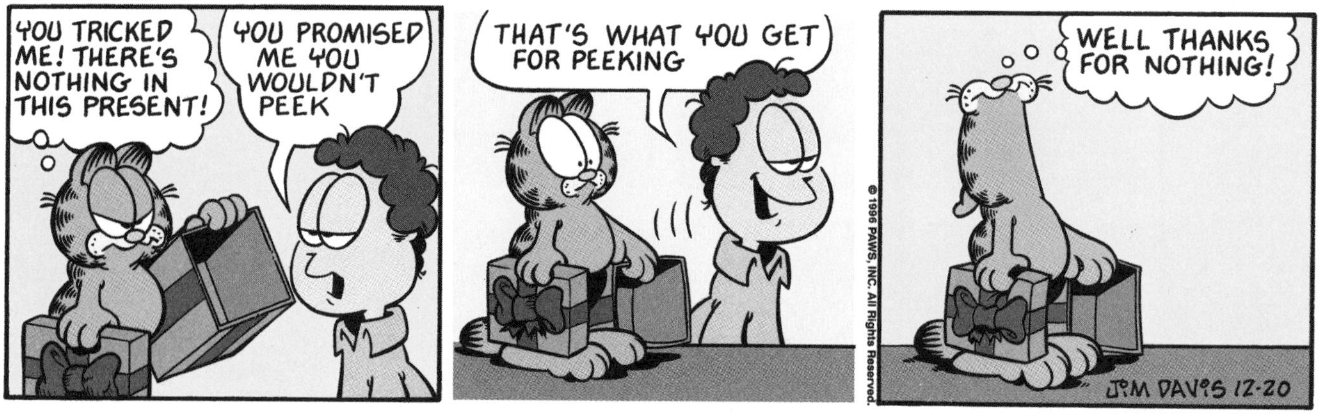
YOU TRICKED ME! THERE'S NOTHING IN THIS PRESENT!
YOU PROMISED ME YOU WOULDN'T PEEK
THAT'S WHAT YOU GET FOR PEEKING
WELL THANKS FOR NOTHING!
© 1996 PAWS, INC. All Rights Reserved.
JIM DAVIS 12-20

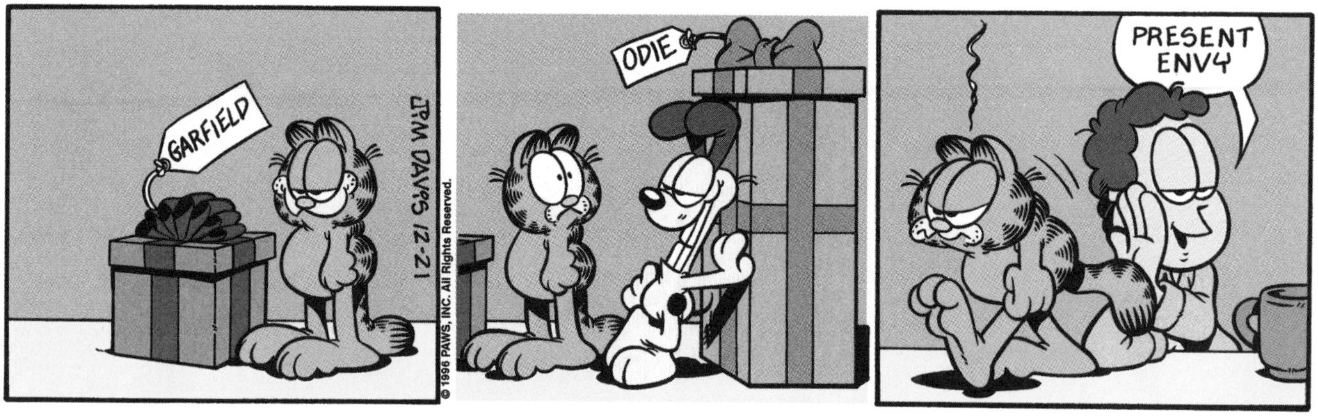
GARFIELD
JIM DAVIS 12-21
© 1996 PAWS, INC. All Rights Reserved.
ODIE
PRESENT ENVY

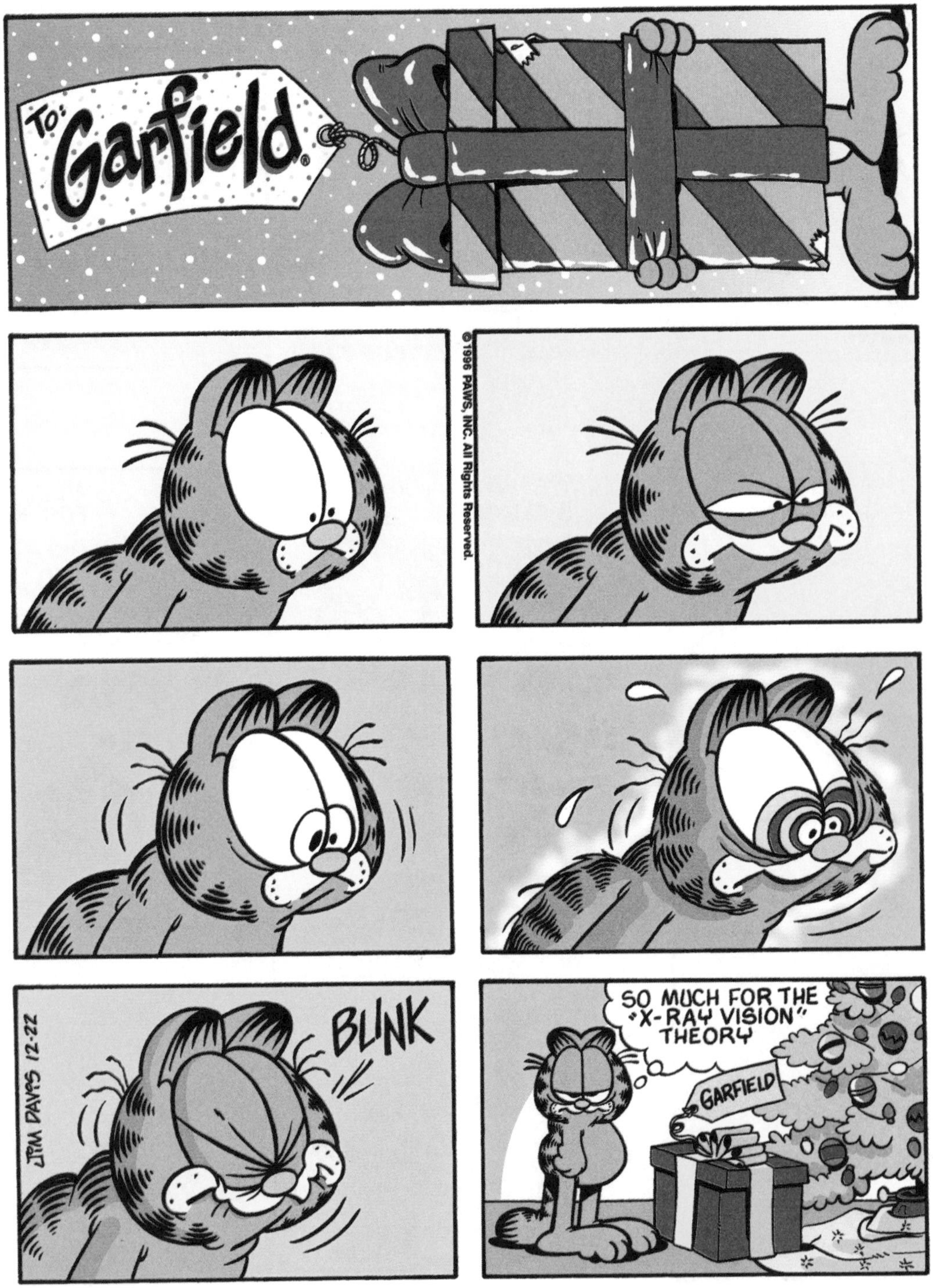
To: Garfield
© 1996 PAWS, INC. All Rights Reserved.
JIM DAVIS 12-22
BLINK
SO MUCH FOR THE "X-RAY VISION" THEORY
GARFIELD

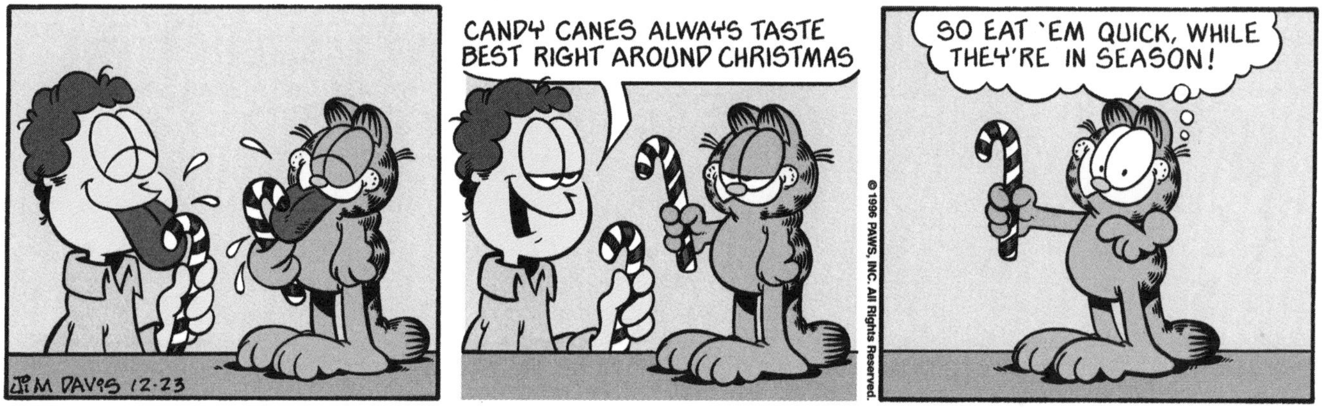
JIM DAVIS 12-23
CANDY CANES ALWAYS TASTE BEST RIGHT AROUND CHRISTMAS
© 1996 PAWS, INC. All Rights Reserved.
SO EAT 'EM QUICK, WHILE THEY'RE IN SEASON!

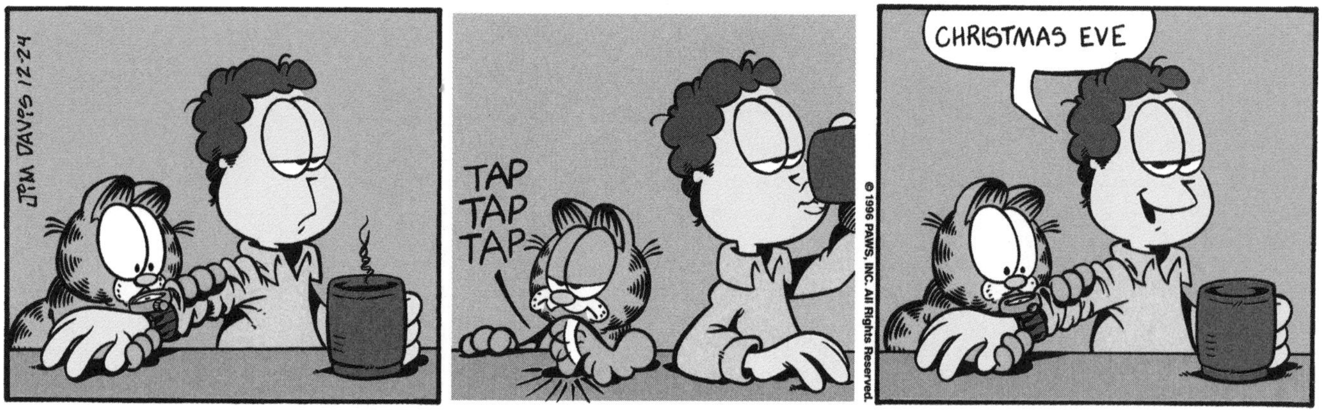
JIM DAVIS 12-24
TAP TAP TAP
© 1996 PAWS, INC. All Rights Reserved.
CHRISTMAS EVE

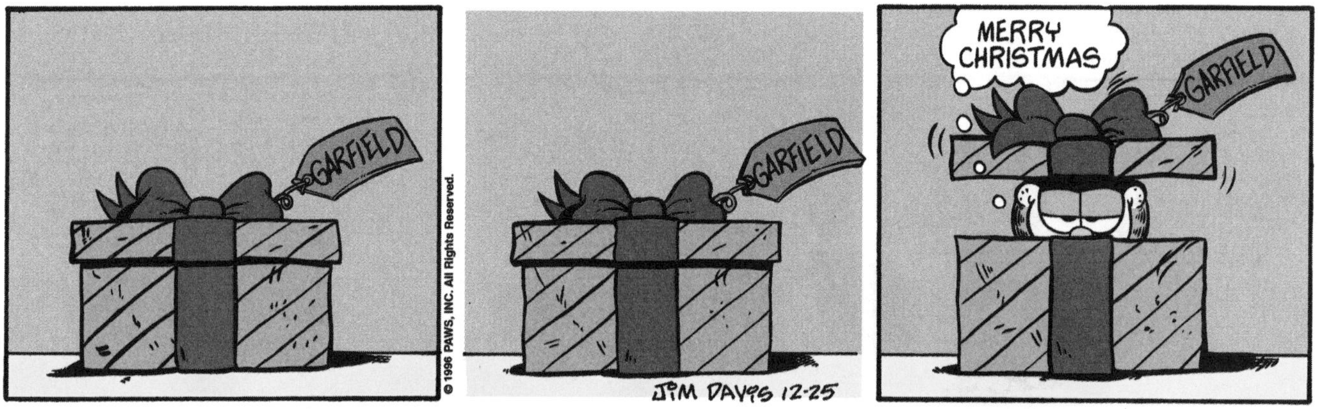
GARFIELD
© 1996 PAWS, INC. All Rights Reserved.
GARFIELD
JIM DAVIS 12-25
MERRY CHRISTMAS
GARFIELD

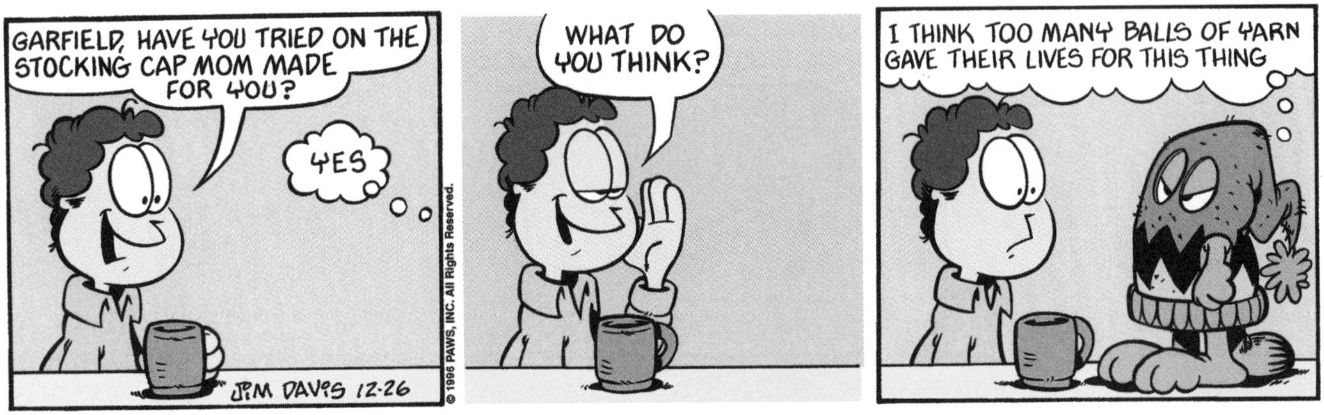
GARFIELD, HAVE YOU TRIED ON THE STOCKING CAP MOM MADE FOR YOU?
YES
JIM DAVIS 12-26
© 1996 PAWS, INC. All Rights Reserved.
WHAT DO YOU THINK?
I THINK TOO MANY BALLS OF YARN GAVE THEIR LIVES FOR THIS THING

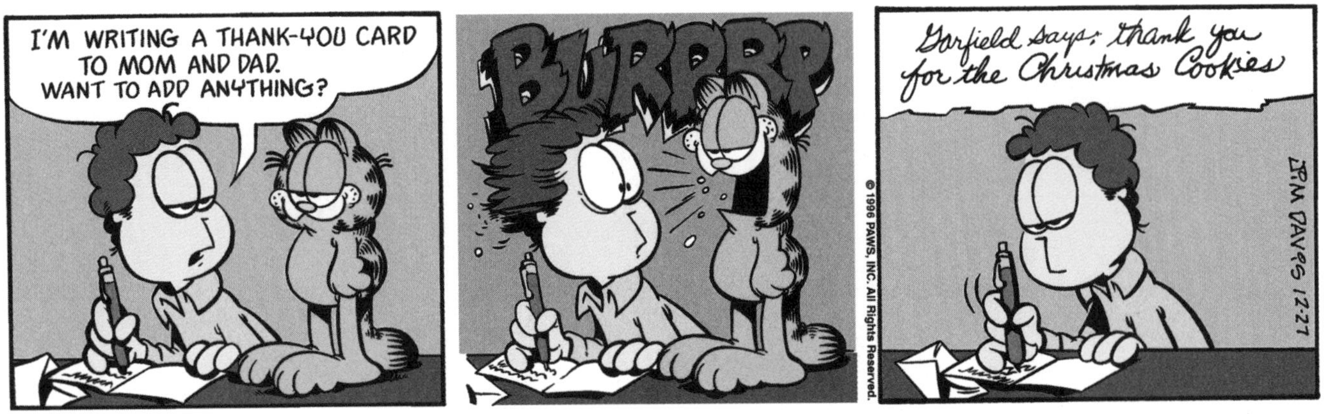
I'M WRITING A THANK-YOU CARD TO MOM AND DAD. WANT TO ADD ANYTHING?
BURPRP
© 1996 PAWS, INC. All Rights Reserved.
Garfield says: thank you for the Christmas Cookies
JIM DAVIS 12-27

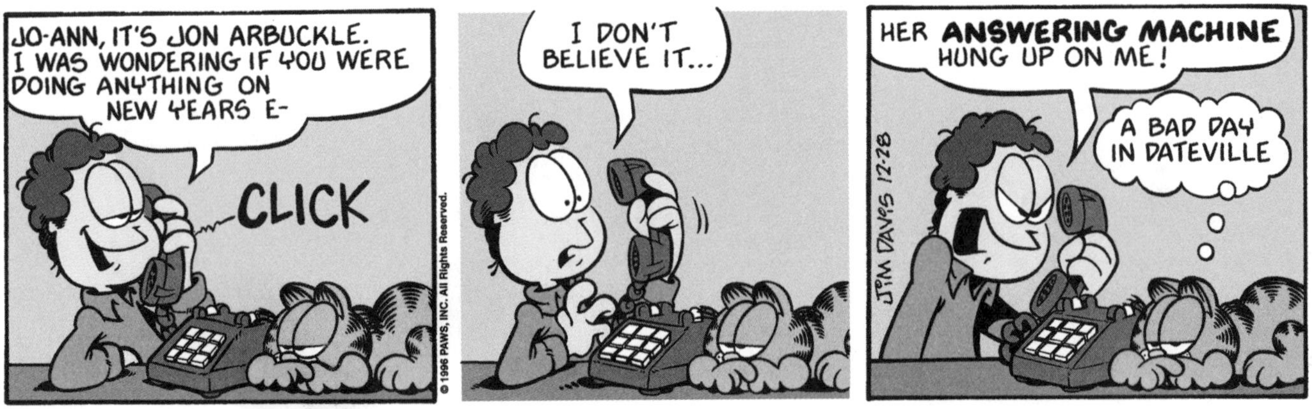
JO-ANN, IT'S JON ARBUCKLE. I WAS WONDERING IF YOU WERE DOING ANYTHING ON NEW YEARS E-
CLICK
© 1996 PAWS, INC. All Rights Reserved.
I DON'T BELIEVE IT...
JIM DAVIS 12-28
HER **ANSWERING MACHINE** HUNG UP ON ME!
A BAD DAY IN DATEVILLE

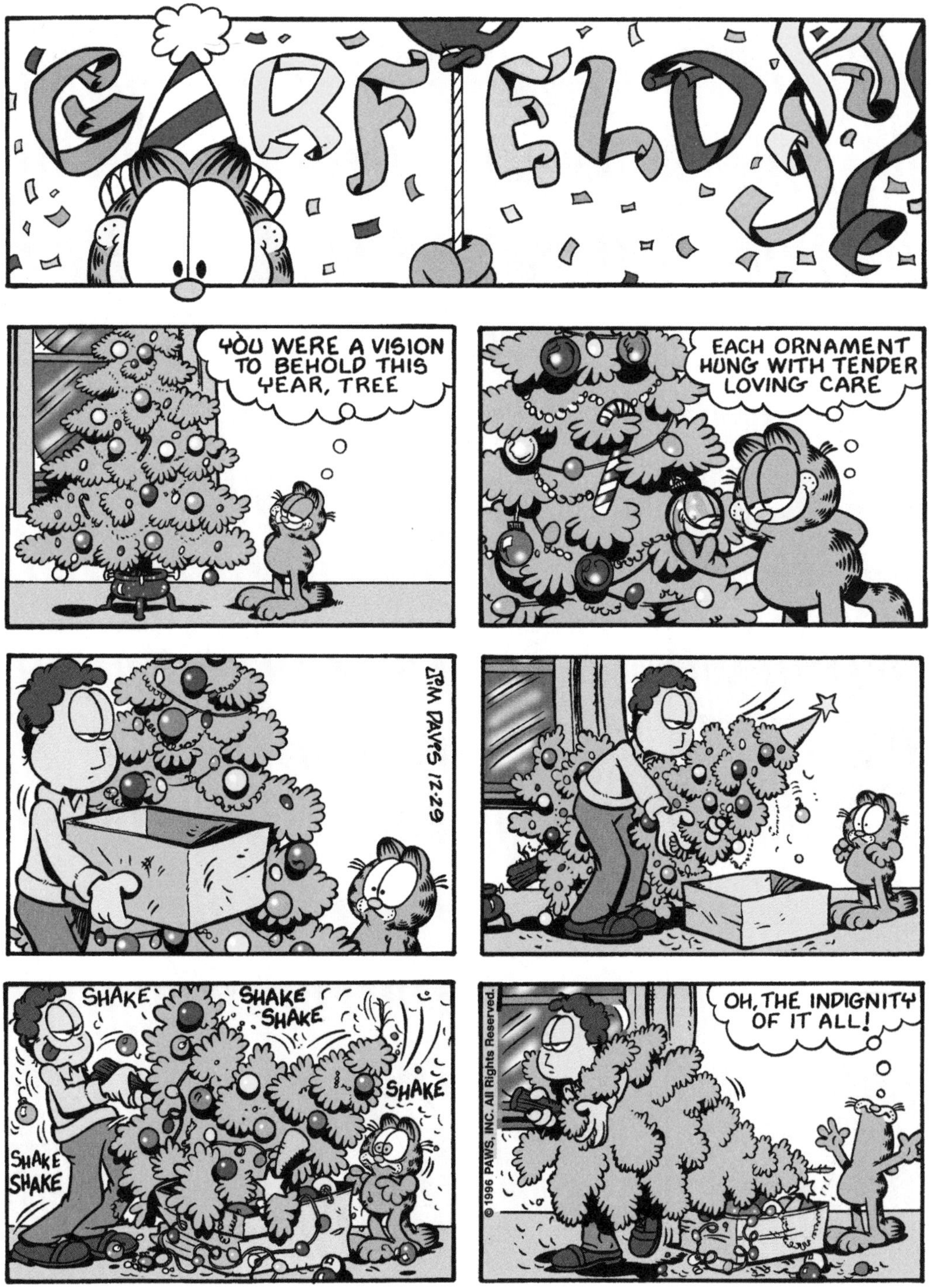
GARFIELD
YOU WERE A VISION TO BEHOLD THIS YEAR, TREE
EACH ORNAMENT HUNG WITH TENDER LOVING CARE
JIM DAVIS 12-29
SHAKE
SHAKE SHAKE
SHAKE
SHAKE SHAKE
© 1996 PAWS, INC. All Rights Reserved.
OH, THE INDIGNITY OF IT ALL!

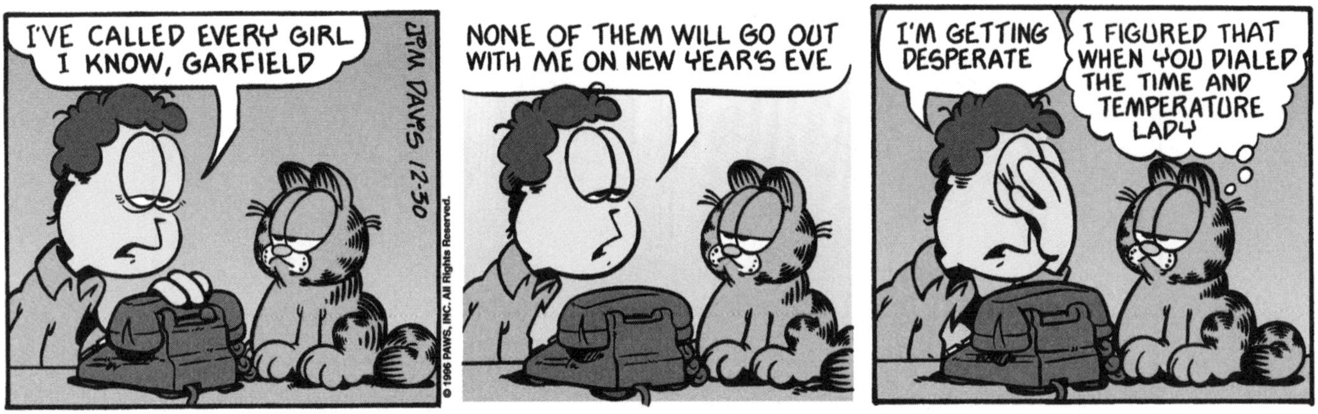

I'VE CALLED EVERY GIRL I KNOW, GARFIELD
JIM DAVIS 12-30
© 1996 PAWS, INC. All Rights Reserved.
NONE OF THEM WILL GO OUT WITH ME ON NEW YEAR'S EVE
I'M GETTING DESPERATE
I FIGURED THAT WHEN YOU DIALED THE TIME AND TEMPERATURE LADY

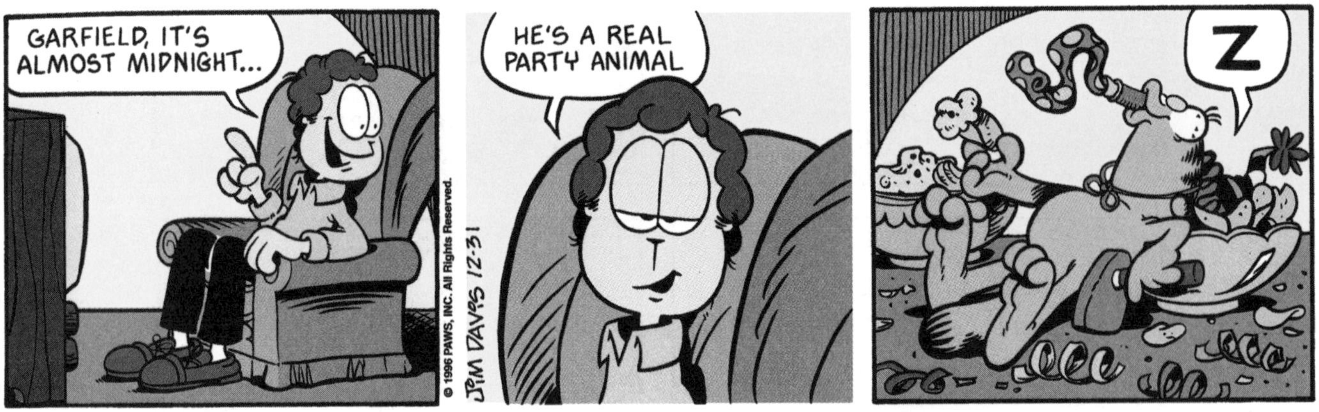

GARFIELD, IT'S ALMOST MIDNIGHT...
© 1996 PAWS, INC. All Rights Reserved.
JIM DAVIS 12-31
HE'S A REAL PARTY ANIMAL
Z

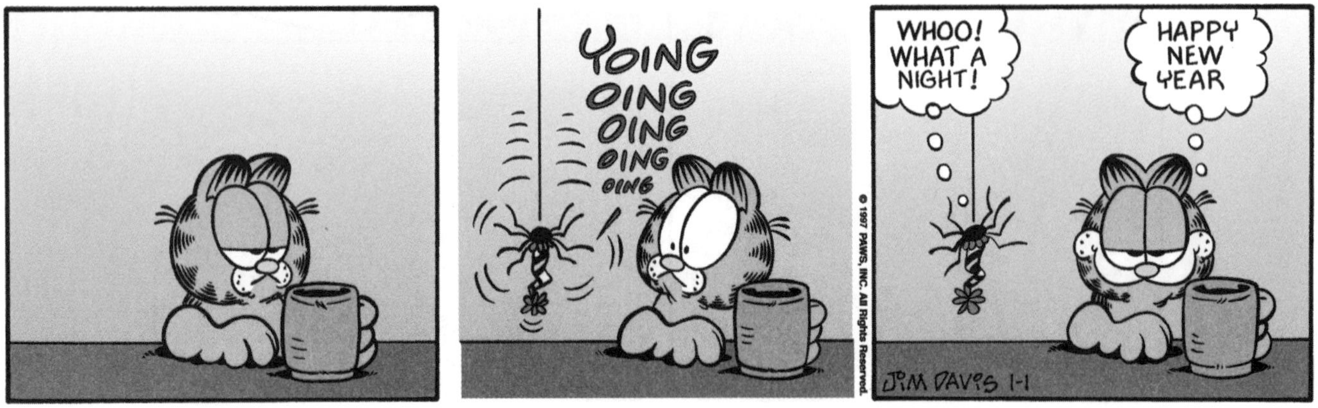

YOING
OING
OING
OING
OING
© 1997 PAWS, INC. All Rights Reserved.
WHOO! WHAT A NIGHT!
HAPPY NEW YEAR
JIM DAVIS 1-1

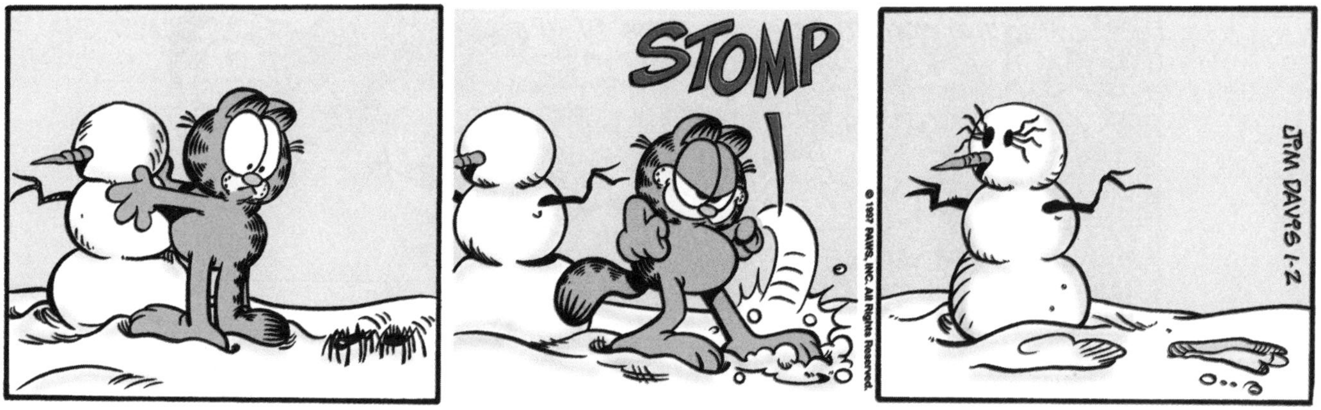
STOMP
© 1997 PAWS, INC. All Rights Reserved.
JIM DAVIS 1-2

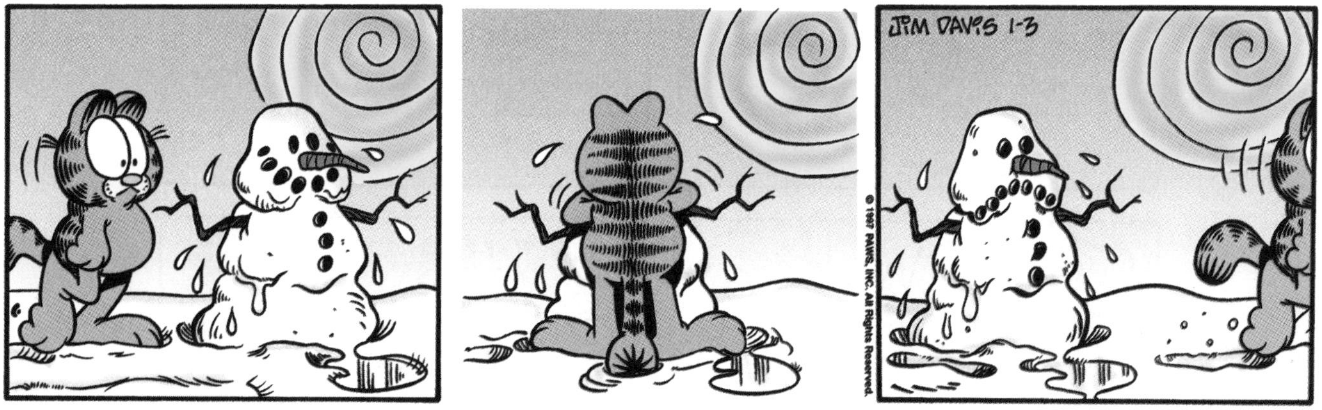
© 1997 PAWS, INC. All Rights Reserved.
JIM DAVIS 1-3

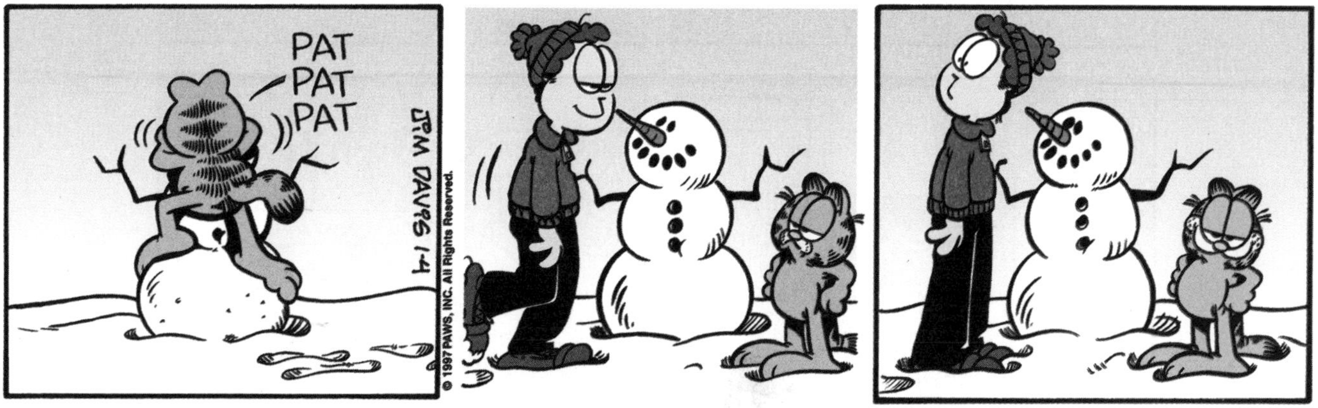
PAT
PAT
PAT
JIM DAVIS 1-4
© 1997 PAWS, INC. All Rights Reserved.

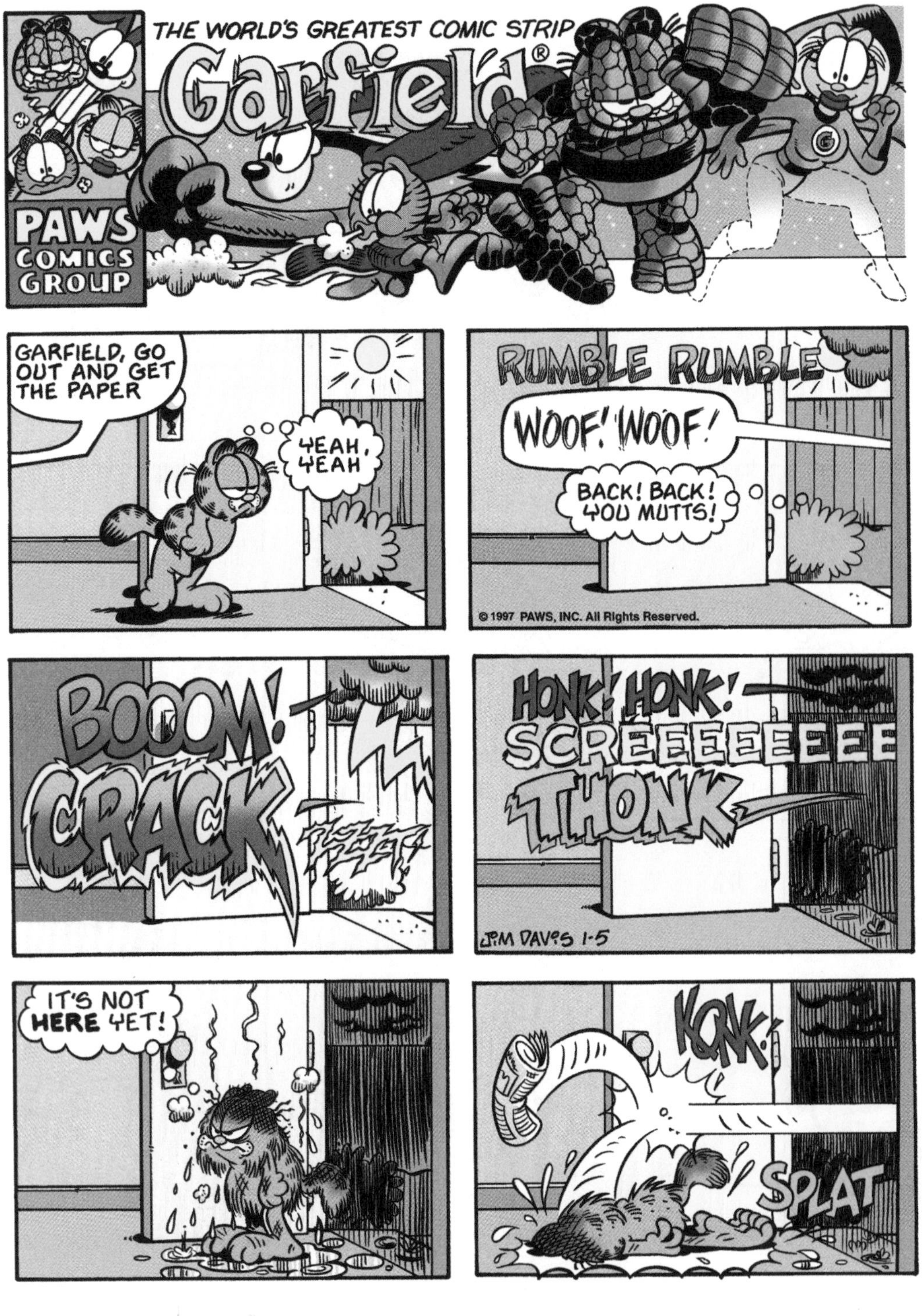

THE WORLD'S GREATEST COMIC STRIP
Garfield®
PAWS COMICS GROUP
GARFIELD, GO OUT AND GET THE PAPER
YEAH, YEAH
RUMBLE RUMBLE
WOOF! WOOF!
BACK! BACK! YOU MUTTS!
© 1997 PAWS, INC. All Rights Reserved.
BOOOM!
CRACK
HONK! HONK!
SCREEEEEEEEE
THONK
JIM DAVIS 1-5
IT'S NOT HERE YET!
KONK!
SPLAT

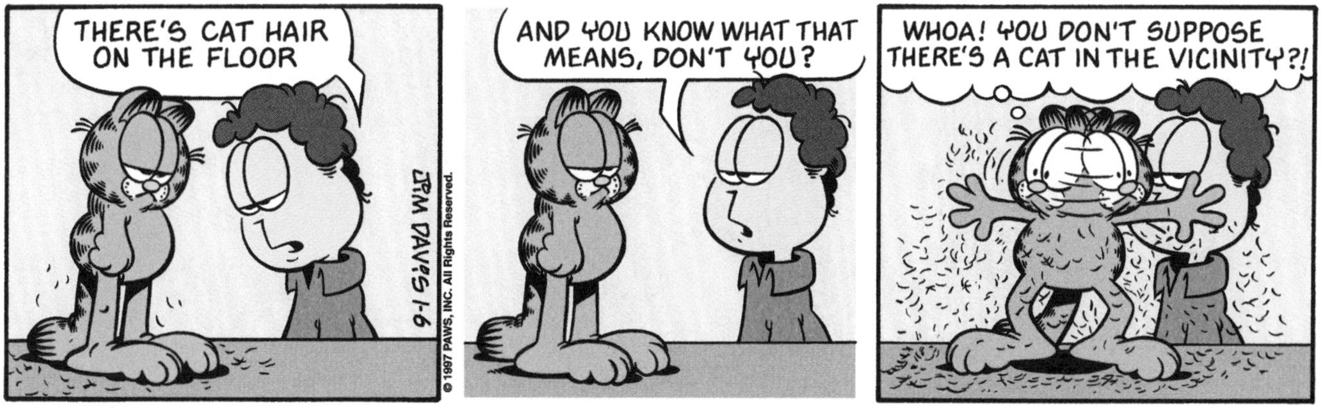
THERE'S CAT HAIR ON THE FLOOR
JIM DAVIS 1-6
© 1997 PAWS, INC. All Rights Reserved.
AND YOU KNOW WHAT THAT MEANS, DON'T YOU?
WHOA! YOU DON'T SUPPOSE THERE'S A CAT IN THE VICINITY?!

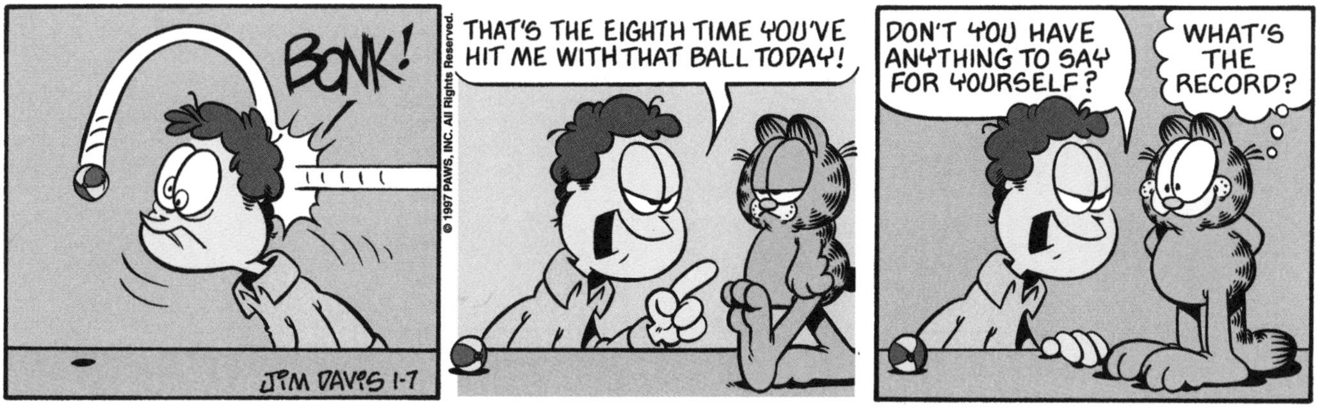
BONK!
JIM DAVIS 1-7
© 1997 PAWS, INC. All Rights Reserved.
THAT'S THE EIGHTH TIME YOU'VE HIT ME WITH THAT BALL TODAY!
DON'T YOU HAVE ANYTHING TO SAY FOR YOURSELF?
WHAT'S THE RECORD?

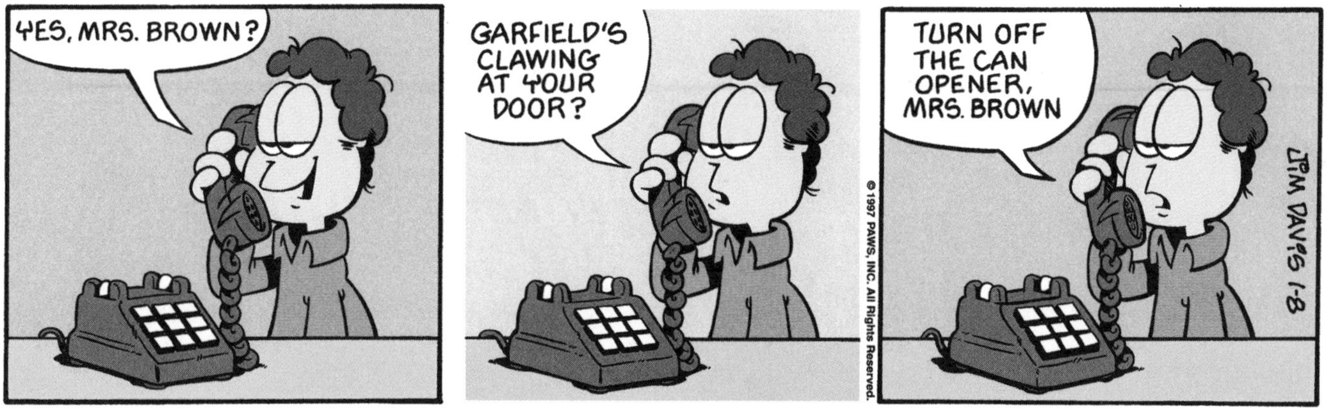
YES, MRS. BROWN?
GARFIELD'S CLAWING AT YOUR DOOR?
© 1997 PAWS, INC. All Rights Reserved.
TURN OFF THE CAN OPENER, MRS. BROWN
JIM DAVIS 1-8

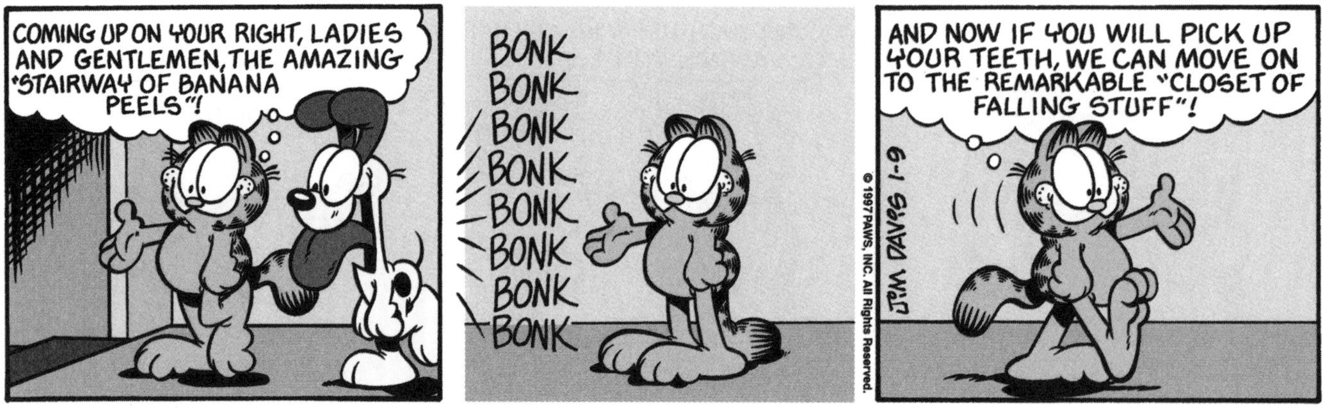
COMING UP ON YOUR RIGHT, LADIES AND GENTLEMEN, THE AMAZING "STAIRWAY OF BANANA PEELS"!
BONK BONK BONK BONK BONK BONK BONK BONK
AND NOW IF YOU WILL PICK UP YOUR TEETH, WE CAN MOVE ON TO THE REMARKABLE "CLOSET OF FALLING STUFF"!
JPM DAVPS 1-9
© 1997 PAWS, INC. All Rights Reserved.

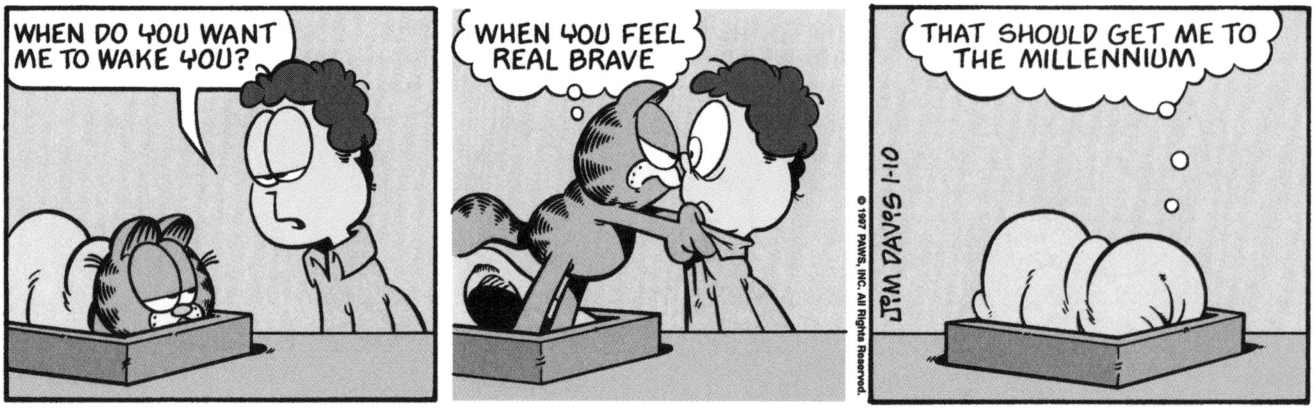
WHEN DO YOU WANT ME TO WAKE YOU?
WHEN YOU FEEL REAL BRAVE
THAT SHOULD GET ME TO THE MILLENNIUM
JPM DAVPS 1-10
© 1997 PAWS, INC. All Rights Reserved.

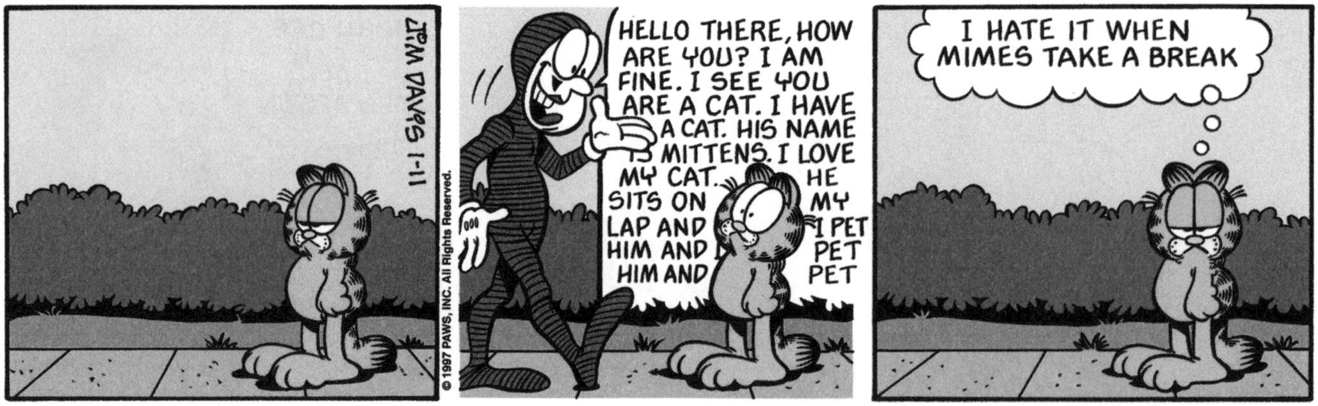
JPM DAVPS 1-11
© 1997 PAWS, INC. All Rights Reserved.
HELLO THERE, HOW
ARE YOU? I AM
FINE. I SEE YOU
ARE A CAT. I HAVE
A CAT. HIS NAME
MITTENS. I LOVE
MY CAT. HE
SITS ON MY
LAP AND I PET
HIM AND PET
HIM AND PET
I HATE IT WHEN MIMES TAKE A BREAK

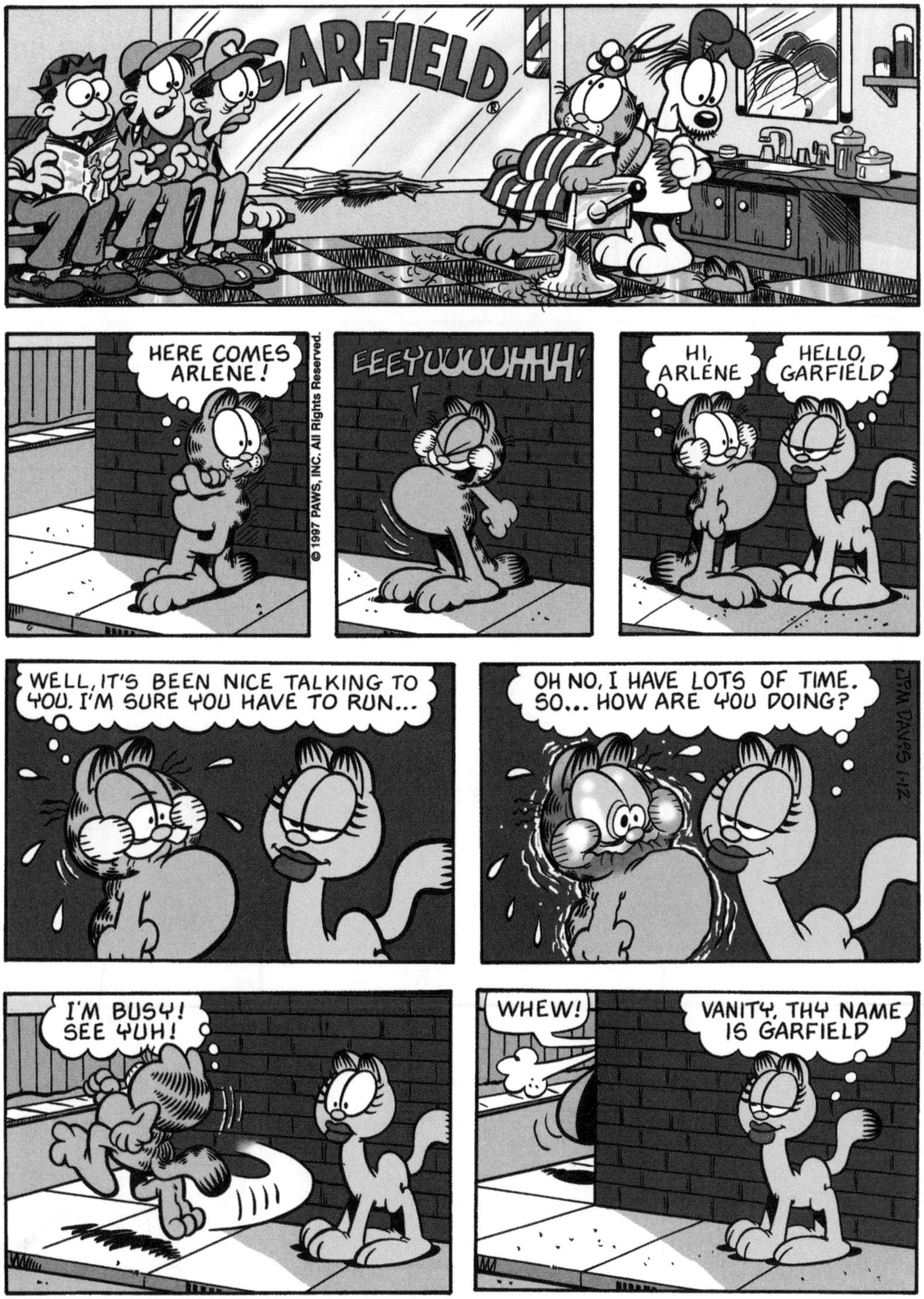
GARFIELD®
© 1997 PAWS, INC. All Rights Reserved.
HERE COMES ARLENE!
EEEYUUUUHHH!
HI, ARLENE
HELLO, GARFIELD
WELL, IT'S BEEN NICE TALKING TO YOU. I'M SURE YOU HAVE TO RUN...
OH NO, I HAVE LOTS OF TIME. SO... HOW ARE YOU DOING?
JPM DAVIS 1-12
I'M BUSY! SEE YUH!
WHEW!
VANITY, THY NAME IS GARFIELD

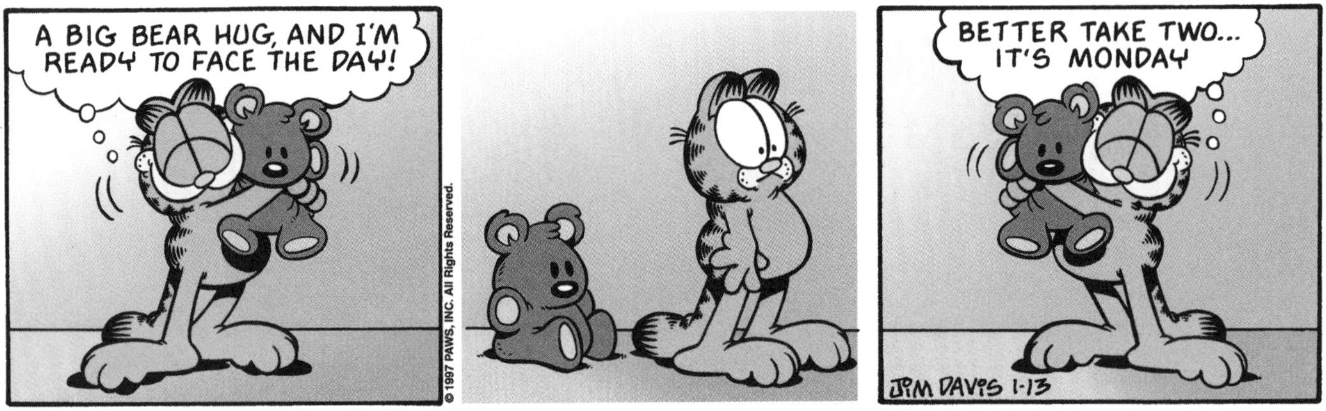
A BIG BEAR HUG, AND I'M READY TO FACE THE DAY!
© 1997 PAWS, INC. All Rights Reserved.
BETTER TAKE TWO... IT'S MONDAY
JIM DAVIS 1-13

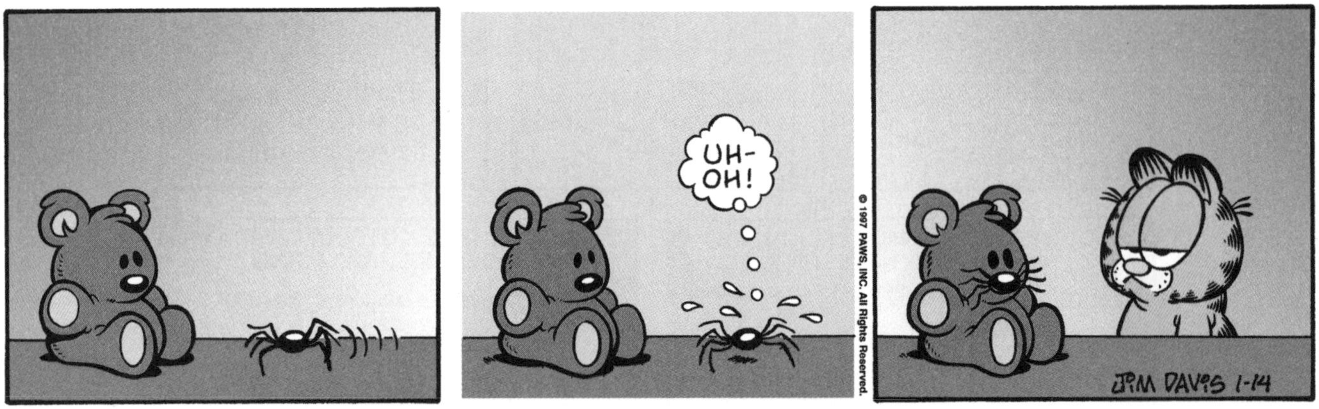
UH-OH!
© 1997 PAWS, INC. All Rights Reserved.
JIM DAVIS 1-14

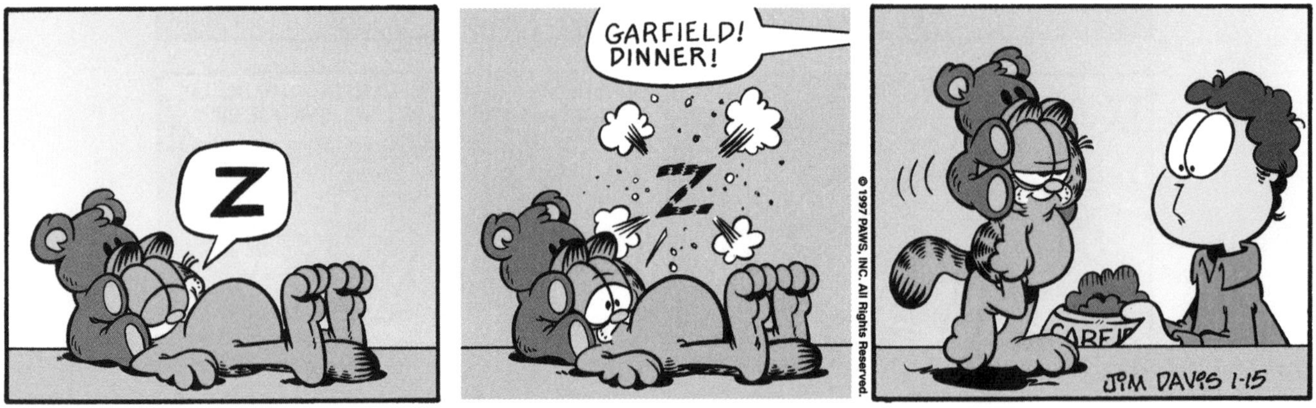
Z
GARFIELD! DINNER!
© 1997 PAWS, INC. All Rights Reserved.
JIM DAVIS 1-15

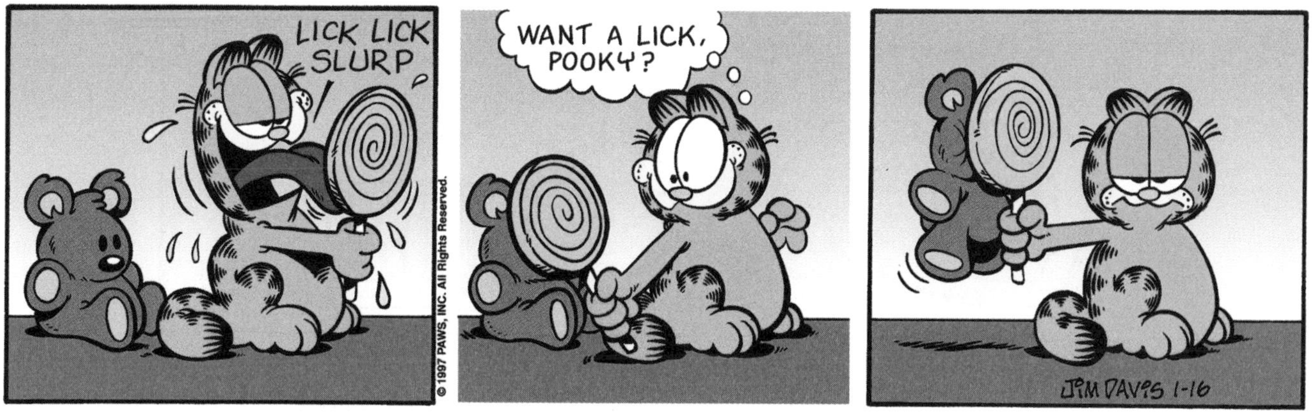
LICK LICK SLURP
© 1997 PAWS, INC. All Rights Reserved.
WANT A LICK, POOKY?
JIM DAVIS 1-16

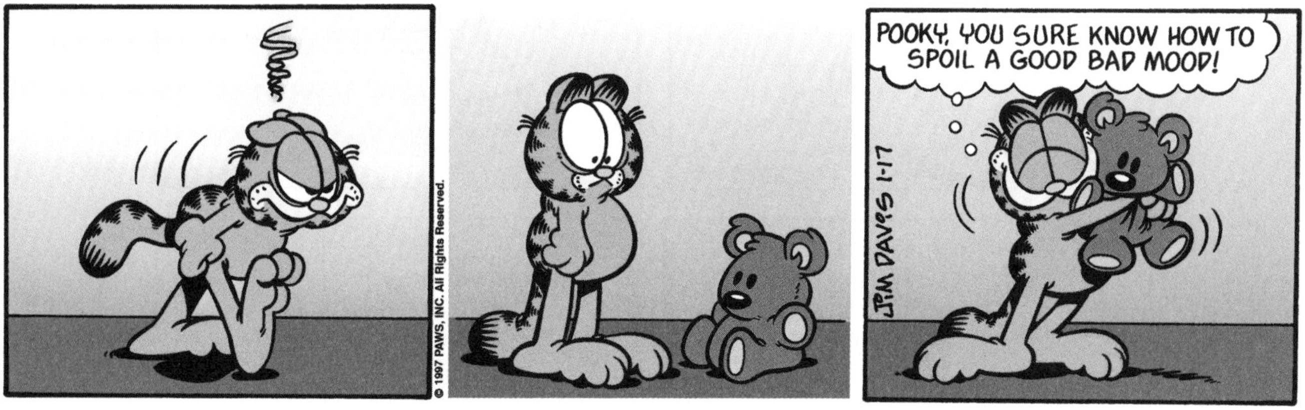
© 1997 PAWS, INC. All Rights Reserved.
JIM DAVIS 1-17
POOKY, YOU SURE KNOW HOW TO SPOIL A GOOD BAD MOOD!

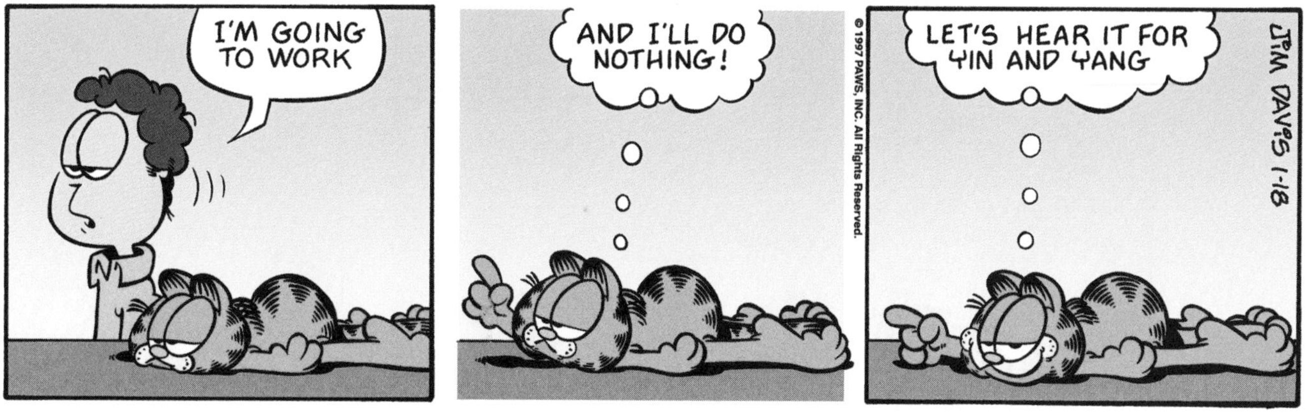
I'M GOING TO WORK
AND I'LL DO NOTHING!
© 1997 PAWS, INC. All Rights Reserved.
LET'S HEAR IT FOR YIN AND YANG
JIM DAVIS 1-18

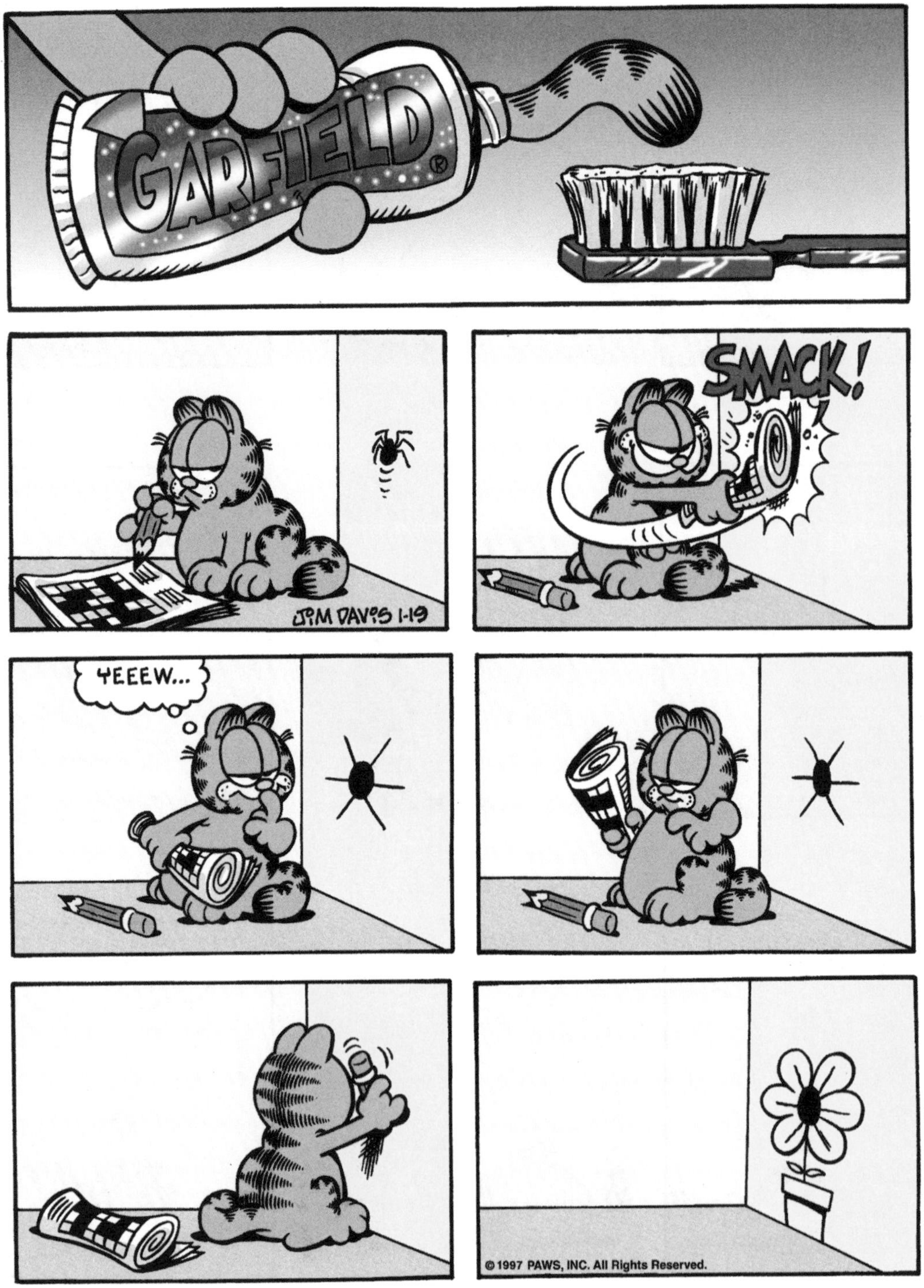
GARFIELD®
JIM DAVIS 1-19
SMACK!
YEEEW...
© 1997 PAWS, INC. All Rights Reserved.

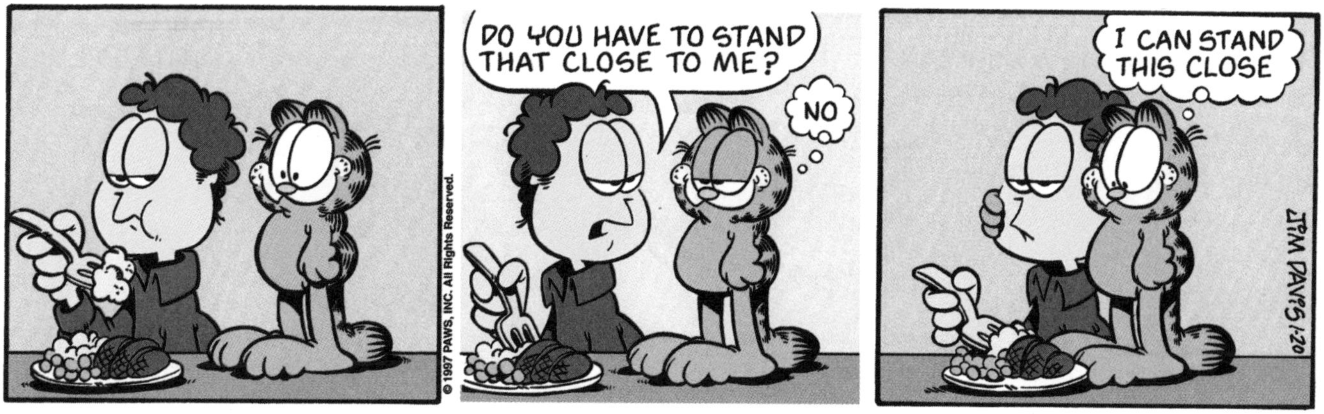
DO YOU HAVE TO STAND THAT CLOSE TO ME?
NO
I CAN STAND THIS CLOSE
© 1997 PAWS, INC. All Rights Reserved.
JIM DAVIS 1-20

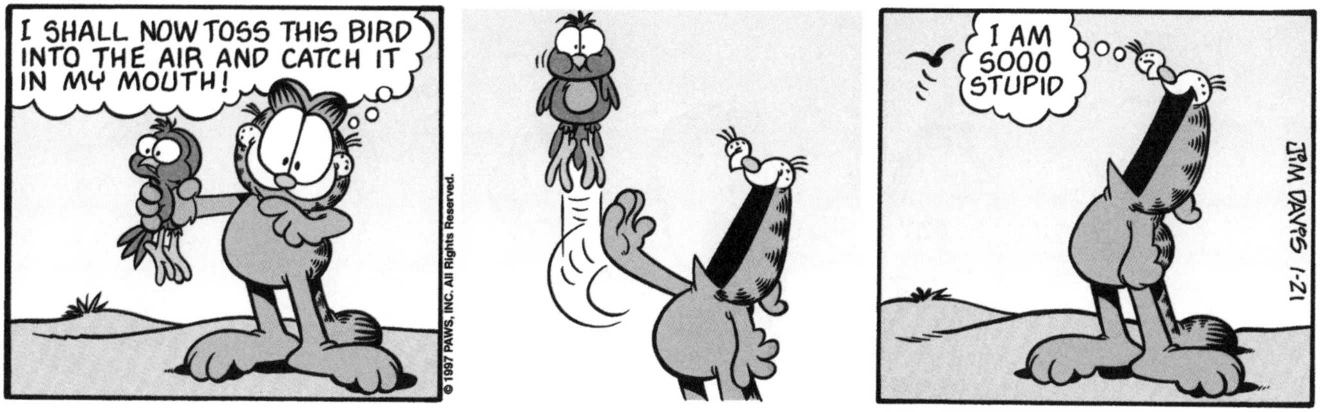
I SHALL NOW TOSS THIS BIRD INTO THE AIR AND CATCH IT IN MY MOUTH!
I AM SOOO STUPID
© 1997 PAWS, INC. All Rights Reserved.
JIM DAVIS 1-21

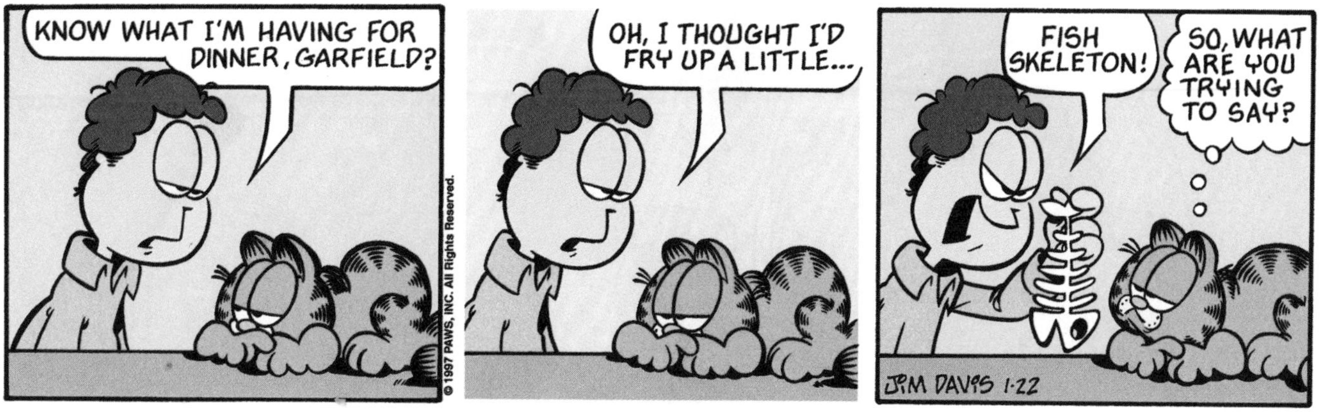
KNOW WHAT I'M HAVING FOR DINNER, GARFIELD?
OH, I THOUGHT I'D FRY UP A LITTLE...
FISH SKELETON!
SO, WHAT ARE YOU TRYING TO SAY?
© 1997 PAWS, INC. All Rights Reserved.
JIM DAVIS 1-22

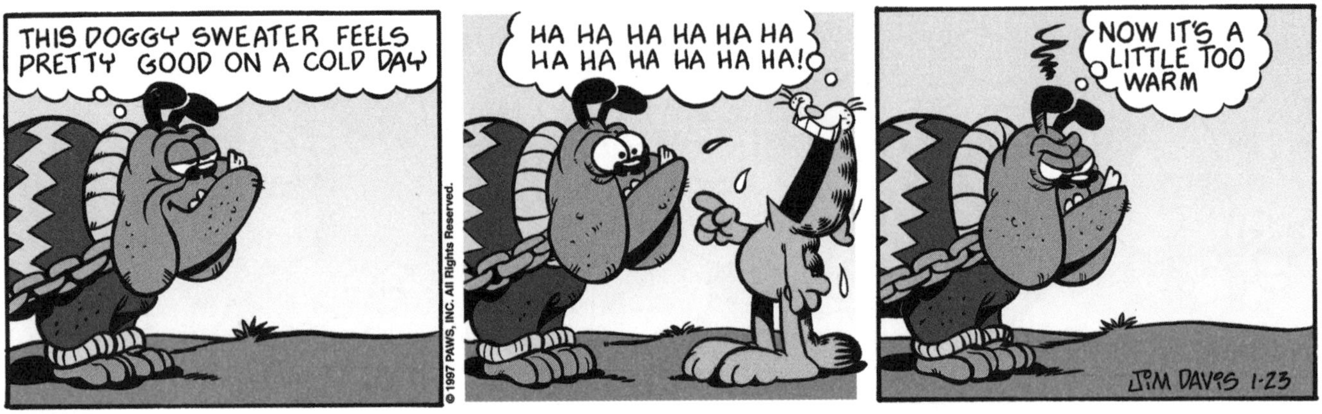
THIS DOGGY SWEATER FEELS PRETTY GOOD ON A COLD DAY
HA HA HA HA HA HA HA HA HA HA HA HA!
NOW IT'S A LITTLE TOO WARM
© 1997 PAWS, INC. All Rights Reserved.
JIM DAVIS 1-23

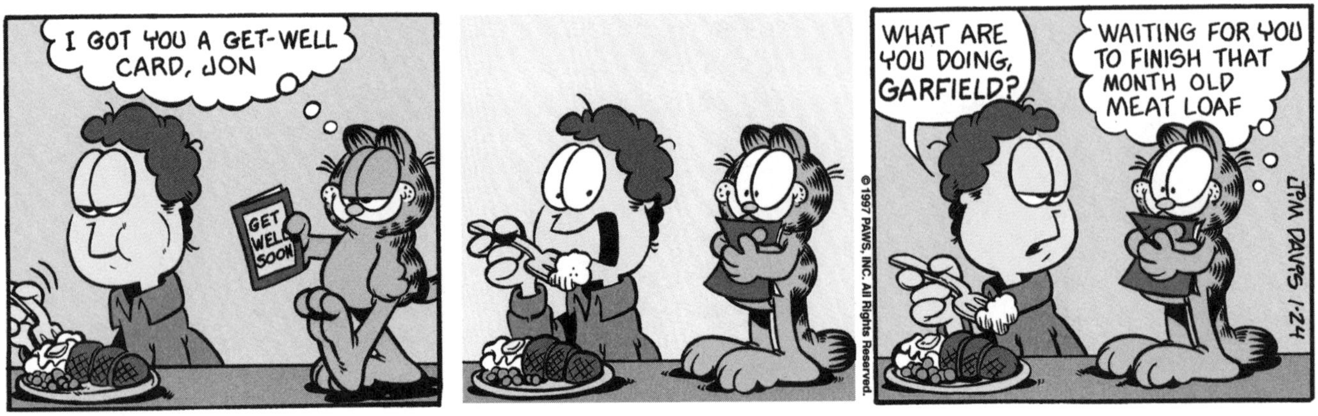
I GOT YOU A GET-WELL CARD, JON
GET WELL SOON
WHAT ARE YOU DOING, GARFIELD?
WAITING FOR YOU TO FINISH THAT MONTH OLD MEAT LOAF
© 1997 PAWS, INC. All Rights Reserved.
JIM DAVIS 1-24

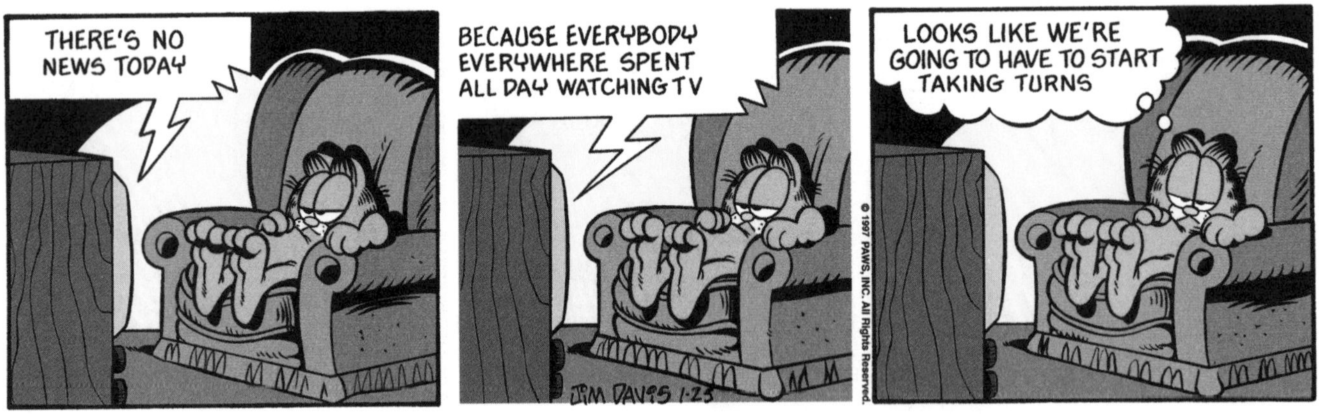
THERE'S NO NEWS TODAY
BECAUSE EVERYBODY EVERYWHERE SPENT ALL DAY WATCHING TV
LOOKS LIKE WE'RE GOING TO HAVE TO START TAKING TURNS
JIM DAVIS 1-25
© 1997 PAWS, INC. All Rights Reserved.

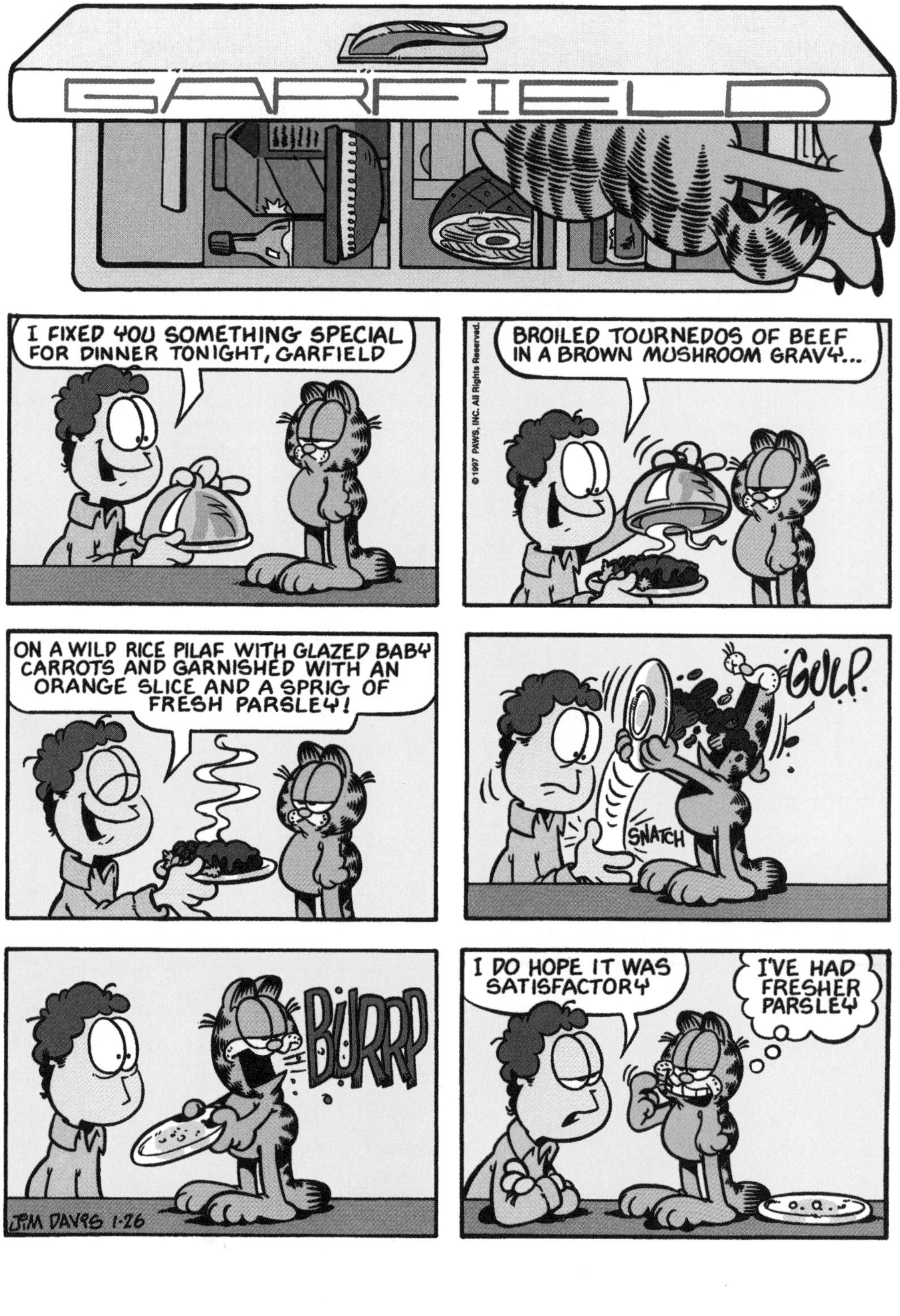
GARFIELD
I FIXED YOU SOMETHING SPECIAL FOR DINNER TONIGHT, GARFIELD
© 1997 PAWS, INC. All Rights Reserved.
BROILED TOURNEDOS OF BEEF IN A BROWN MUSHROOM GRAVY...
ON A WILD RICE PILAF WITH GLAZED BABY CARROTS AND GARNISHED WITH AN ORANGE SLICE AND A SPRIG OF FRESH PARSLEY!
GULP
SNATCH
BURRP
JIM DAVIS 1-26
I DO HOPE IT WAS SATISFACTORY
I'VE HAD FRESHER PARSLEY

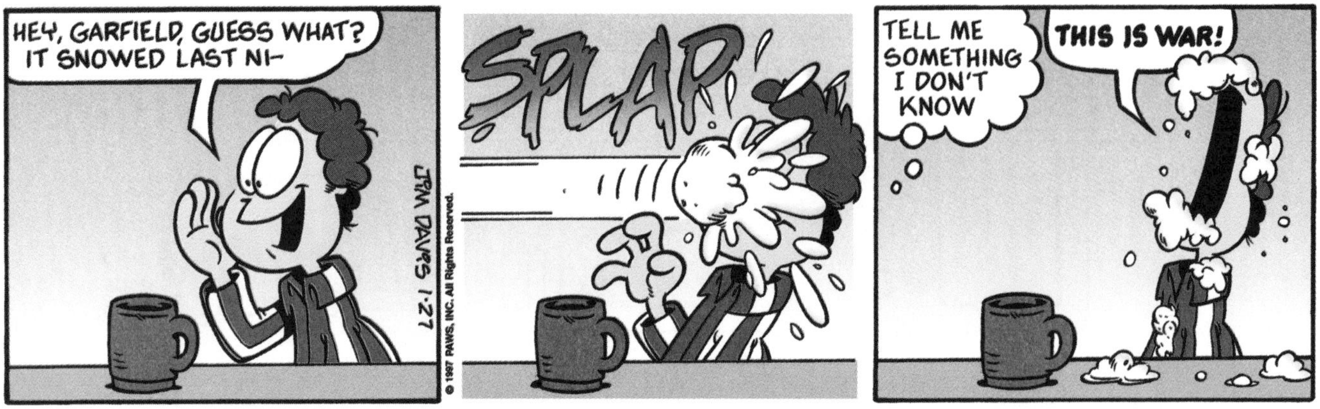
HEY, GARFIELD, GUESS WHAT? IT SNOWED LAST NI–
JIM DAVIS 1-27
SPLAP!
© 1997 PAWS, INC. All Rights Reserved.
TELL ME SOMETHING I DON'T KNOW
THIS IS WAR!

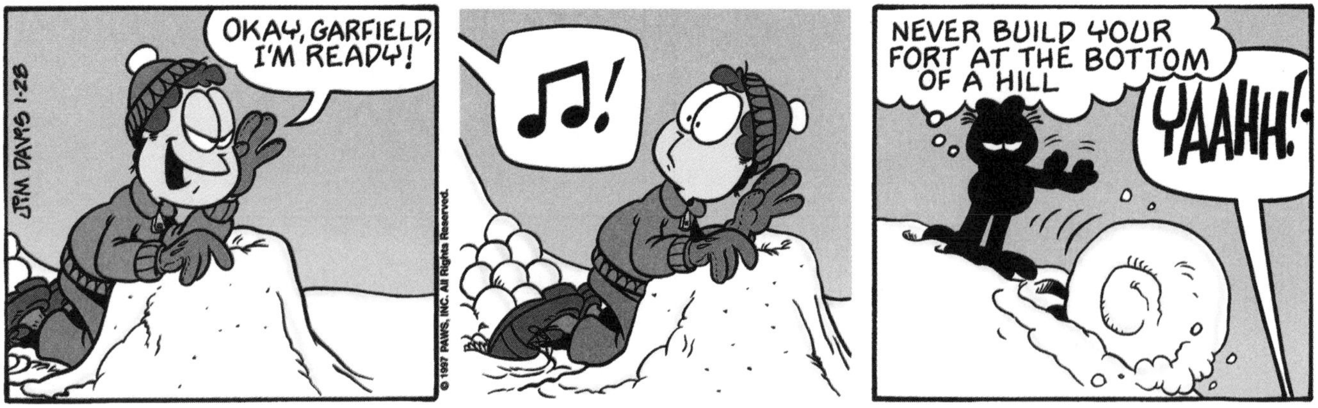
OKAY, GARFIELD, I'M READY!
JIM DAVIS 1-28
© 1997 PAWS, INC. All Rights Reserved.
♫!
NEVER BUILD YOUR FORT AT THE BOTTOM OF A HILL
YAAHH!

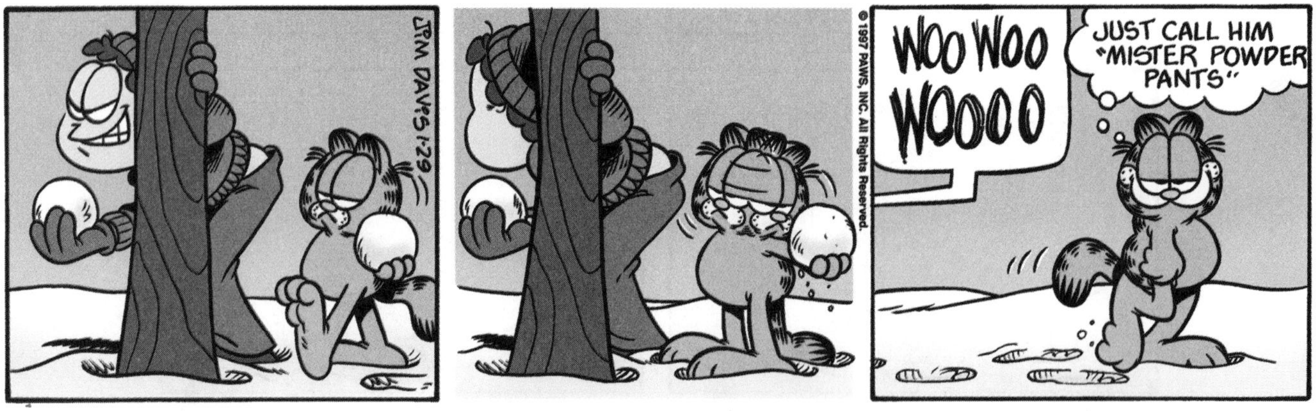
JIM DAVIS 1-29
© 1997 PAWS, INC. All Rights Reserved.
WOO WOO WOOOO
JUST CALL HIM "MISTER POWDER PANTS"

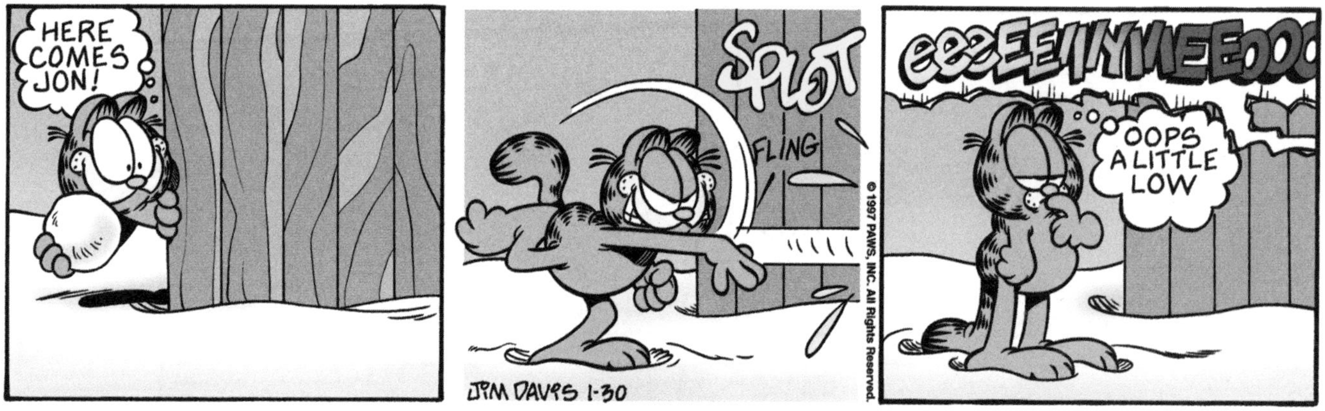
HERE COMES JON!
SPLOT
FLING
JIM DAVIS 1-30
© 1997 PAWS, INC. All Rights Reserved.
OOPS A LITTLE LOW

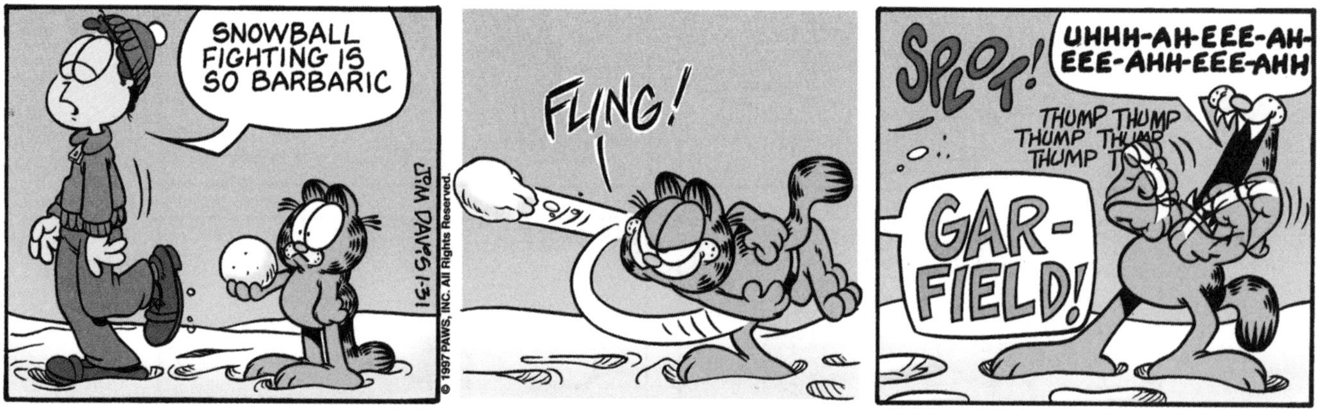
SNOWBALL FIGHTING IS SO BARBARIC
JIM DAVIS 1-31
© 1997 PAWS, INC. All Rights Reserved.
FLING!
SPLOT!
UHHH-AH-EEE-AH-EEE-AHH-EEE-AHH
THUMP THUMP THUMP
GAR-FIELD!

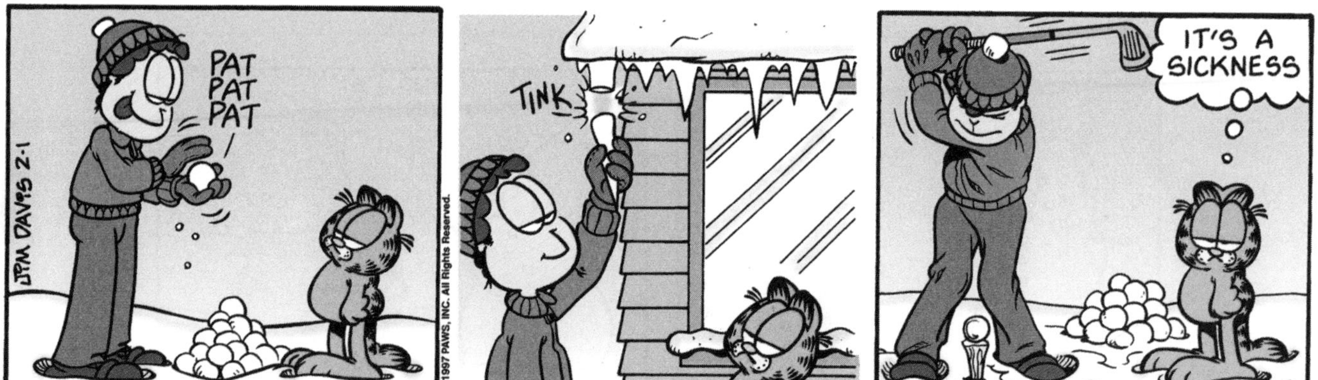
JIM DAVIS 2-1
PAT PAT PAT
© 1997 PAWS, INC. All Rights Reserved.
TINK
IT'S A SICKNESS

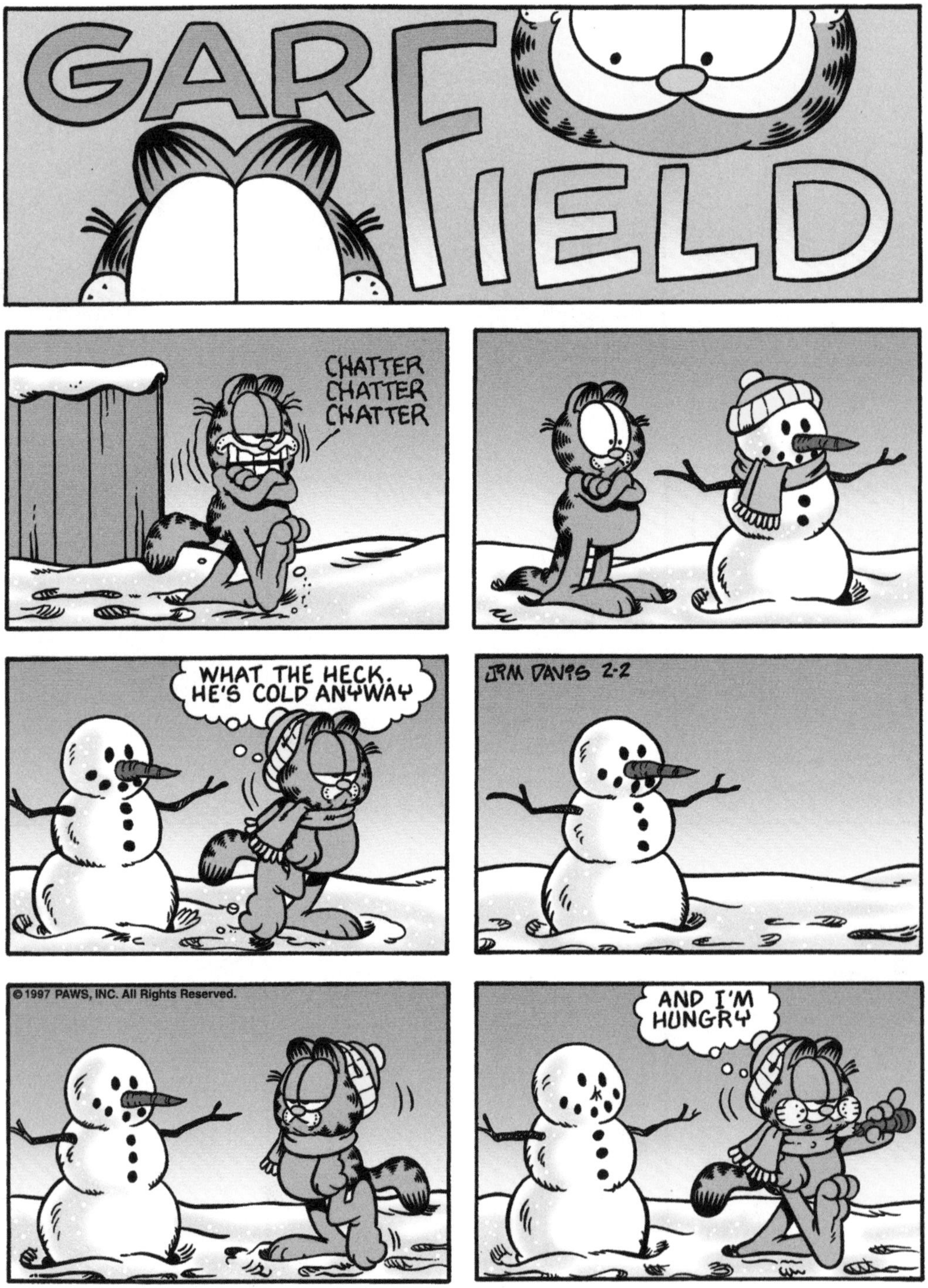
GARFIELD
CHATTER CHATTER CHATTER
WHAT THE HECK. HE'S COLD ANYWAY
JIM DAVIS 2-2
©1997 PAWS, INC. All Rights Reserved.
AND I'M HUNGRY

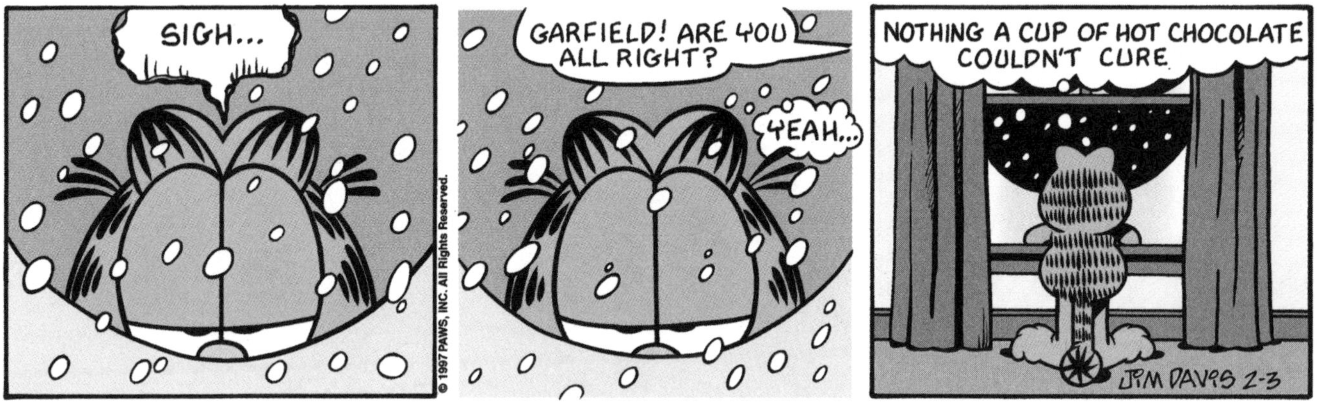
SIGH...
GARFIELD! ARE YOU ALL RIGHT?
YEAH...
NOTHING A CUP OF HOT CHOCOLATE COULDN'T CURE
JIM DAVIS 2-3
© 1997 PAWS, INC. All Rights Reserved.

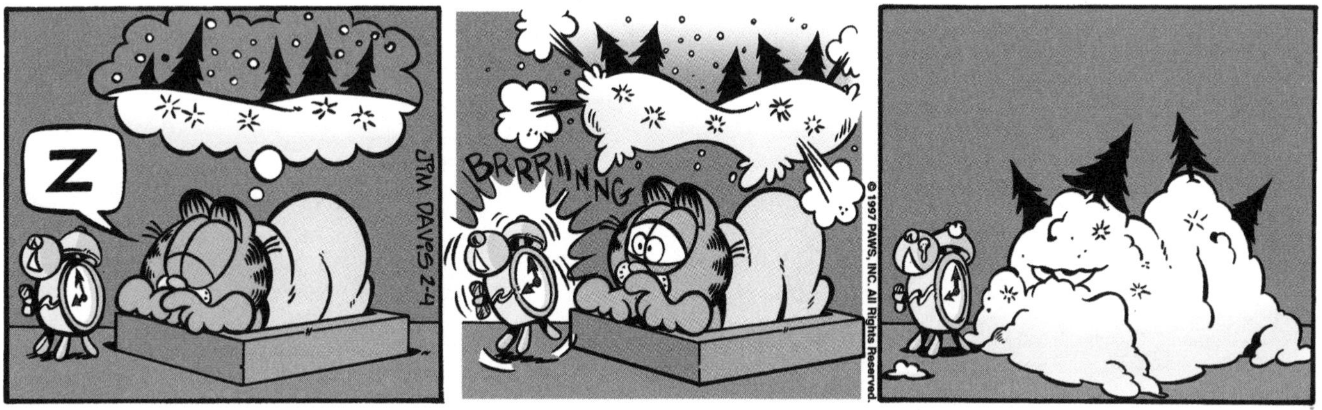
Z
JIM DAVIS 2-4
BRRRIINNG
© 1997 PAWS, INC. All Rights Reserved.

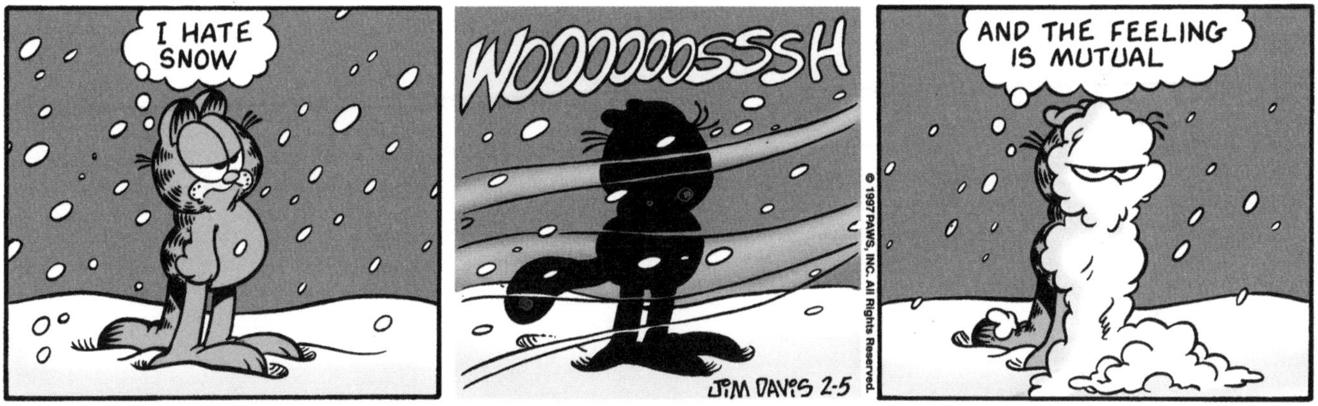
I HATE SNOW
WOOOOOOOSSSH
JIM DAVIS 2-5
© 1997 PAWS, INC. All Rights Reserved.
AND THE FEELING IS MUTUAL

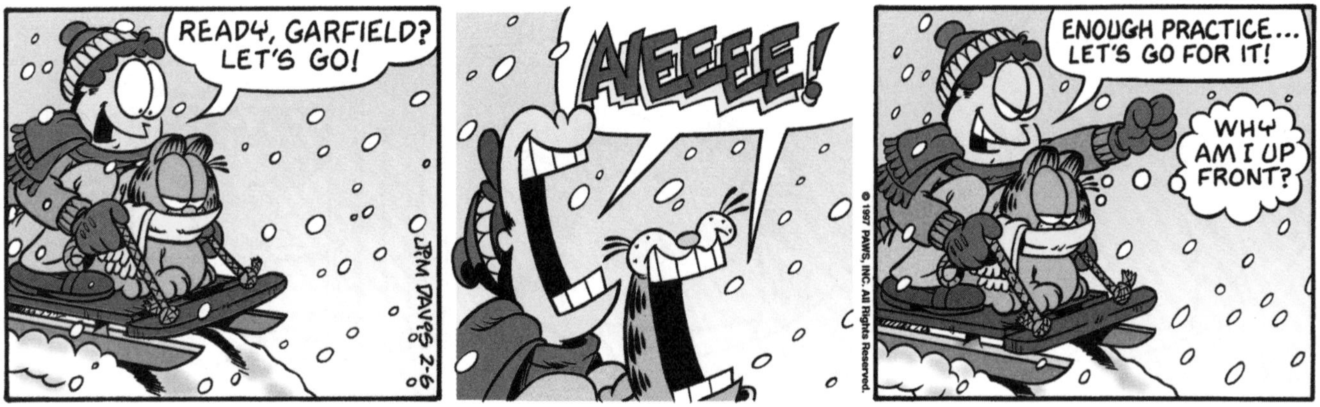
READY, GARFIELD? LET'S GO!
JIM DAVIS 2-6
AIEEEE!
© 1997 PAWS, INC. All Rights Reserved.
ENOUGH PRACTICE... LET'S GO FOR IT!
WHY AM I UP FRONT?

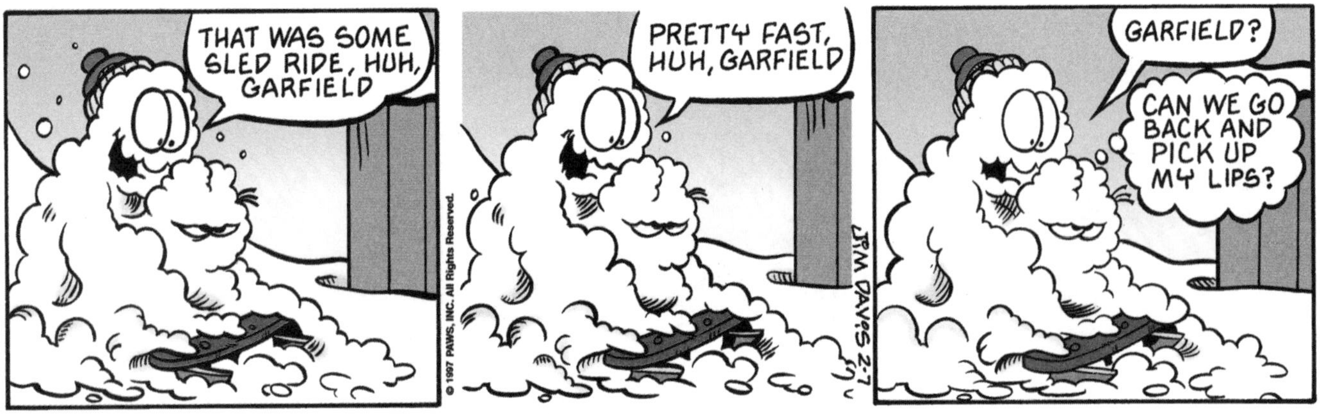
THAT WAS SOME SLED RIDE, HUH, GARFIELD
© 1997 PAWS, INC. All Rights Reserved.
PRETTY FAST, HUH, GARFIELD
JIM DAVIS 2-7
GARFIELD?
CAN WE GO BACK AND PICK UP MY LIPS?

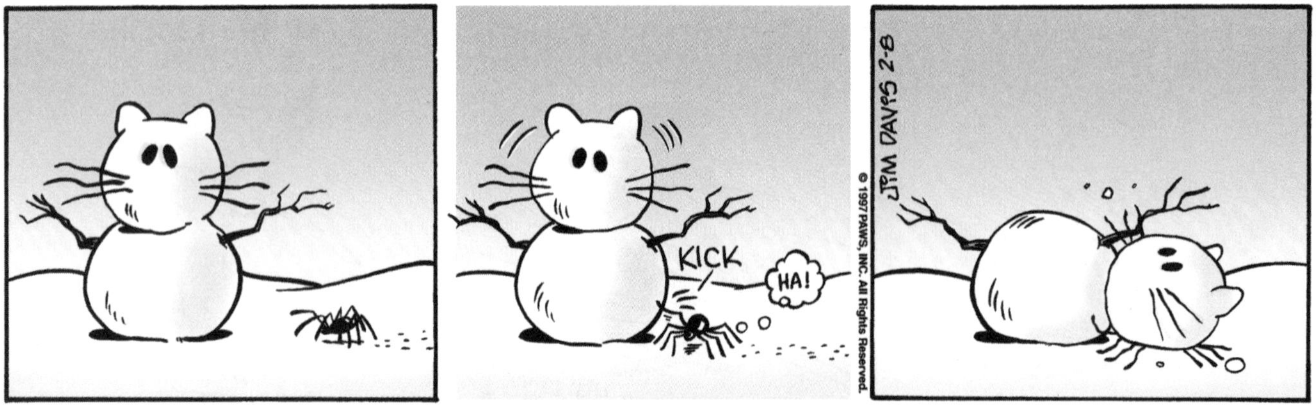
KICK
HA!
© 1997 PAWS, INC. All Rights Reserved.
JIM DAVIS 2-8

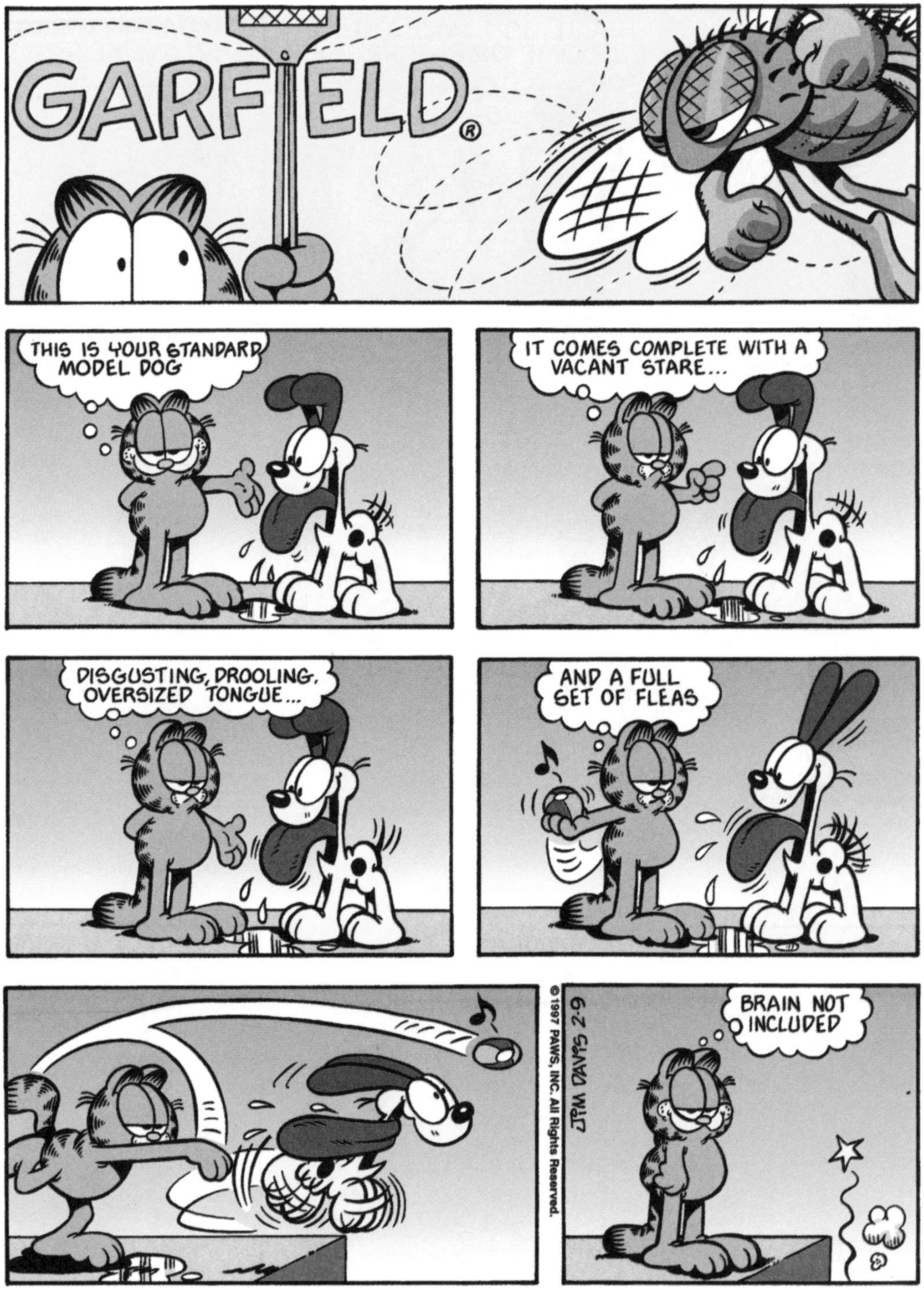
GARFIELD®
THIS IS YOUR STANDARD MODEL DOG
IT COMES COMPLETE WITH A VACANT STARE...
DISGUSTING, DROOLING, OVERSIZED TONGUE...
AND A FULL SET OF FLEAS
© 1997 PAWS, INC. All Rights Reserved.
JPM DAVIS 2-9
BRAIN NOT INCLUDED

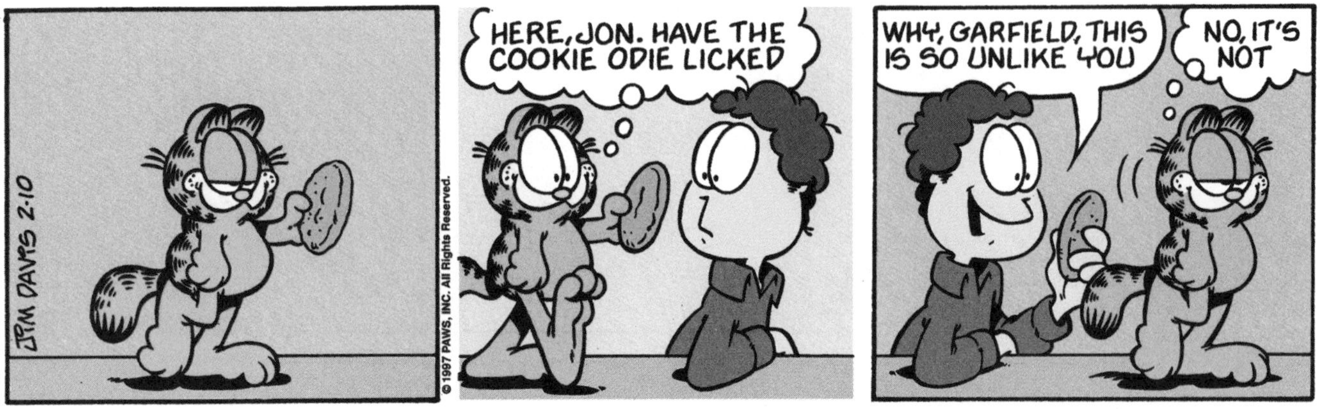
JIM DAVIS 2-10
HERE, JON. HAVE THE COOKIE ODIE LICKED
© 1997 PAWS, INC. All Rights Reserved.
WHY, GARFIELD, THIS IS SO UNLIKE YOU
NO, IT'S NOT

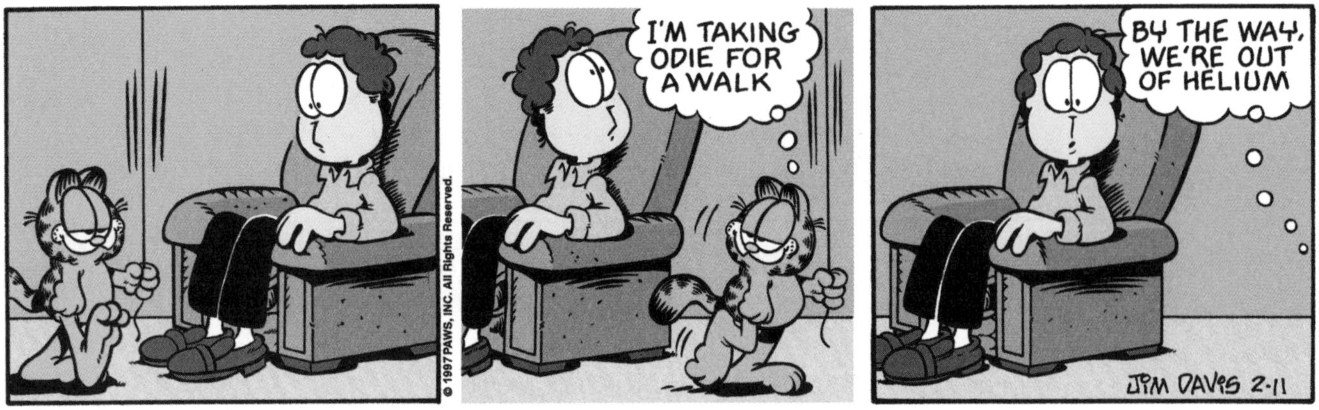
© 1997 PAWS, INC. All Rights Reserved.
I'M TAKING ODIE FOR A WALK
BY THE WAY, WE'RE OUT OF HELIUM
JIM DAVIS 2-11

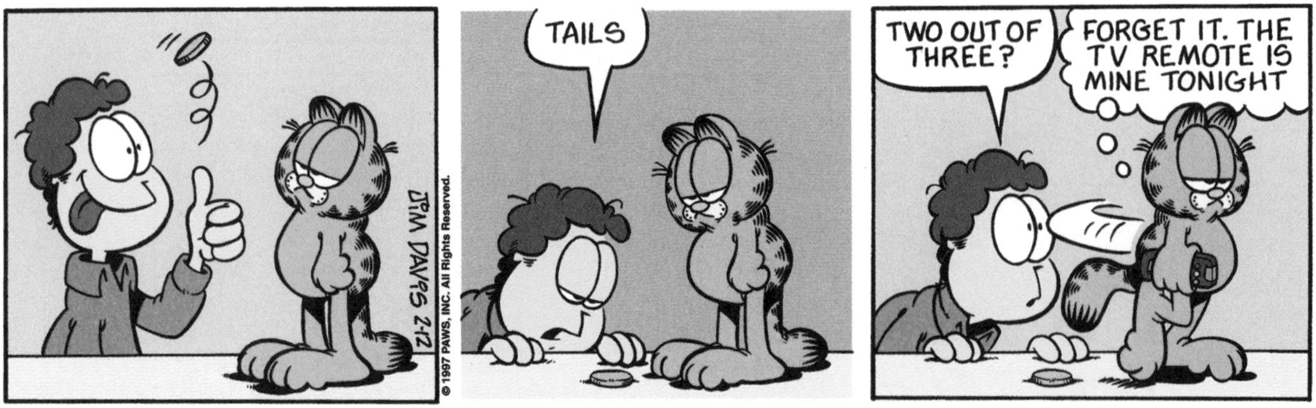
JIM DAVIS 2-12
© 1997 PAWS, INC. All Rights Reserved.
TAILS
TWO OUT OF THREE?
FORGET IT. THE TV REMOTE IS MINE TONIGHT

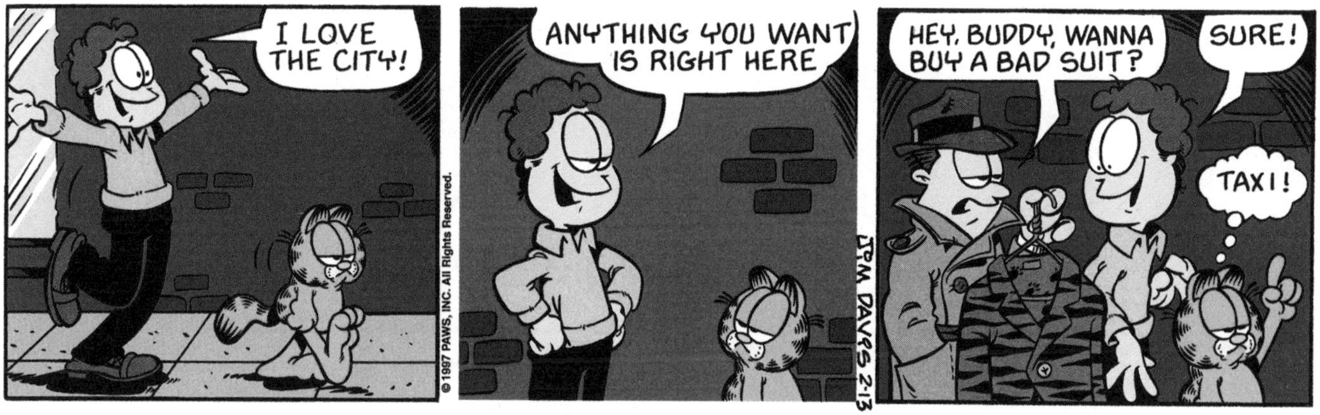
I LOVE THE CITY!
© 1997 PAWS, INC. All Rights Reserved.
ANYTHING YOU WANT IS RIGHT HERE
JIM DAVIS 2-13
HEY, BUDDY, WANNA BUY A BAD SUIT?
SURE!
TAXI!

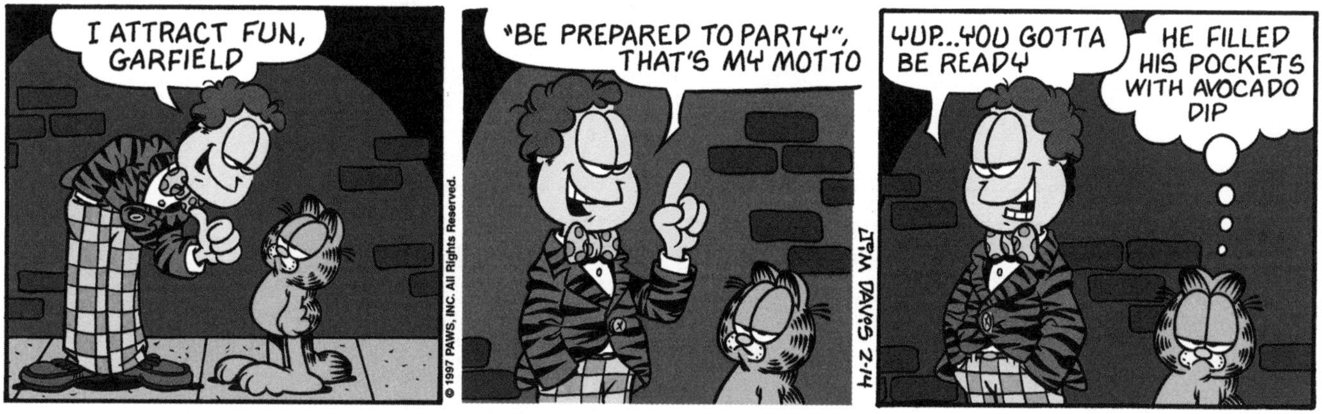
I ATTRACT FUN, GARFIELD
© 1997 PAWS, INC. All Rights Reserved.
"BE PREPARED TO PARTY", THAT'S MY MOTTO
JIM DAVIS 2-14
YUP...YOU GOTTA BE READY
HE FILLED HIS POCKETS WITH AVOCADO DIP

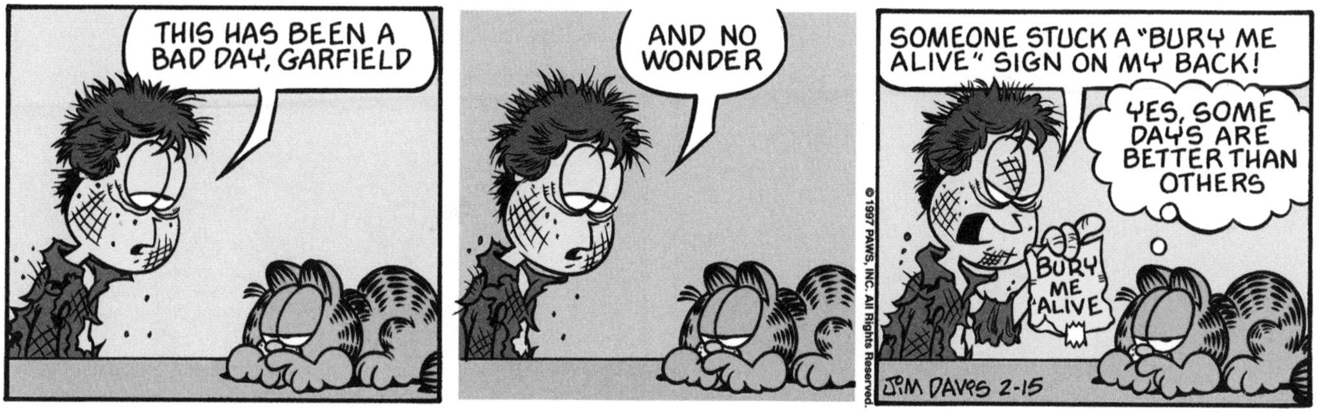
THIS HAS BEEN A BAD DAY, GARFIELD
AND NO WONDER
© 1997 PAWS, INC. All Rights Reserved.
SOMEONE STUCK A "BURY ME ALIVE" SIGN ON MY BACK!
BURY ME ALIVE
YES, SOME DAYS ARE BETTER THAN OTHERS
JIM DAVIS 2-15

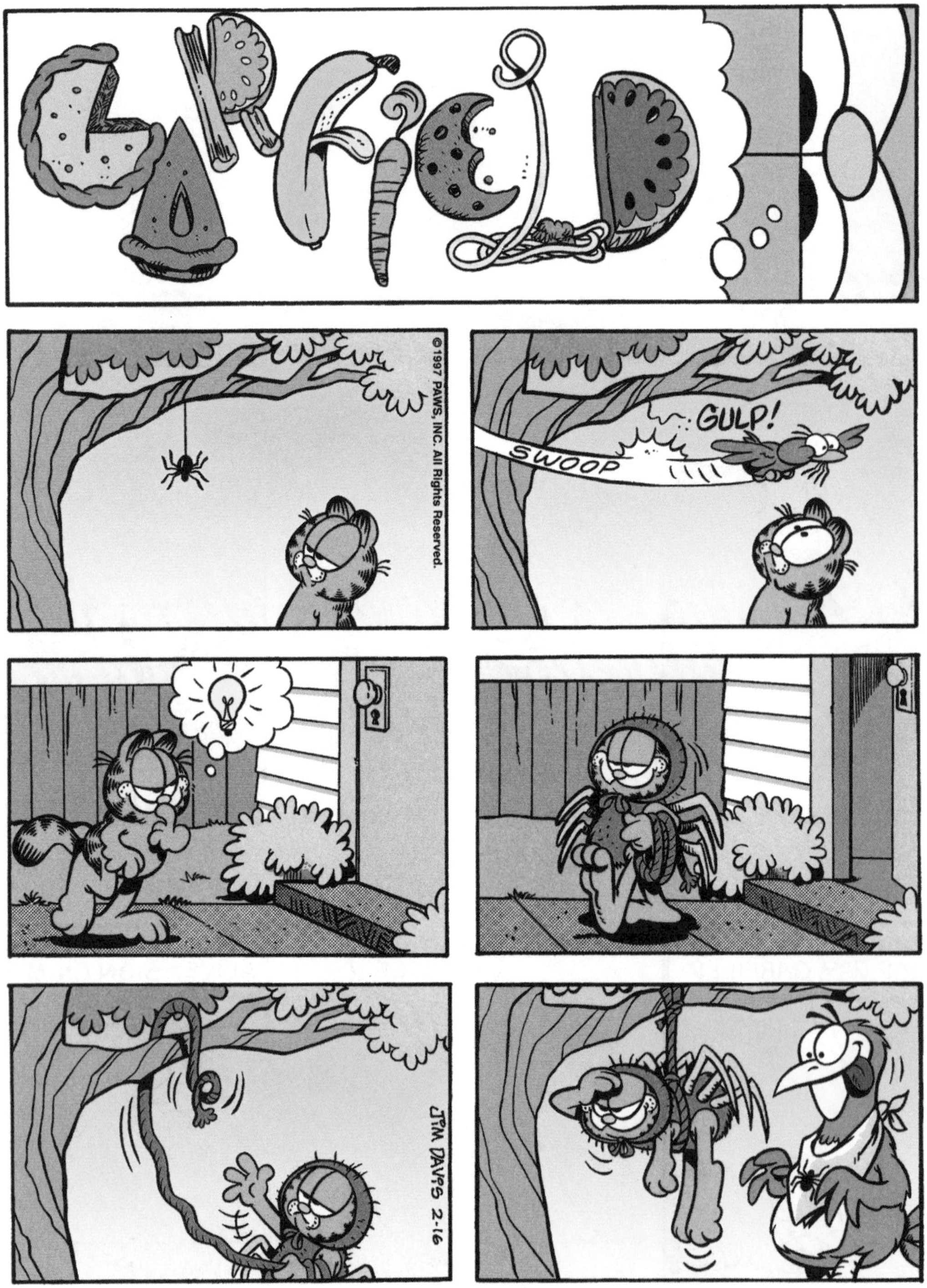
GARFIELD
© 1997 PAWS, INC. All Rights Reserved.
SWOOP
GULP!
JIM DAVIS 2-16

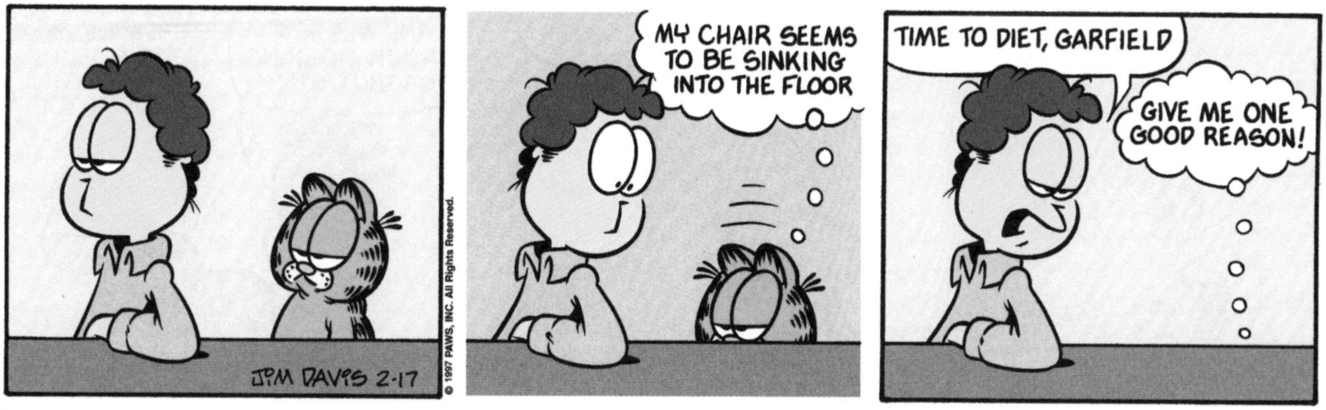
JIM DAVIS 2-17
© 1997 PAWS, INC. All Rights Reserved.
MY CHAIR SEEMS TO BE SINKING INTO THE FLOOR
TIME TO DIET, GARFIELD
GIVE ME ONE GOOD REASON!

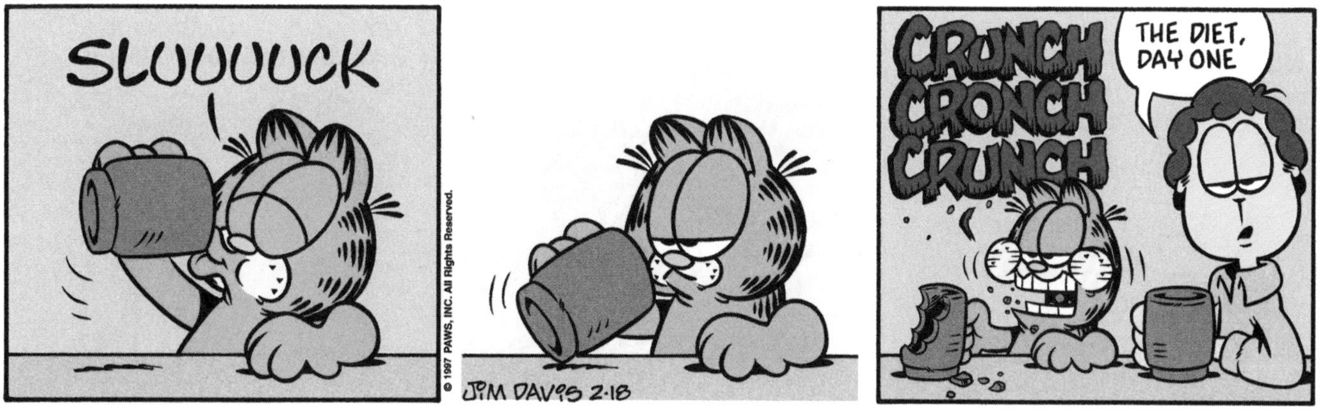
SLUUUUCK
© 1997 PAWS, INC. All Rights Reserved.
JIM DAVIS 2-18
CRUNCH
CRONCH
CRUNCH
THE DIET, DAY ONE

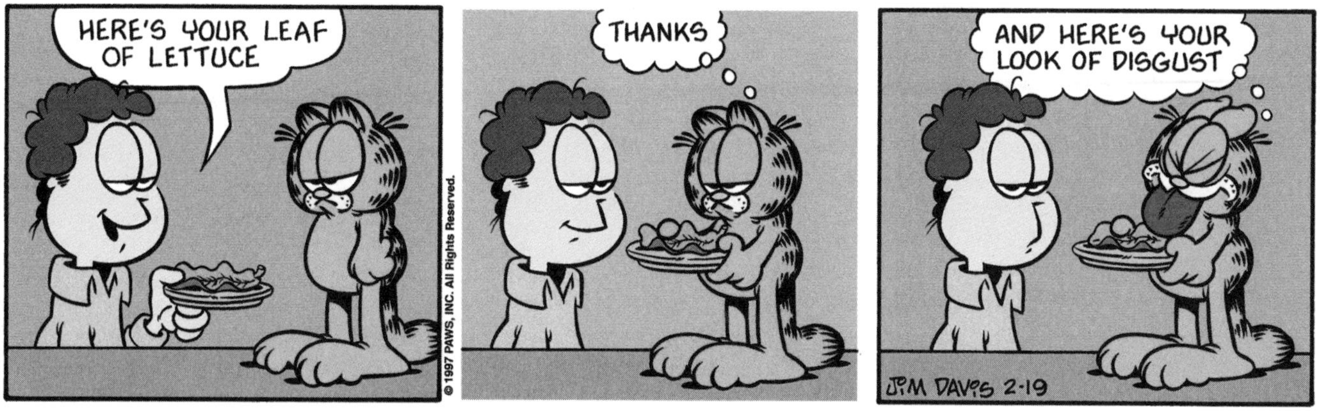
HERE'S YOUR LEAF OF LETTUCE
© 1997 PAWS, INC. All Rights Reserved.
THANKS
AND HERE'S YOUR LOOK OF DISGUST
JIM DAVIS 2-19

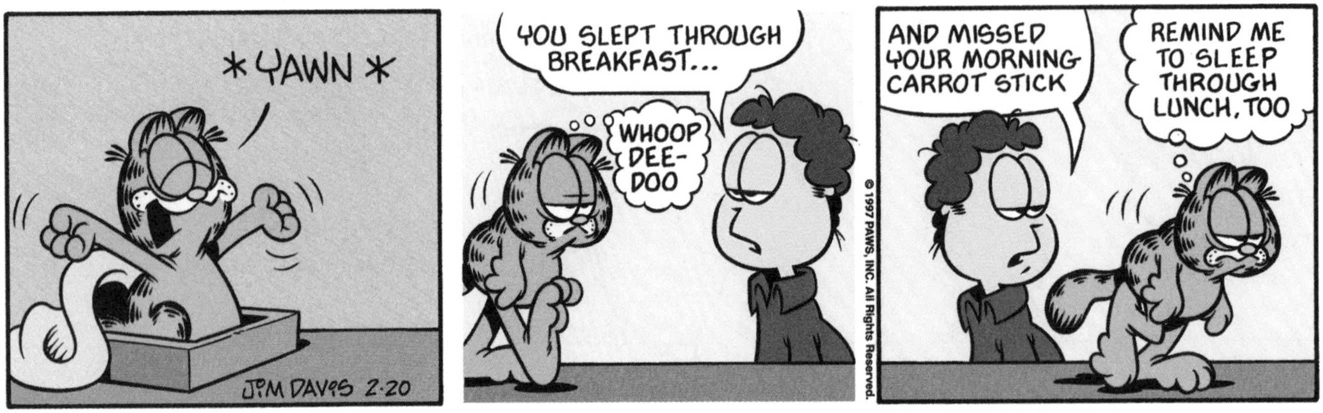
YAWN
JIM DAVIS 2-20
YOU SLEPT THROUGH BREAKFAST...
WHOOP DEE-DOO
© 1997 PAWS, INC. All Rights Reserved.
AND MISSED YOUR MORNING CARROT STICK
REMIND ME TO SLEEP THROUGH LUNCH, TOO

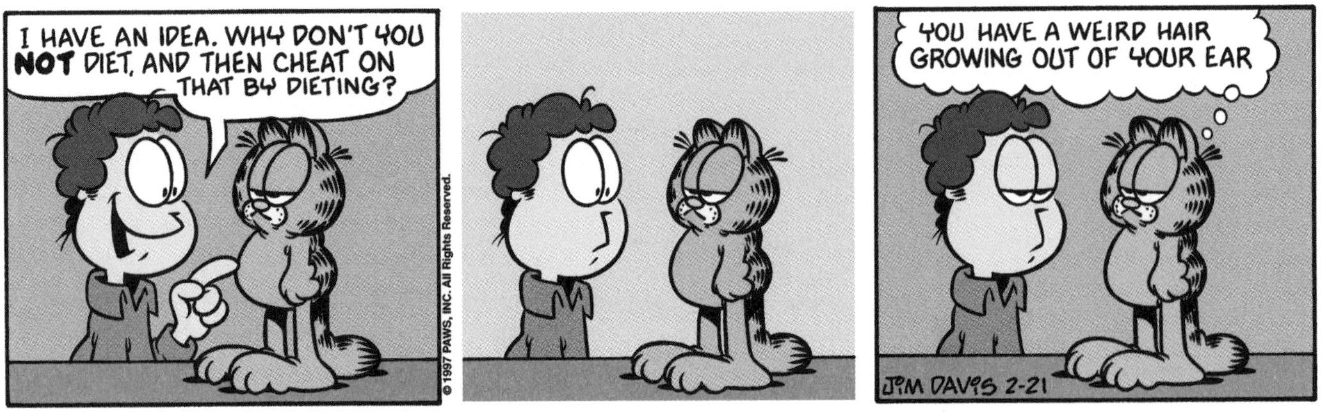
I HAVE AN IDEA. WHY DON'T YOU **NOT** DIET, AND THEN CHEAT ON THAT BY DIETING?
© 1997 PAWS, INC. All Rights Reserved.
YOU HAVE A WEIRD HAIR GROWING OUT OF YOUR EAR
JIM DAVIS 2-21

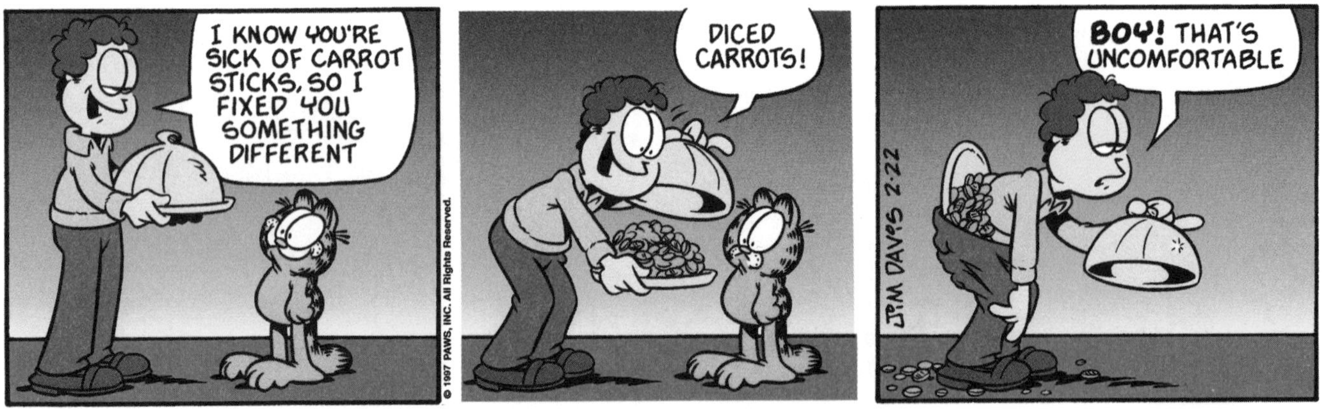
I KNOW YOU'RE SICK OF CARROT STICKS, SO I FIXED YOU SOMETHING DIFFERENT
© 1997 PAWS, INC. All Rights Reserved.
DICED CARROTS!
BOY! THAT'S UNCOMFORTABLE
JIM DAVIS 2-22

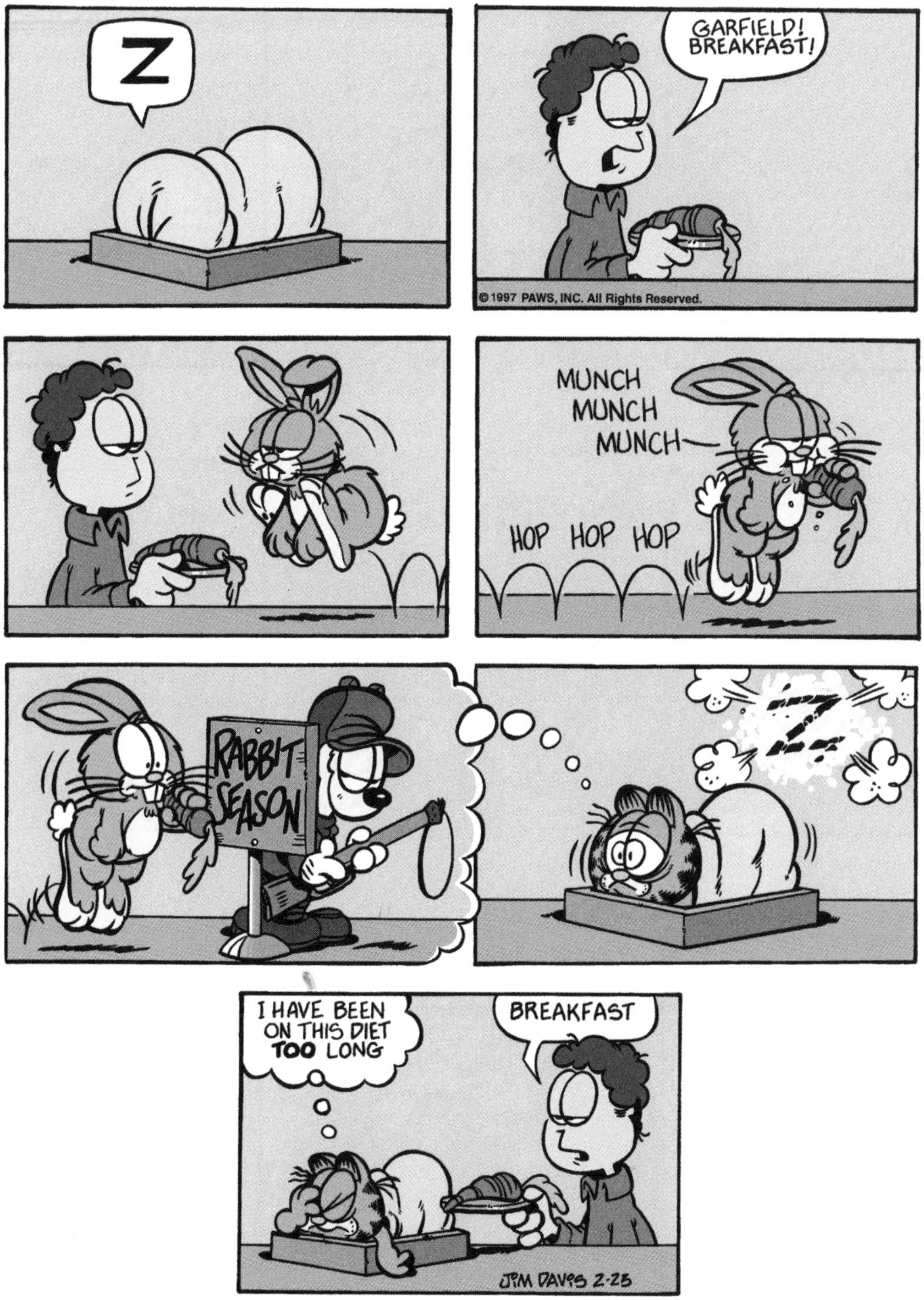
Z
GARFIELD! BREAKFAST!
© 1997 PAWS, INC. All Rights Reserved.
MUNCH MUNCH MUNCH
HOP HOP HOP
RABBIT SEASON
I HAVE BEEN ON THIS DIET **TOO** LONG
BREAKFAST
JIM DAVIS 2-23

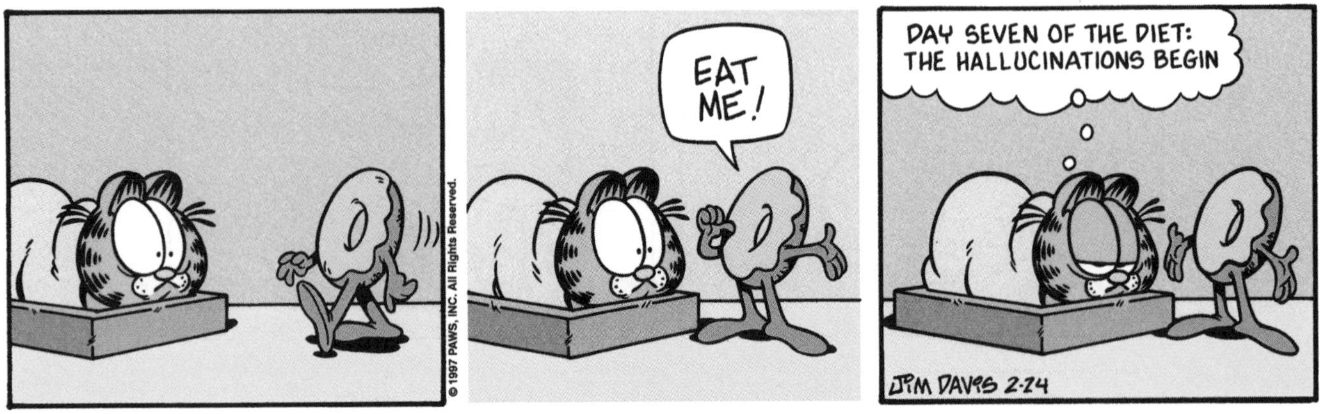
© 1997 PAWS, INC. All Rights Reserved.
EAT ME!
DAY SEVEN OF THE DIET: THE HALLUCINATIONS BEGIN
JIM DAVIS 2-24

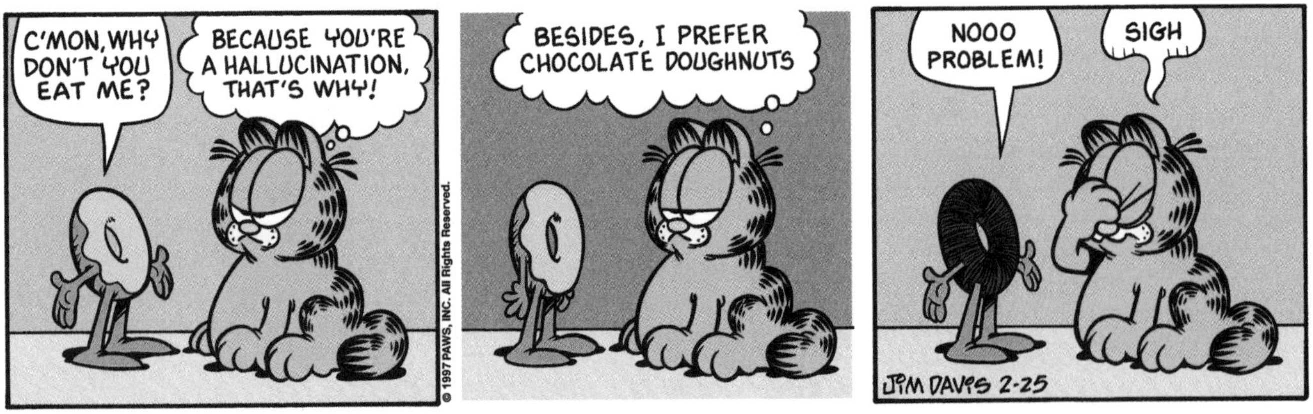
C'MON, WHY DON'T YOU EAT ME?
BECAUSE YOU'RE A HALLUCINATION, THAT'S WHY!
© 1997 PAWS, INC. All Rights Reserved.
BESIDES, I PREFER CHOCOLATE DOUGHNUTS
NOOO PROBLEM!
SIGH
JIM DAVIS 2-25

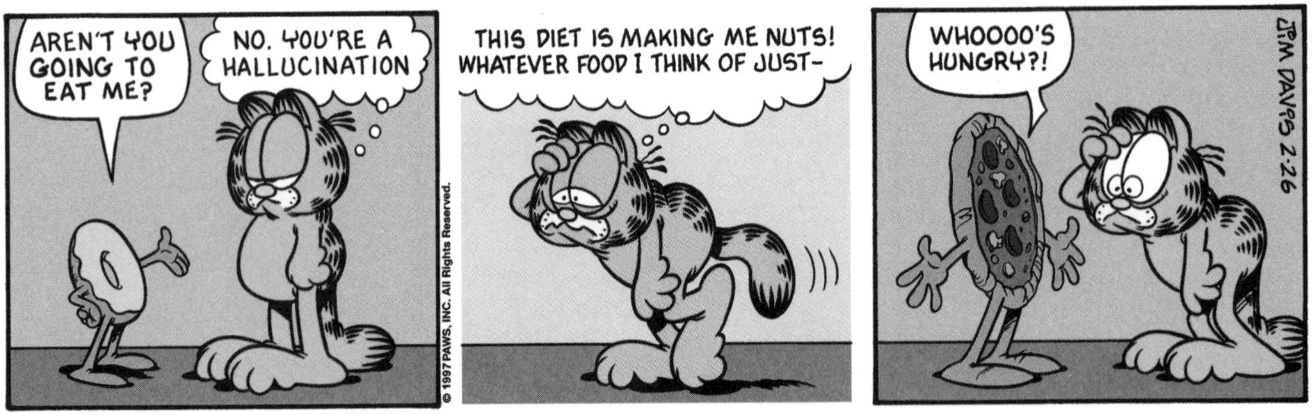
AREN'T YOU GOING TO EAT ME?
NO. YOU'RE A HALLUCINATION
© 1997 PAWS, INC. All Rights Reserved.
THIS DIET IS MAKING ME NUTS! WHATEVER FOOD I THINK OF JUST-
WHOOOO'S HUNGRY?!
JIM DAVIS 2-26

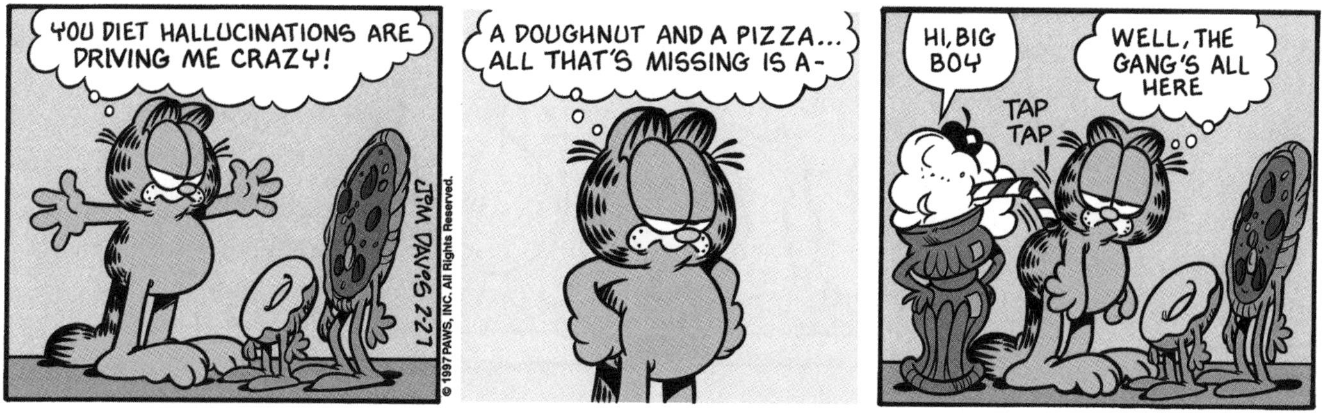
YOU DIET HALLUCINATIONS ARE DRIVING ME CRAZY!
JPM DAVPS 2-27
© 1997 PAWS, INC. All Rights Reserved.
A DOUGHNUT AND A PIZZA... ALL THAT'S MISSING IS A-
HI, BIG BOY
TAP TAP
WELL, THE GANG'S ALL HERE

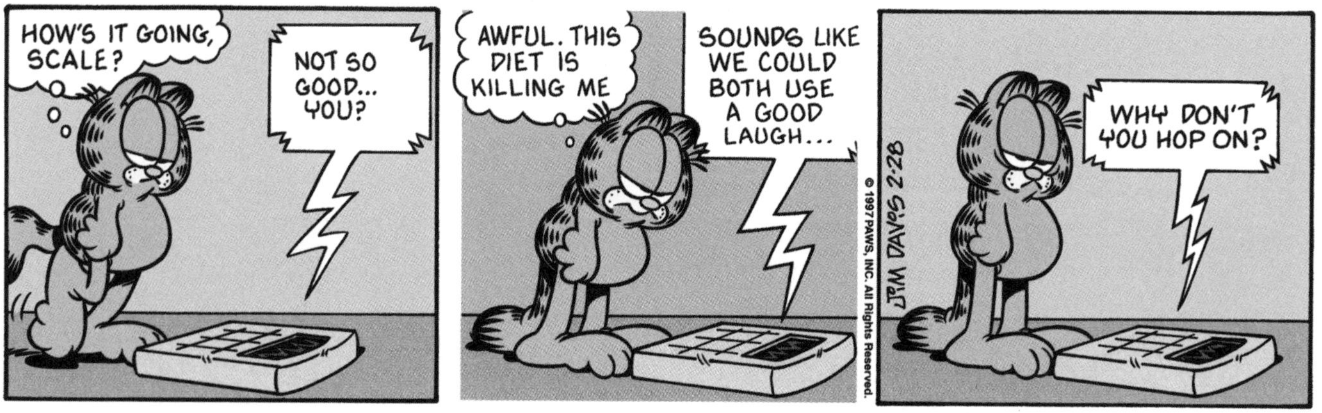
HOW'S IT GOING, SCALE?
NOT SO GOOD... YOU?
AWFUL. THIS DIET IS KILLING ME
SOUNDS LIKE WE COULD BOTH USE A GOOD LAUGH...
© 1997 PAWS, INC. All Rights Reserved.
JPM DAVPS 2-28
WHY DON'T YOU HOP ON?

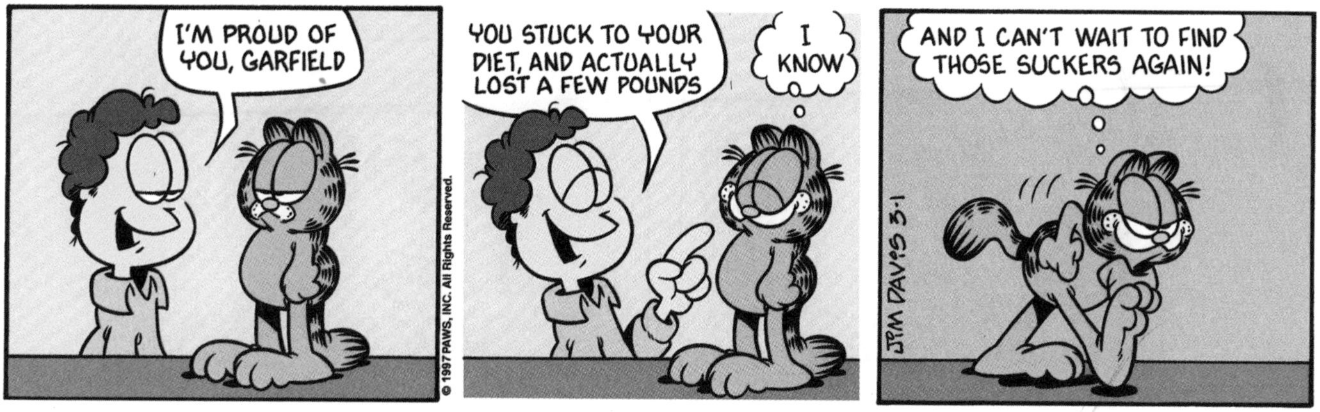
I'M PROUD OF YOU, GARFIELD
© 1997 PAWS, INC. All Rights Reserved.
YOU STUCK TO YOUR DIET, AND ACTUALLY LOST A FEW POUNDS
I KNOW
AND I CAN'T WAIT TO FIND THOSE SUCKERS AGAIN!
JPM DAVPS 3-1

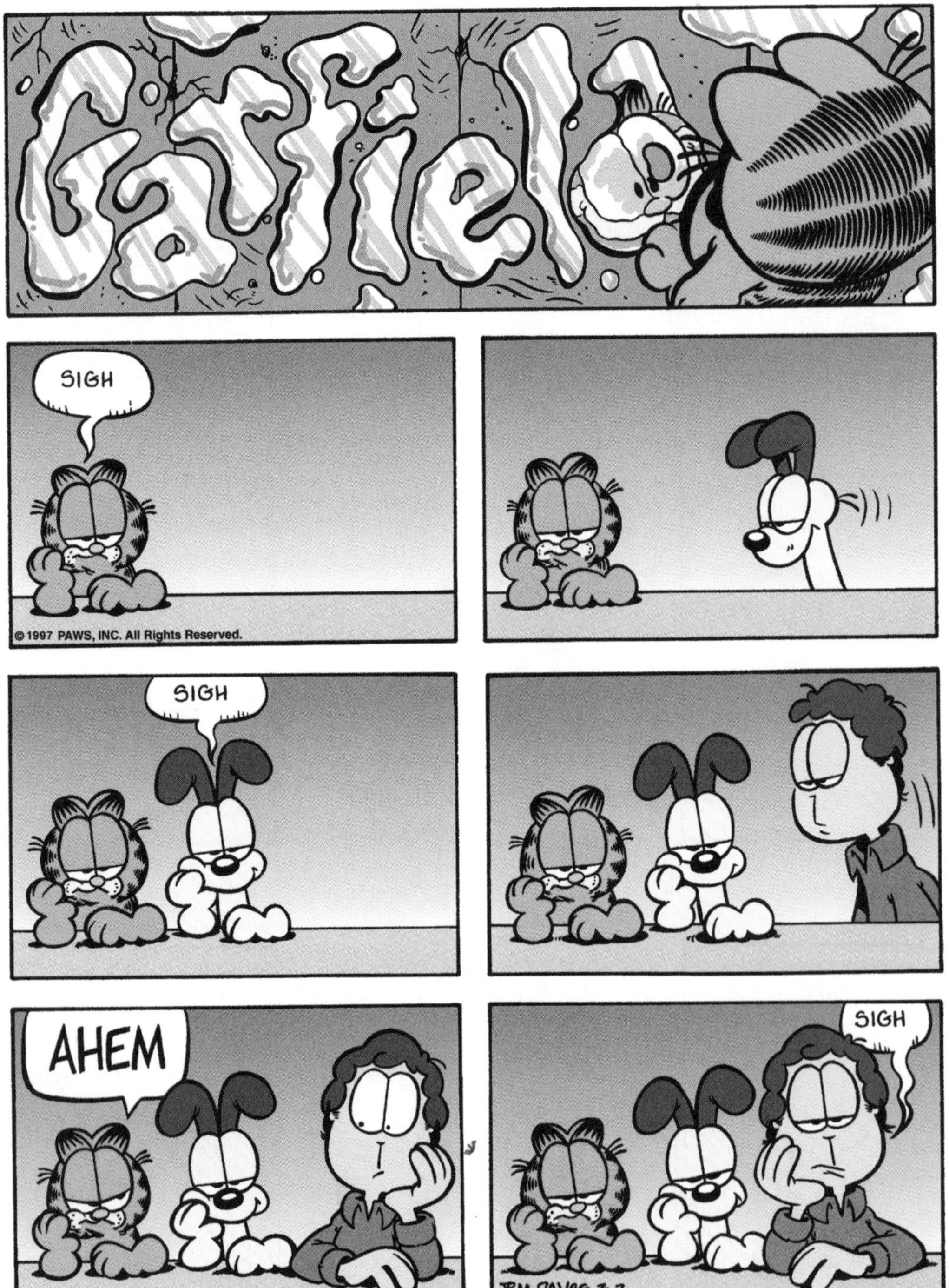
GARFIELD
SIGH
© 1997 PAWS, INC. All Rights Reserved.
SIGH
AHEM
SIGH
JIM DAVIS 3-2

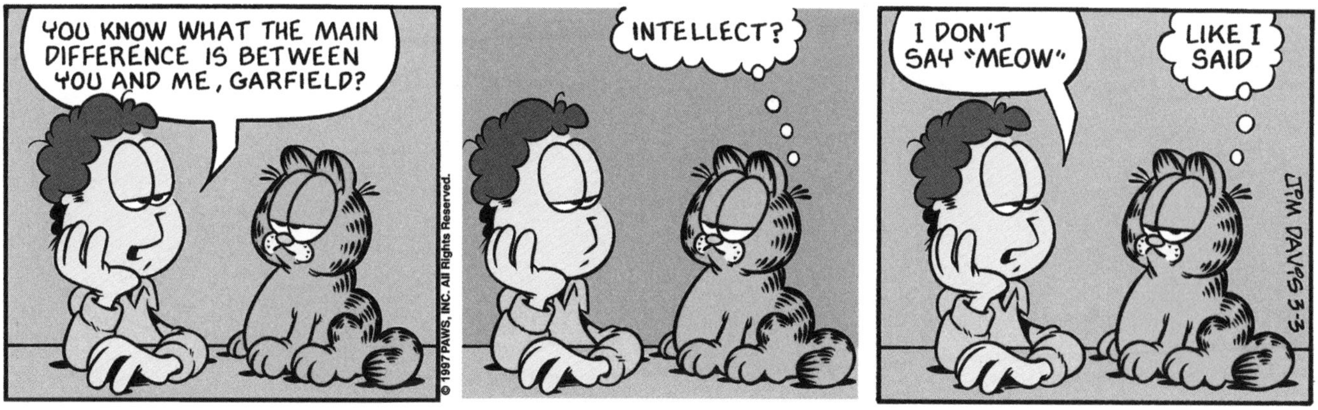
YOU KNOW WHAT THE MAIN DIFFERENCE IS BETWEEN YOU AND ME, GARFIELD?
© 1997 PAWS, INC. All Rights Reserved.
INTELLECT?
I DON'T SAY "MEOW"
LIKE I SAID
JIM DAVIS 3-3

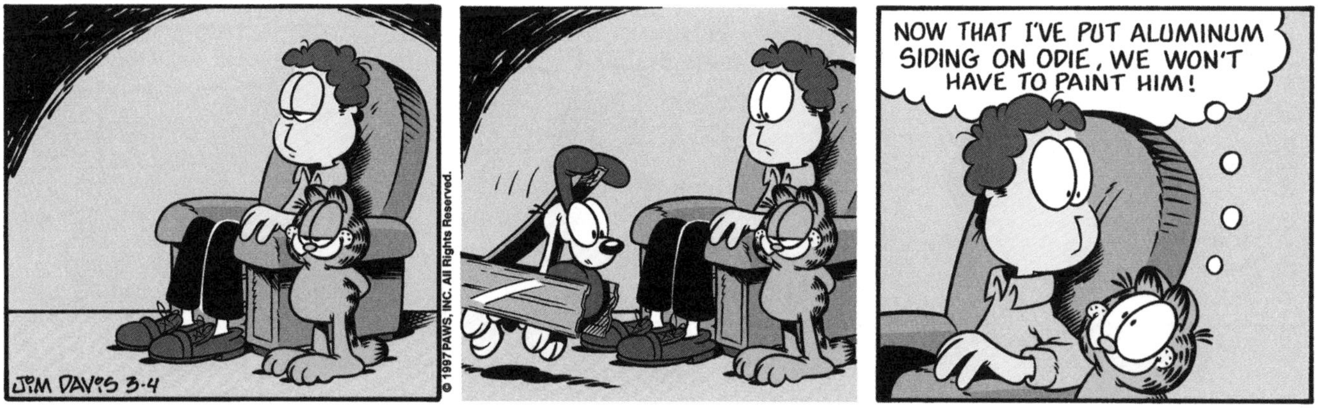
JIM DAVIS 3-4
© 1997 PAWS, INC. All Rights Reserved.
NOW THAT I'VE PUT ALUMINUM SIDING ON ODIE, WE WON'T HAVE TO PAINT HIM!

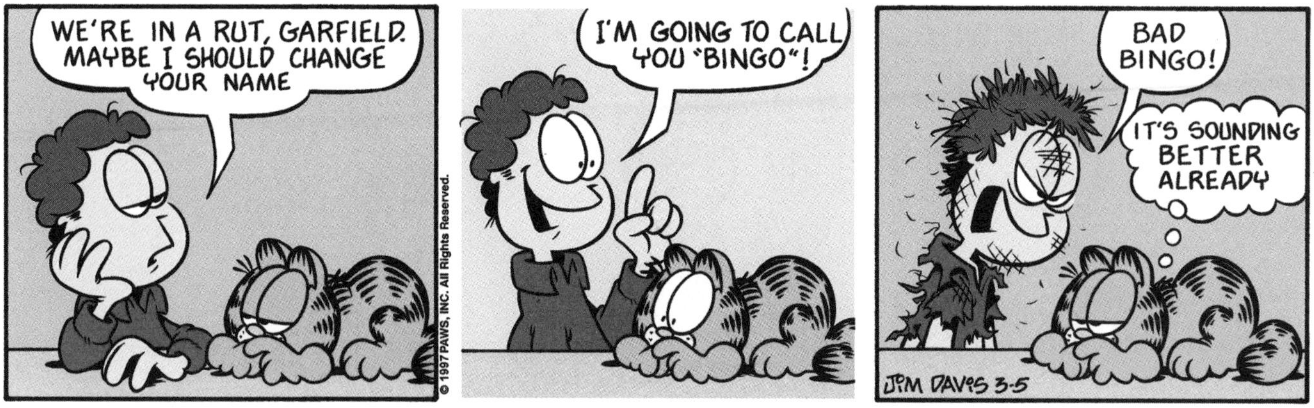
WE'RE IN A RUT, GARFIELD. MAYBE I SHOULD CHANGE YOUR NAME
© 1997 PAWS, INC. All Rights Reserved.
I'M GOING TO CALL YOU "BINGO"!
BAD BINGO!
IT'S SOUNDING BETTER ALREADY
JIM DAVIS 3-5

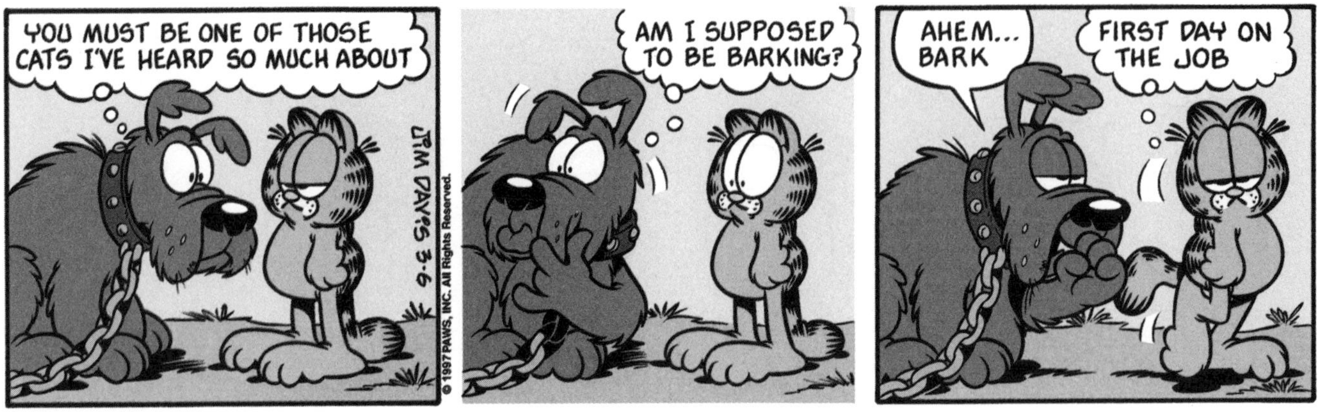
YOU MUST BE ONE OF THOSE CATS I'VE HEARD SO MUCH ABOUT
JIM DAVIS 3-6
© 1997 PAWS, INC. All Rights Reserved.
AM I SUPPOSED TO BE BARKING?
AHEM... BARK
FIRST DAY ON THE JOB

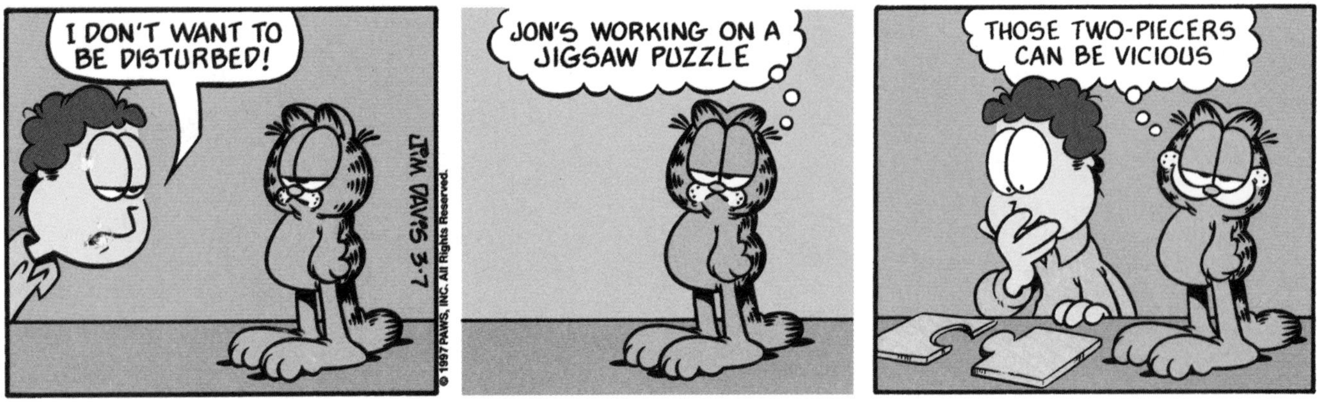
I DON'T WANT TO BE DISTURBED!
JIM DAVIS 3-7
© 1997 PAWS, INC. All Rights Reserved.
JON'S WORKING ON A JIGSAW PUZZLE
THOSE TWO-PIECERS CAN BE VICIOUS

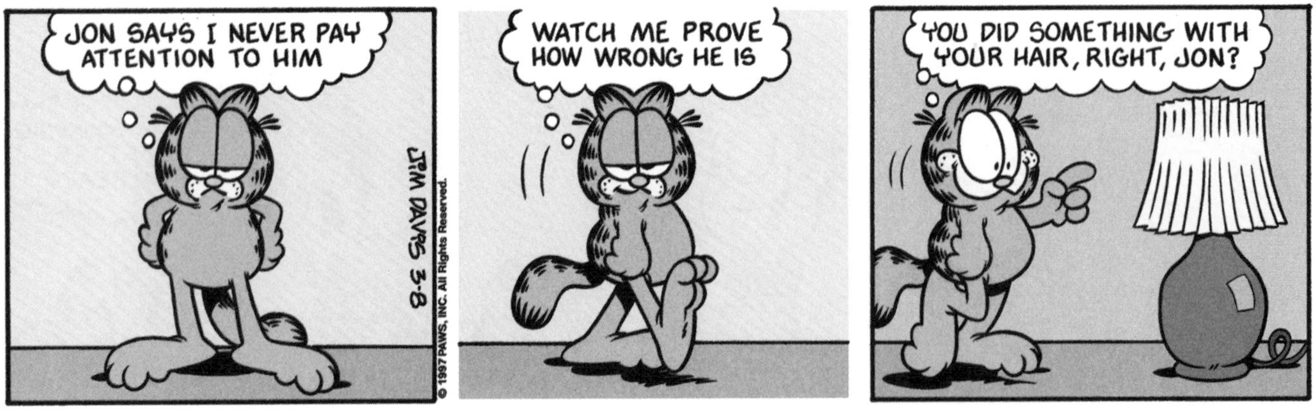
JON SAYS I NEVER PAY ATTENTION TO HIM
JIM DAVIS 3-8
© 1997 PAWS, INC. All Rights Reserved.
WATCH ME PROVE HOW WRONG HE IS
YOU DID SOMETHING WITH YOUR HAIR, RIGHT, JON?

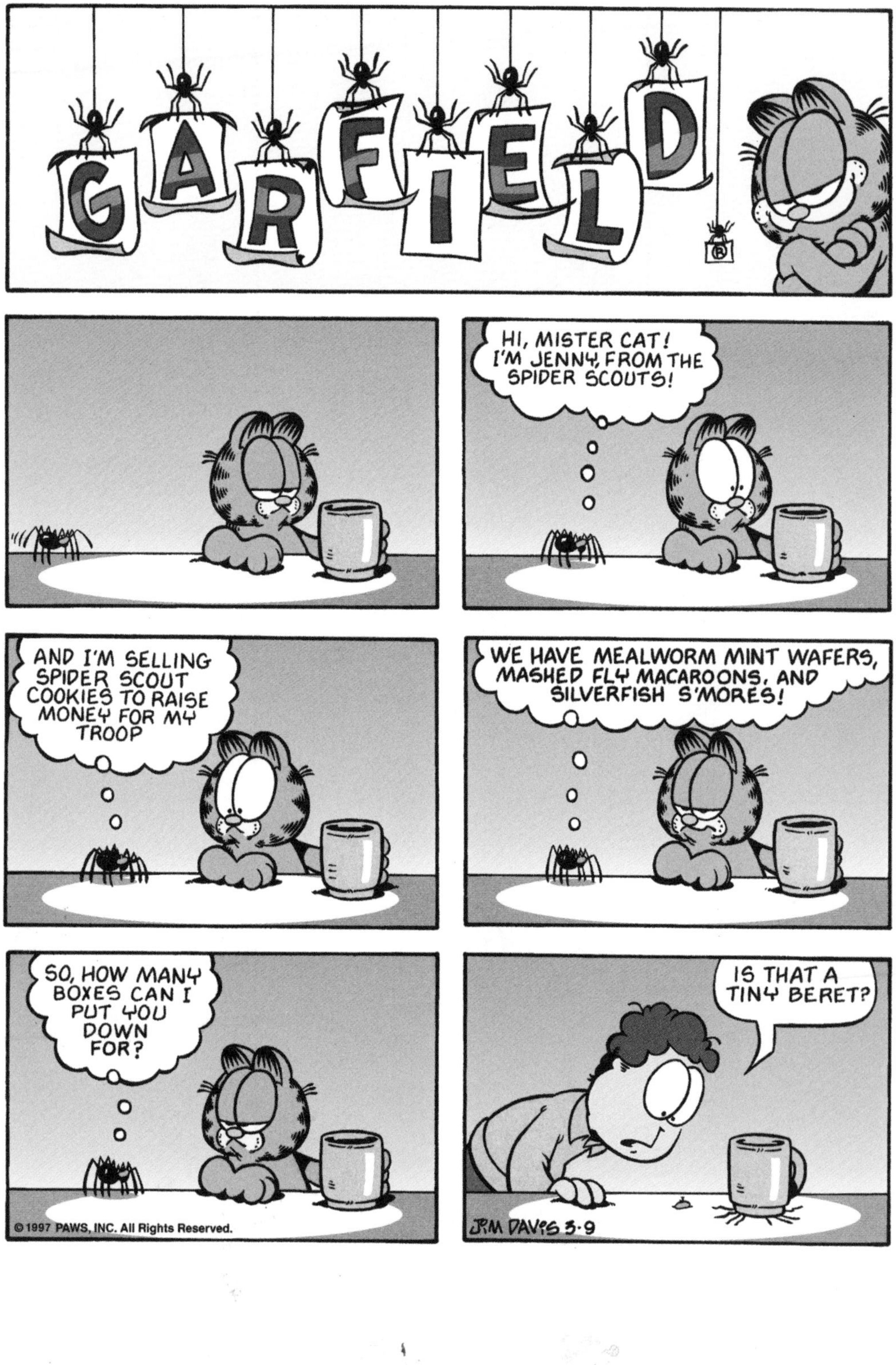
GARFIELD
HI, MISTER CAT! I'M JENNY, FROM THE SPIDER SCOUTS!
AND I'M SELLING SPIDER SCOUT COOKIES TO RAISE MONEY FOR MY TROOP
WE HAVE MEALWORM MINT WAFERS, MASHED FLY MACAROONS, AND SILVERFISH S'MORES!
SO, HOW MANY BOXES CAN I PUT YOU DOWN FOR?
IS THAT A TINY BERET?
© 1997 PAWS, INC. All Rights Reserved.
JPM DAVIS 3-9

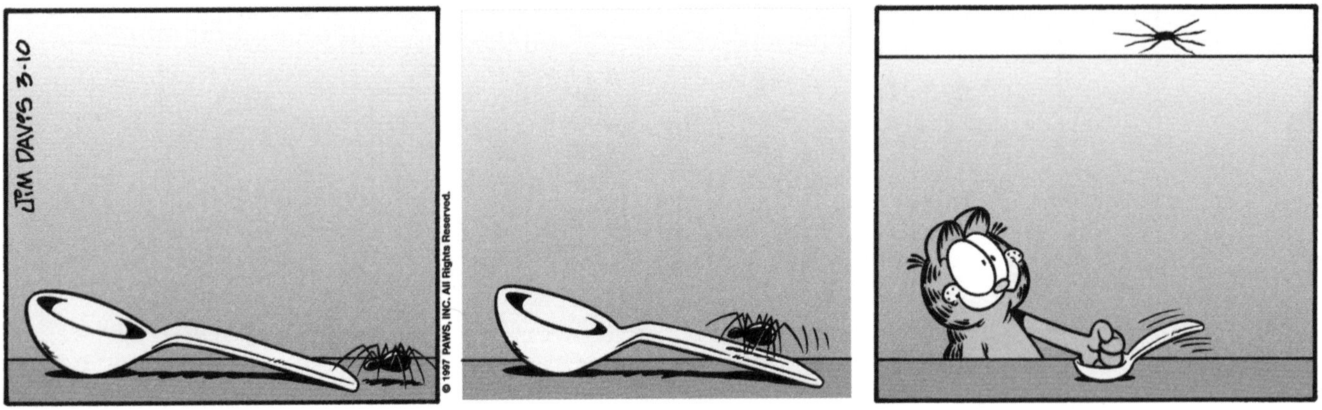
JIM DAVIS 3-10
© 1997 PAWS, INC. All Rights Reserved.

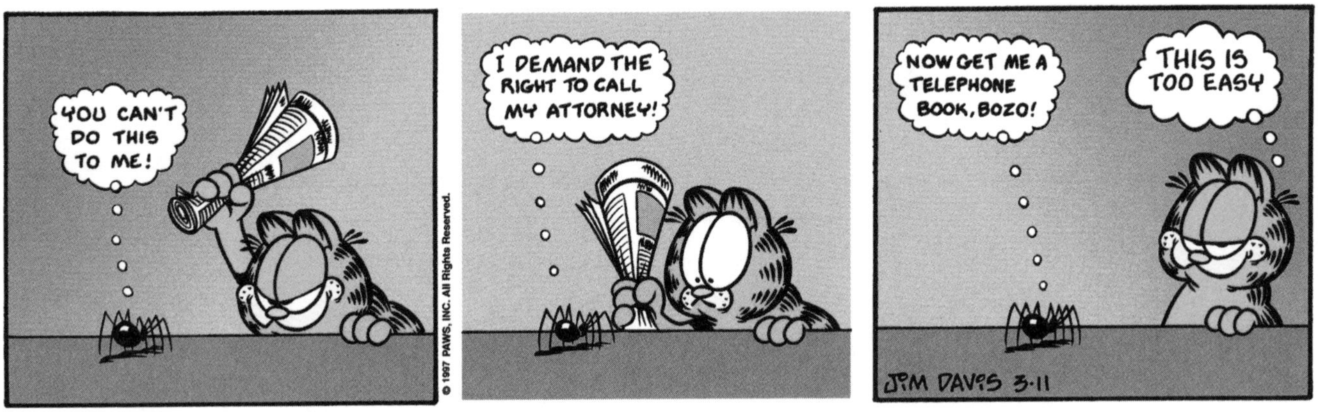
YOU CAN'T DO THIS TO ME!
© 1997 PAWS, INC. All Rights Reserved.
I DEMAND THE RIGHT TO CALL MY ATTORNEY!
NOW GET ME A TELEPHONE BOOK, BOZO!
THIS IS TOO EASY
JIM DAVIS 3-11

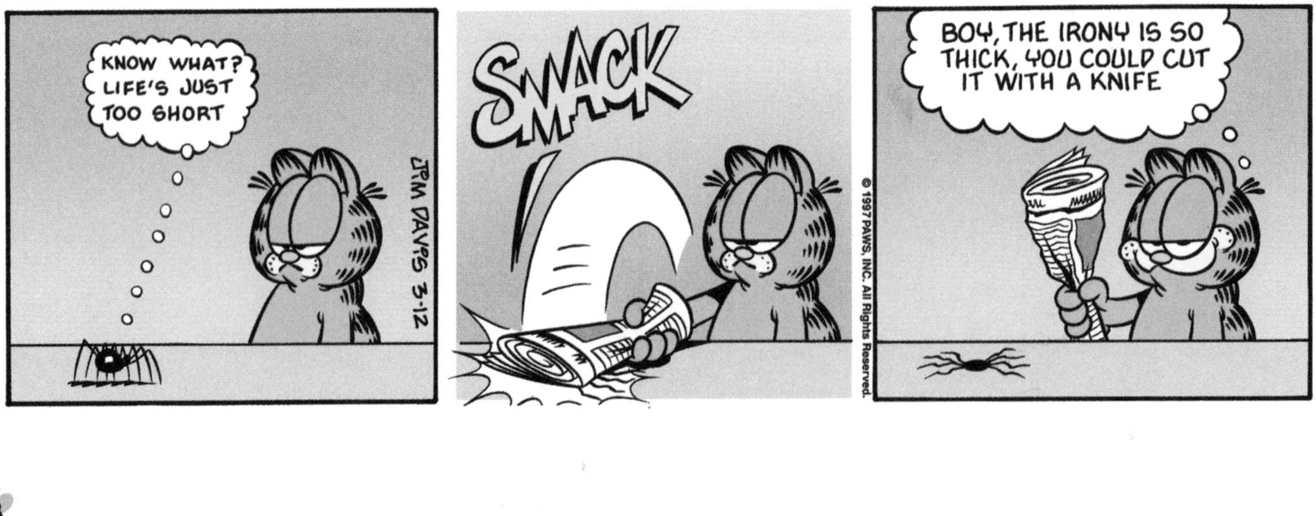
KNOW WHAT? LIFE'S JUST TOO SHORT
JIM DAVIS 3-12
SMACK
© 1997 PAWS, INC. All Rights Reserved.
BOY, THE IRONY IS SO THICK, YOU COULD CUT IT WITH A KNIFE

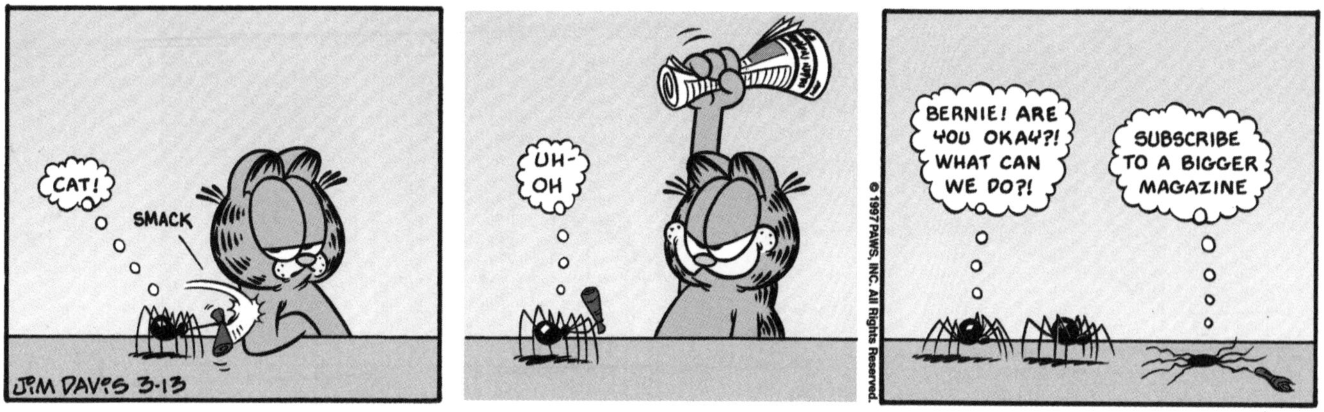
CAT!
SMACK
JIM DAVIS 3-13
UH-OH
BERNIE! ARE YOU OKAY?! WHAT CAN WE DO?!
SUBSCRIBE TO A BIGGER MAGAZINE

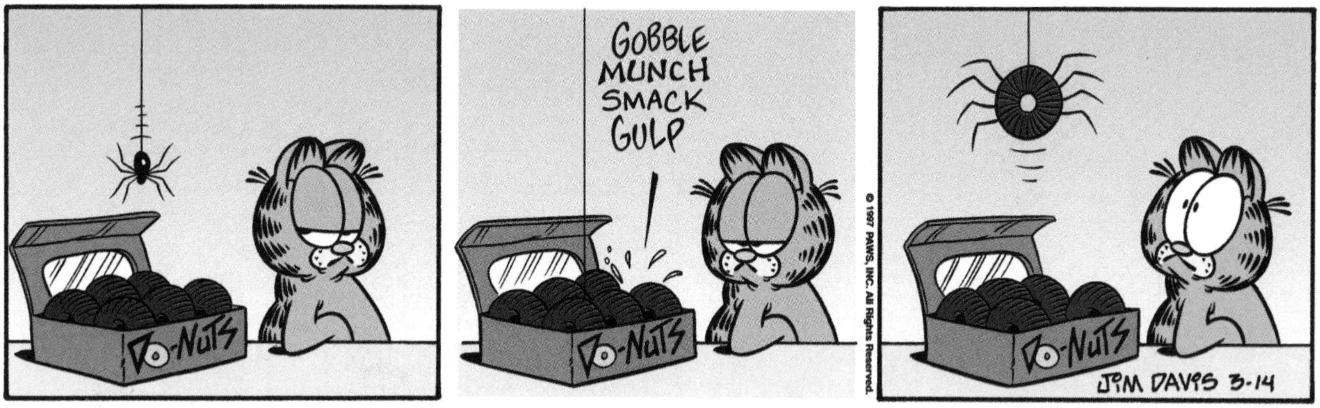
DO-NUTS
GOBBLE MUNCH SMACK GULP
JIM DAVIS 3-14

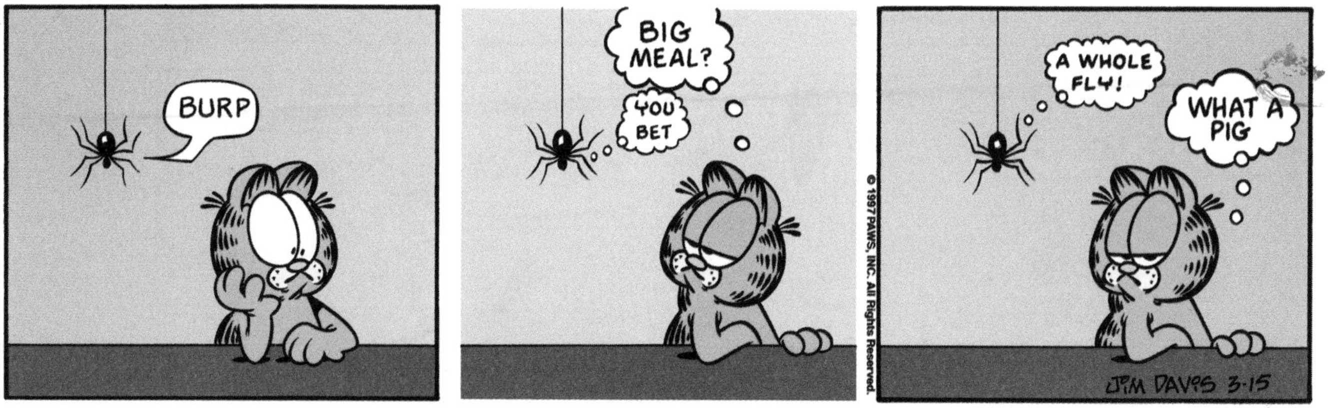
BURP
BIG MEAL?
YOU BET
A WHOLE FLY!
WHAT A PIG
JIM DAVIS 3-15

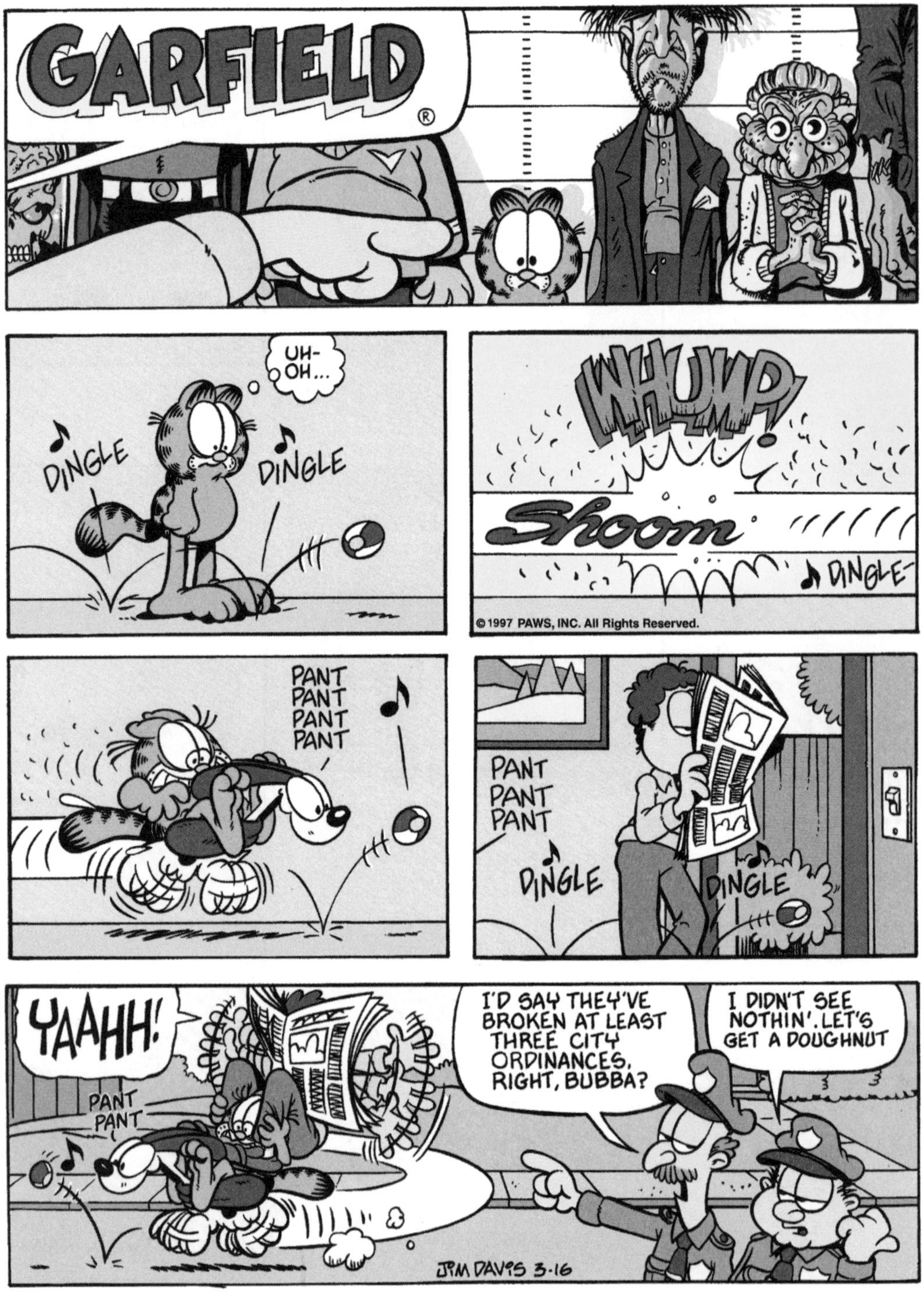
GARFIELD®
UH-OH...
DINGLE
DINGLE
WHUMP!
Shoom
DINGLE-
© 1997 PAWS, INC. All Rights Reserved.
PANT PANT PANT PANT
PANT PANT PANT
DINGLE
DINGLE
YAAHH!
PANT PANT
I'D SAY THEY'VE BROKEN AT LEAST THREE CITY ORDINANCES, RIGHT, BUBBA?
I DIDN'T SEE NOTHIN'. LET'S GET A DOUGHNUT
JIM DAVIS 3-16

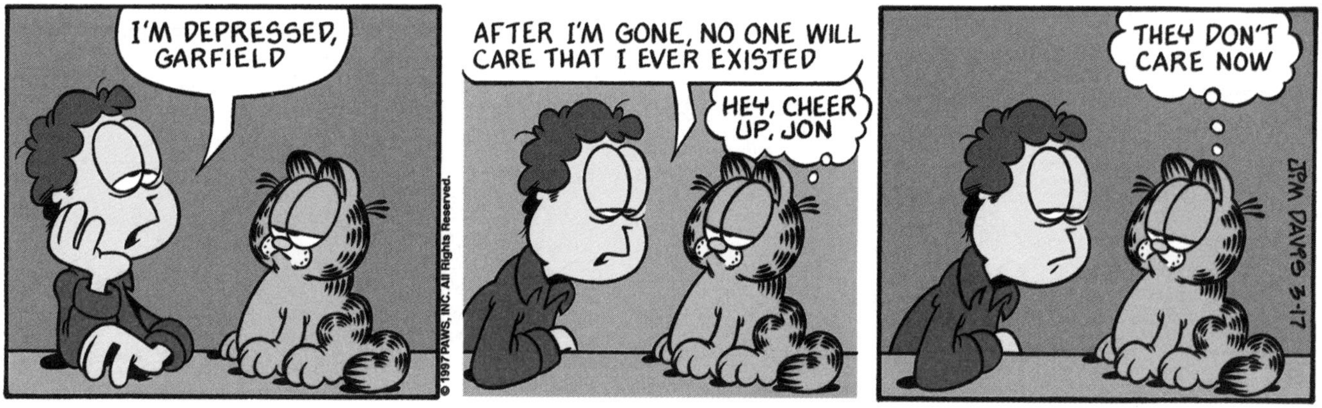
I'M DEPRESSED, GARFIELD
© 1997 PAWS, INC. All Rights Reserved.
AFTER I'M GONE, NO ONE WILL CARE THAT I EVER EXISTED
HEY, CHEER UP, JON
THEY DON'T CARE NOW
JIM DAVIS 3-17

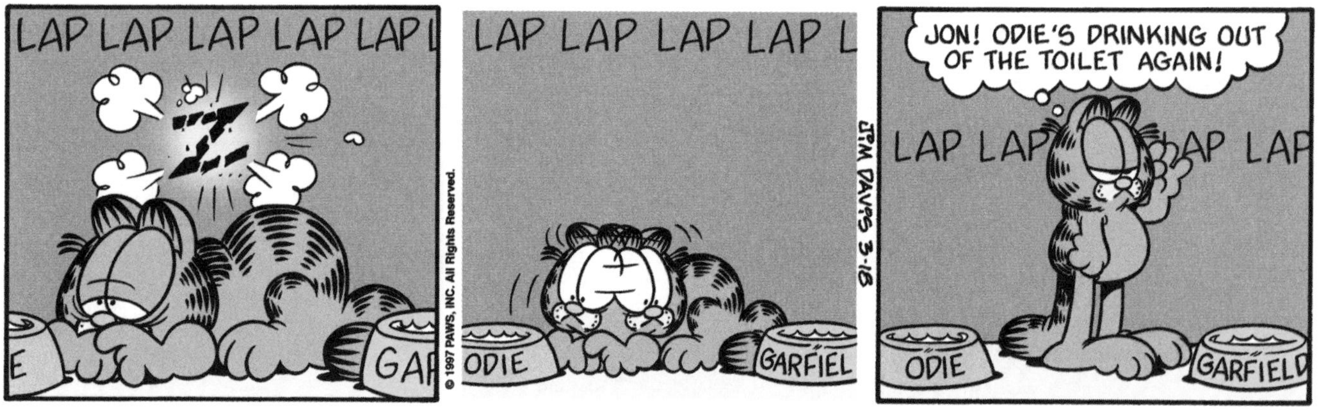
LAP LAP LAP LAP LAP
E
GAR
© 1997 PAWS, INC. All Rights Reserved.
LAP LAP LAP LAP
ODIE
GARFIEL
JIM DAVIS 3-18
JON! ODIE'S DRINKING OUT OF THE TOILET AGAIN!
LAP LAP
AP LAP
ODIE
GARFIELD

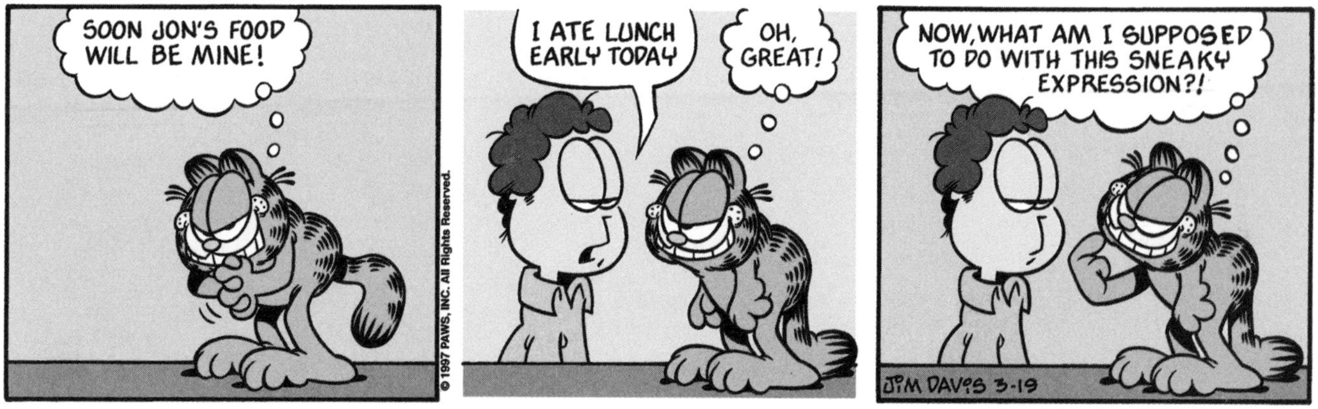
SOON JON'S FOOD WILL BE MINE!
© 1997 PAWS, INC. All Rights Reserved.
I ATE LUNCH EARLY TODAY
OH, GREAT!
NOW, WHAT AM I SUPPOSED TO DO WITH THIS SNEAKY EXPRESSION?!
JIM DAVIS 3-19

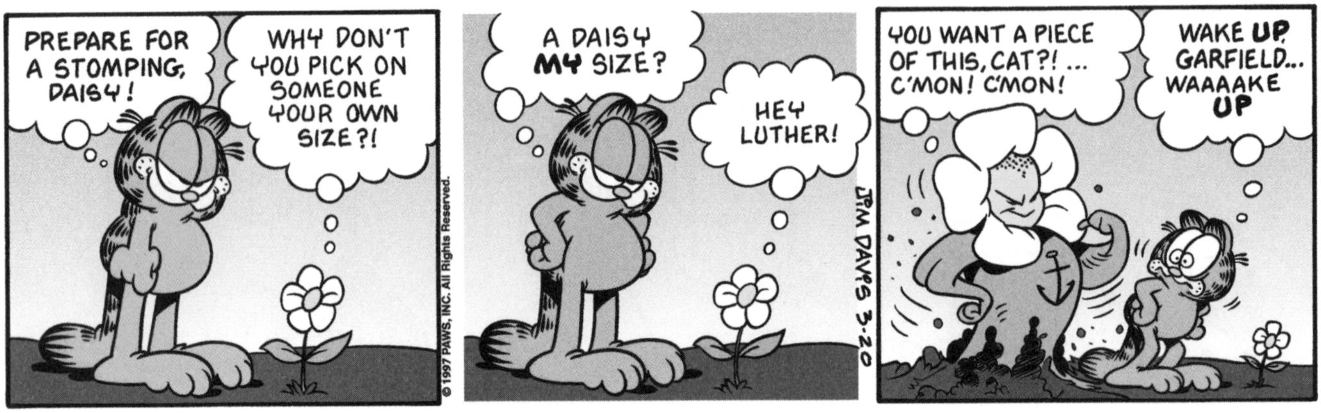
PREPARE FOR A STOMPING, DAISY!
WHY DON'T YOU PICK ON SOMEONE YOUR OWN SIZE?!
© 1997 PAWS, INC. All Rights Reserved.
A DAISY MY SIZE?
HEY LUTHER!
JIM DAVIS 3-20
YOU WANT A PIECE OF THIS, CAT?! ... C'MON! C'MON!
WAKE UP, GARFIELD... WAAAAKE UP

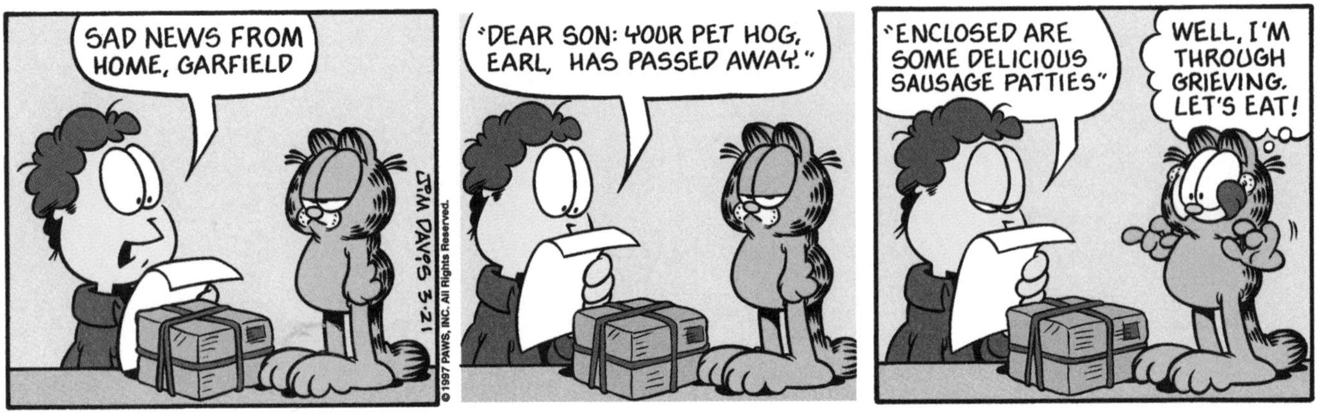
SAD NEWS FROM HOME, GARFIELD
JIM DAVIS 3-21
© 1997 PAWS, INC. All Rights Reserved.
"DEAR SON: YOUR PET HOG, EARL, HAS PASSED AWAY."
"ENCLOSED ARE SOME DELICIOUS SAUSAGE PATTIES"
WELL, I'M THROUGH GRIEVING. LET'S EAT!

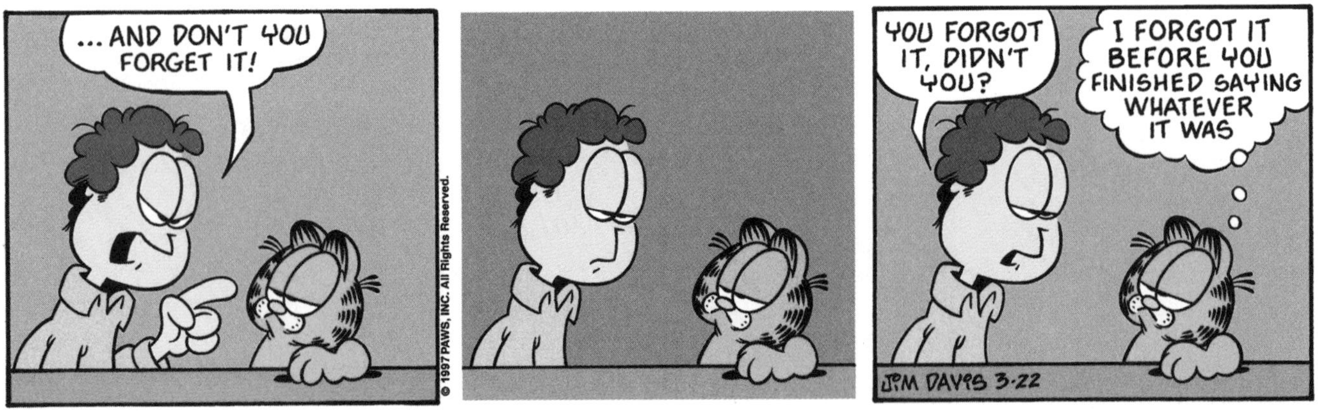
... AND DON'T YOU FORGET IT!
© 1997 PAWS, INC. All Rights Reserved.
YOU FORGOT IT, DIDN'T YOU?
I FORGOT IT BEFORE YOU FINISHED SAYING WHATEVER IT WAS
JIM DAVIS 3-22

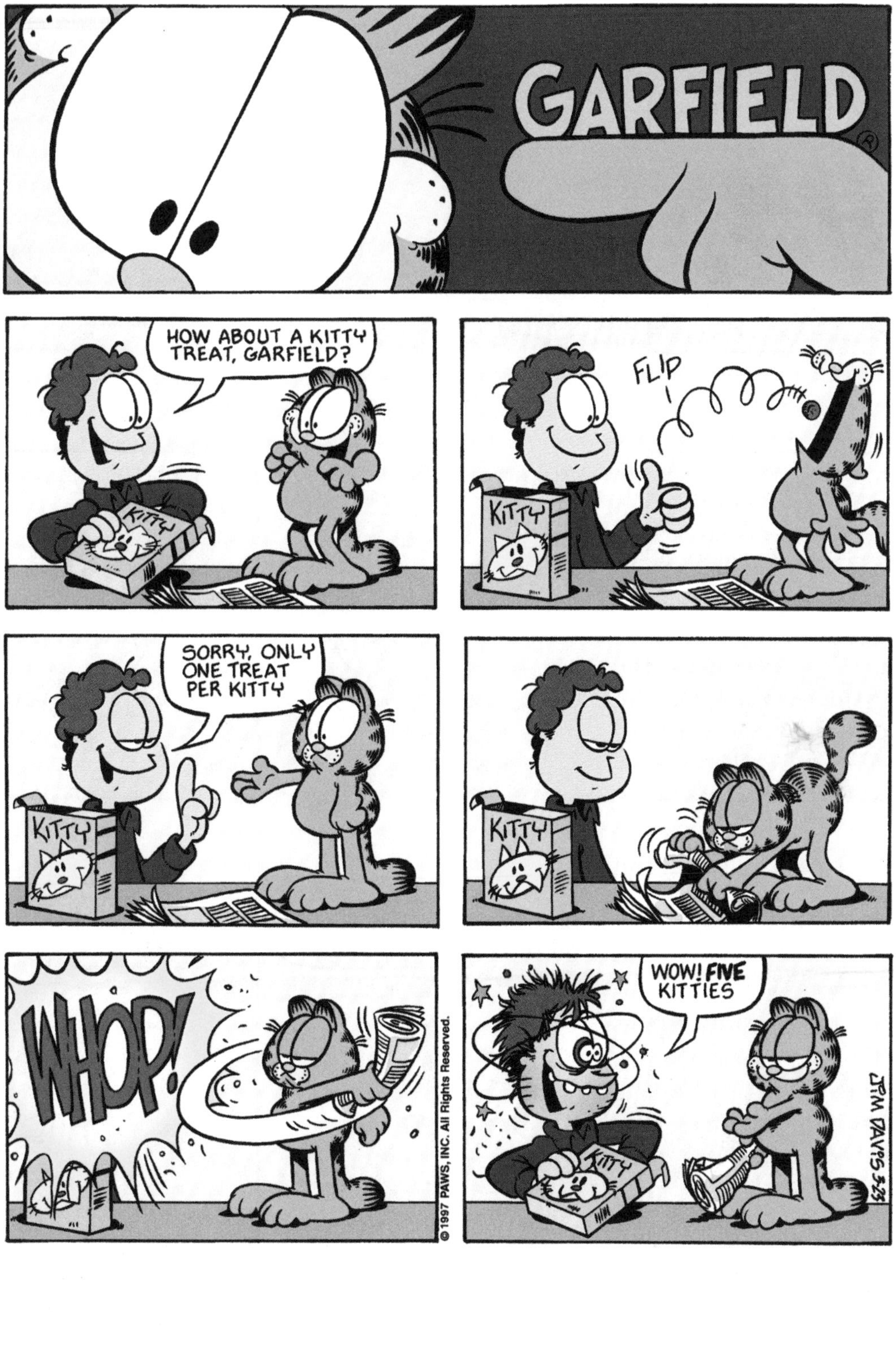
GARFIELD
HOW ABOUT A KITTY TREAT, GARFIELD?
KITTY
FLIP
KITTY
SORRY, ONLY ONE TREAT PER KITTY
KITTY
KITTY
WHOP!
WOW! **FIVE** KITTIES
KITTY
JIM DAVIS 3-23

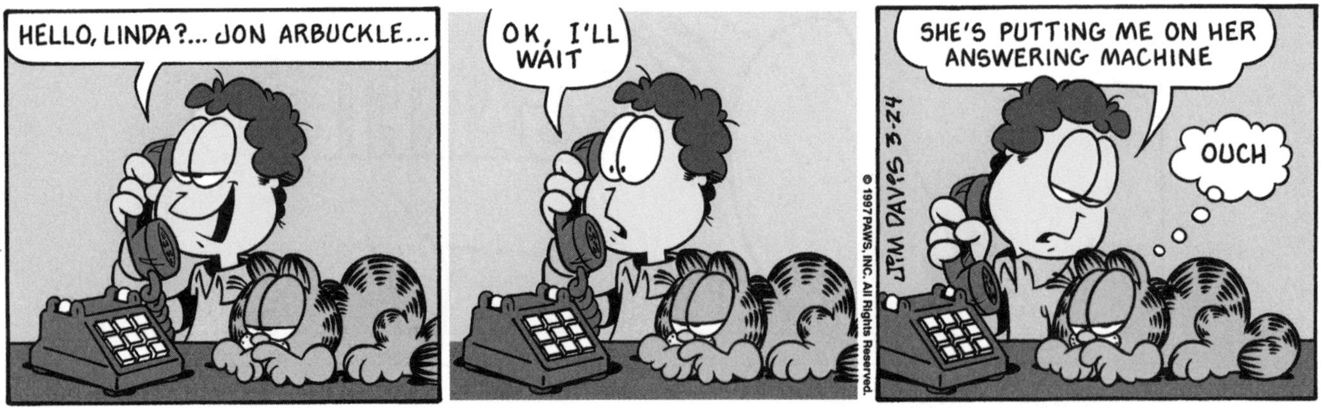
HELLO, LINDA?... JON ARBUCKLE...
OK, I'LL WAIT
SHE'S PUTTING ME ON HER ANSWERING MACHINE
OUCH
JIM DAVIS 3-24
© 1997 PAWS, INC. All Rights Reserved.

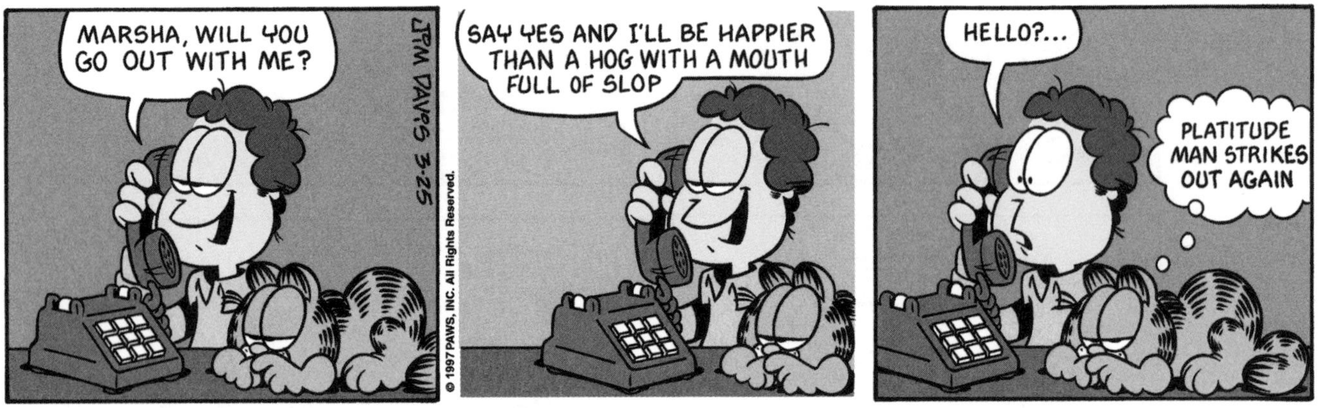
MARSHA, WILL YOU GO OUT WITH ME?
SAY YES AND I'LL BE HAPPIER THAN A HOG WITH A MOUTH FULL OF SLOP
HELLO?...
PLATITUDE MAN STRIKES OUT AGAIN
JIM DAVIS 3-25
© 1997 PAWS, INC. All Rights Reserved.

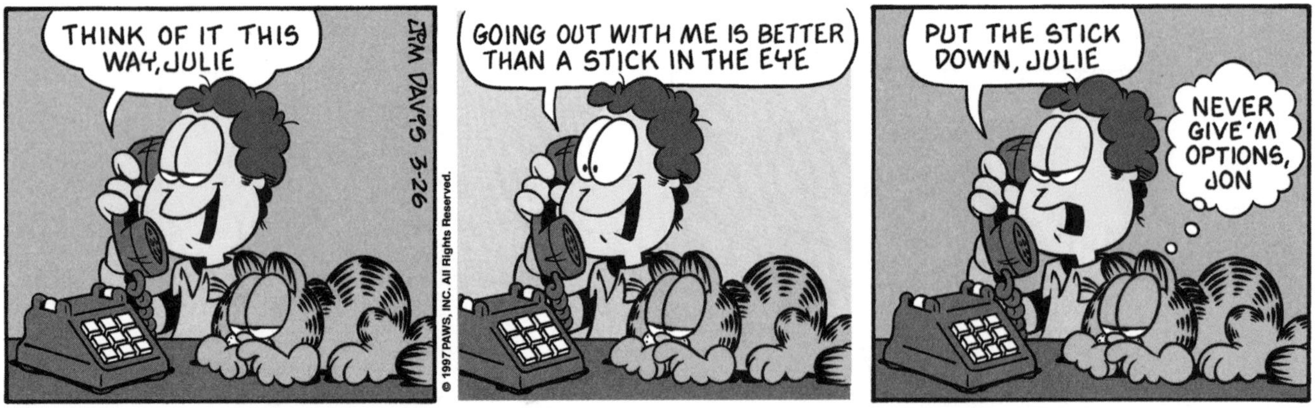
THINK OF IT THIS WAY, JULIE
GOING OUT WITH ME IS BETTER THAN A STICK IN THE EYE
PUT THE STICK DOWN, JULIE
NEVER GIVE'M OPTIONS, JON
JIM DAVIS 3-26
© 1997 PAWS, INC. All Rights Reserved.

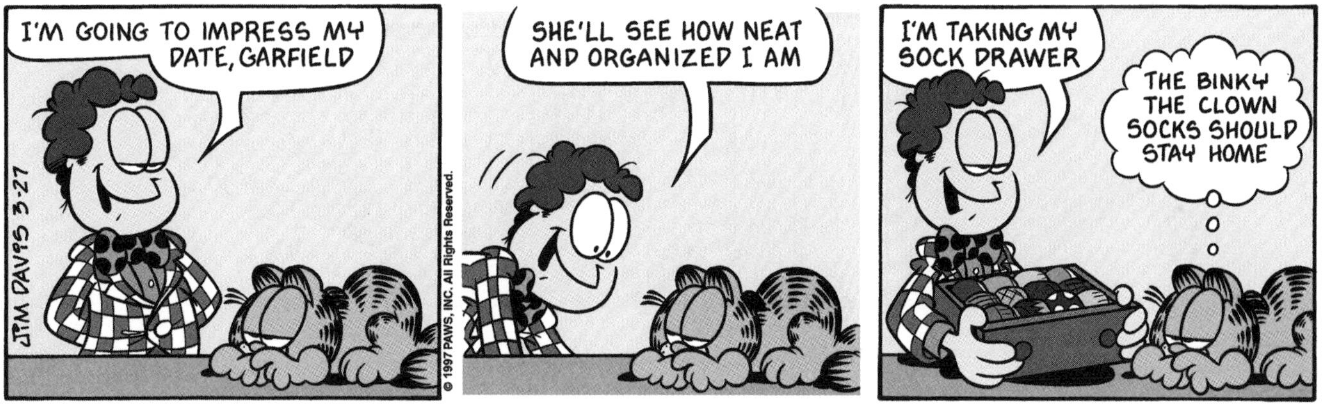
I'M GOING TO IMPRESS MY DATE, GARFIELD
JIM DAVIS 3-27
© 1997 PAWS, INC. All Rights Reserved.
SHE'LL SEE HOW NEAT AND ORGANIZED I AM
I'M TAKING MY SOCK DRAWER
THE BINKY THE CLOWN SOCKS SHOULD STAY HOME

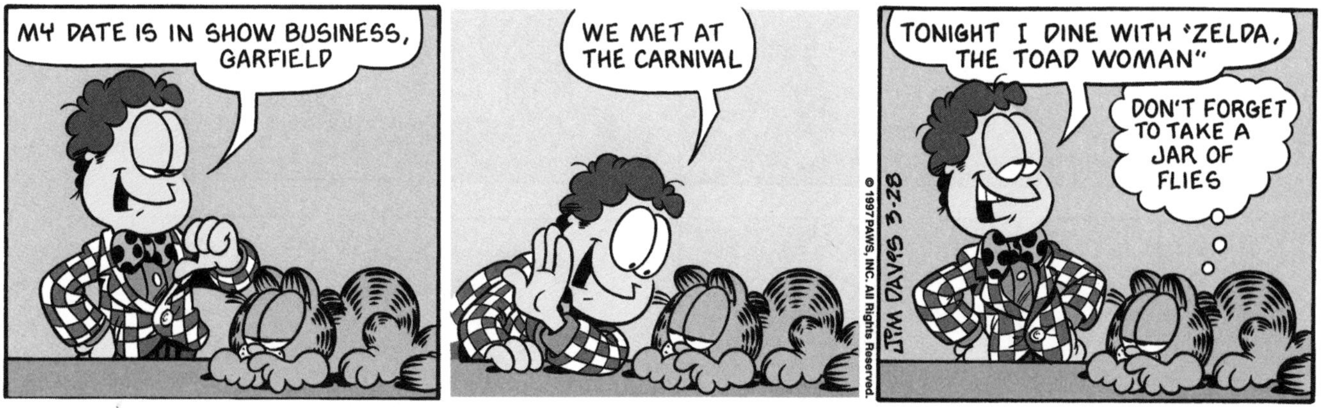
MY DATE IS IN SHOW BUSINESS, GARFIELD
WE MET AT THE CARNIVAL
TONIGHT I DINE WITH "ZELDA, THE TOAD WOMAN"
DON'T FORGET TO TAKE A JAR OF FLIES
© 1997 PAWS, INC. All Rights Reserved.
JIM DAVIS 3-28

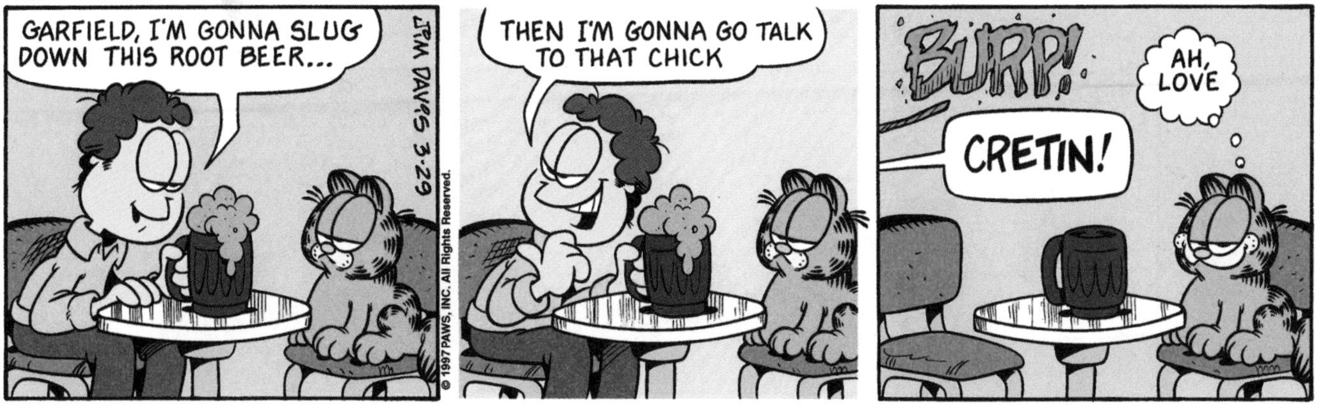
GARFIELD, I'M GONNA SLUG DOWN THIS ROOT BEER...
JIM DAVIS 3-29
© 1997 PAWS, INC. All Rights Reserved.
THEN I'M GONNA GO TALK TO THAT CHICK
BURP!
CRETIN!
AH, LOVE

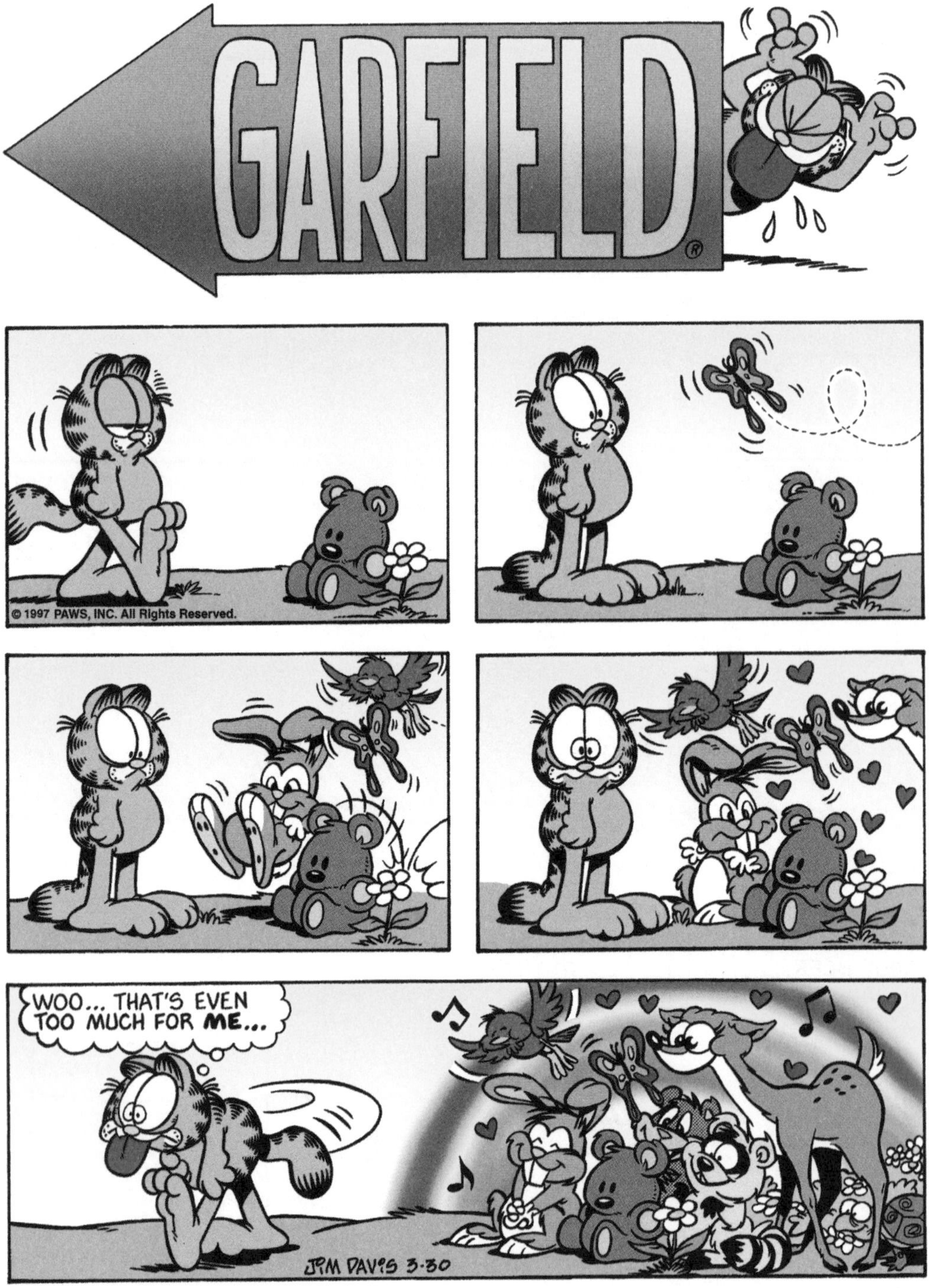
GARFIELD
© 1997 PAWS, INC. All Rights Reserved.
WOO... THAT'S EVEN TOO MUCH FOR ME...
JIM DAVIS 3-30

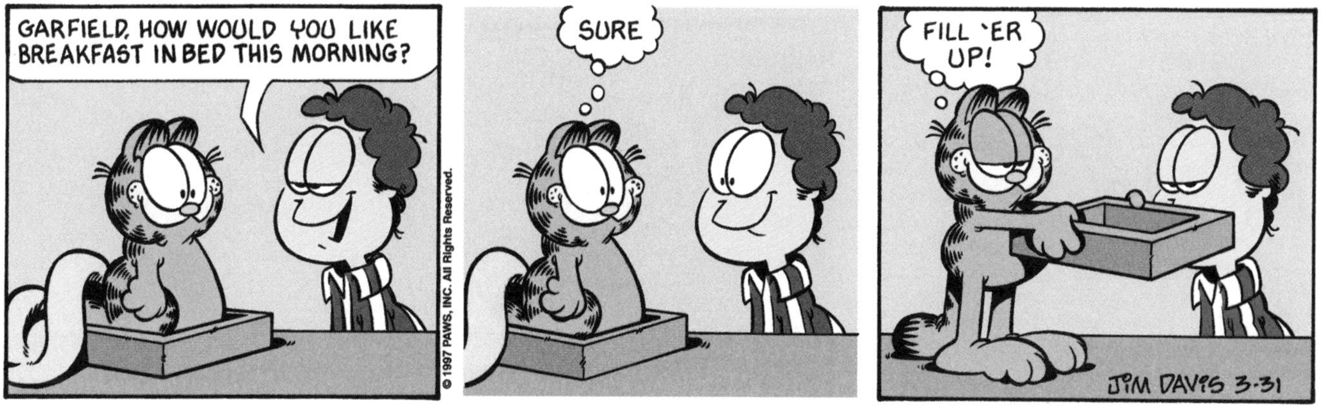
GARFIELD, HOW WOULD YOU LIKE BREAKFAST IN BED THIS MORNING?
SURE
FILL 'ER UP!
JIM DAVIS 3-31
© 1997 PAWS, INC. All Rights Reserved.

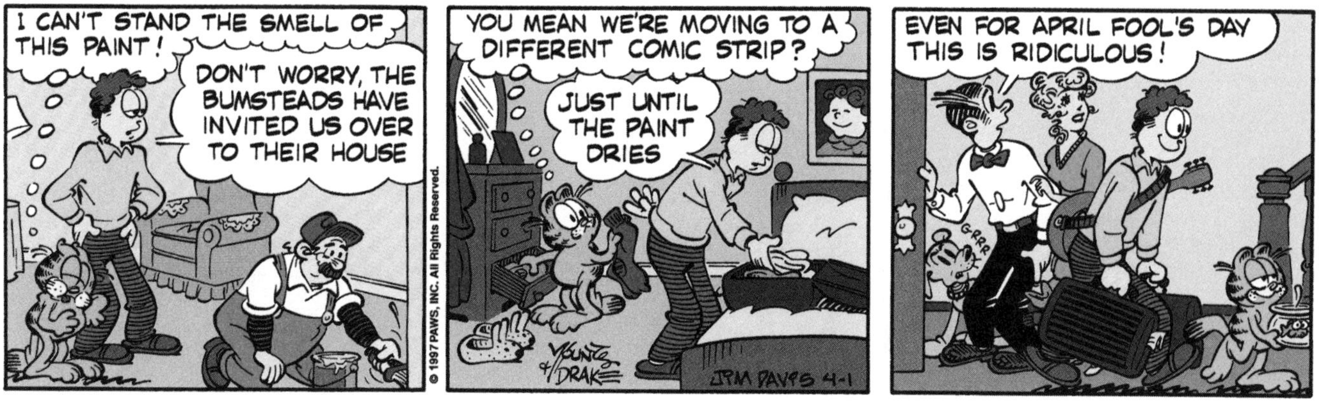
I CAN'T STAND THE SMELL OF THIS PAINT!
DON'T WORRY, THE BUMSTEADS HAVE INVITED US OVER TO THEIR HOUSE
YOU MEAN WE'RE MOVING TO A DIFFERENT COMIC STRIP?
JUST UNTIL THE PAINT DRIES
YOUNG & DRAKE
JIM DAVIS 4-1
EVEN FOR APRIL FOOL'S DAY THIS IS RIDICULOUS!
G-RRR
© 1997 PAWS, INC. All Rights Reserved.

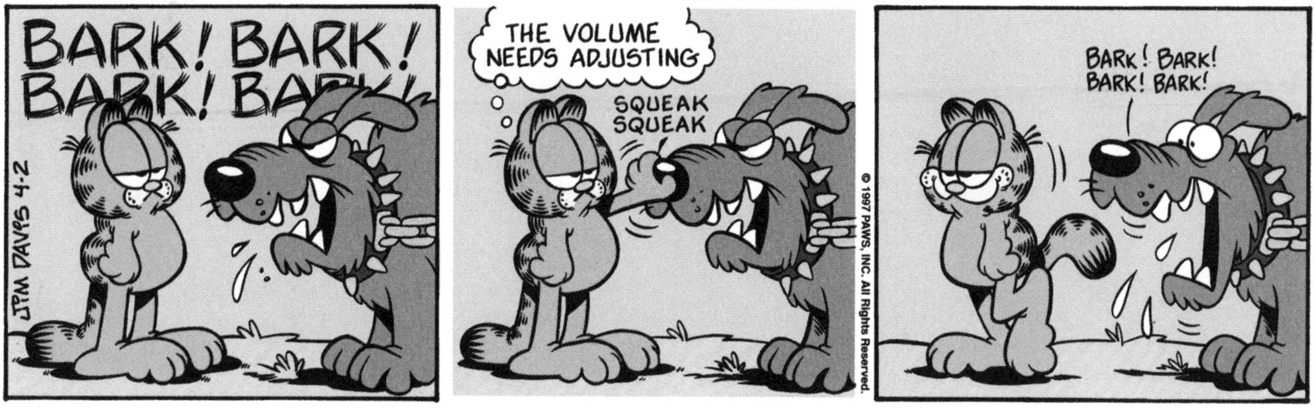
BARK! BARK! BARK! BARK!
JIM DAVIS 4-2
THE VOLUME NEEDS ADJUSTING
SQUEAK SQUEAK
BARK! BARK! BARK! BARK!
© 1997 PAWS, INC. All Rights Reserved.

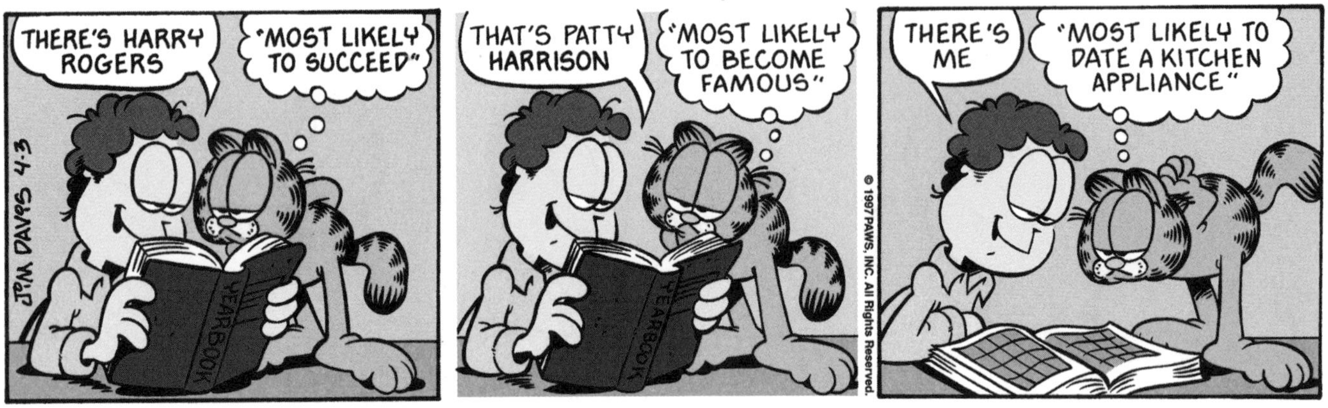
JIM DAVIS 4-3
THERE'S HARRY ROGERS
"MOST LIKELY TO SUCCEED"
YEARBOOK
THAT'S PATTY HARRISON
"MOST LIKELY TO BECOME FAMOUS"
YEARBOOK
THERE'S ME
"MOST LIKELY TO DATE A KITCHEN APPLIANCE"

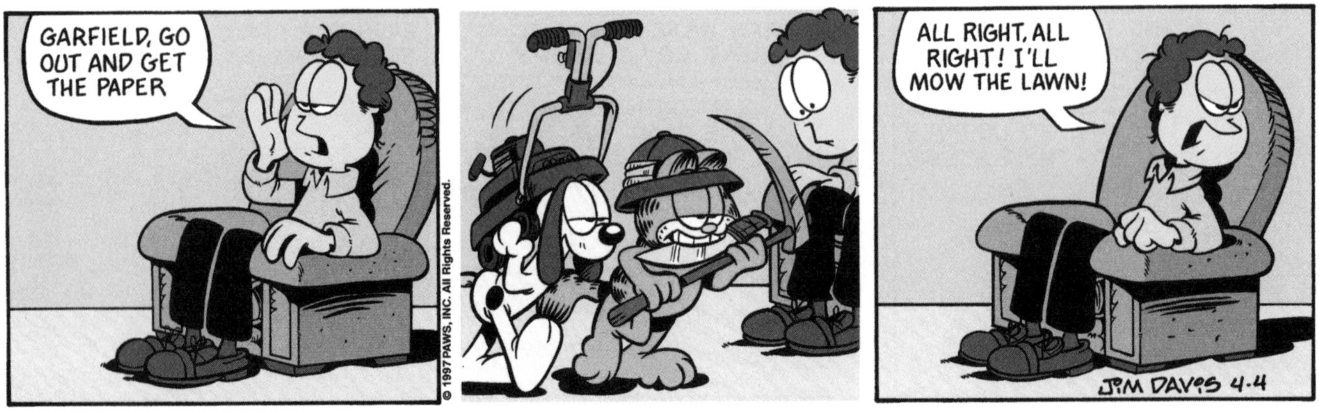
GARFIELD, GO OUT AND GET THE PAPER
ALL RIGHT, ALL RIGHT! I'LL MOW THE LAWN!
JIM DAVIS 4-4

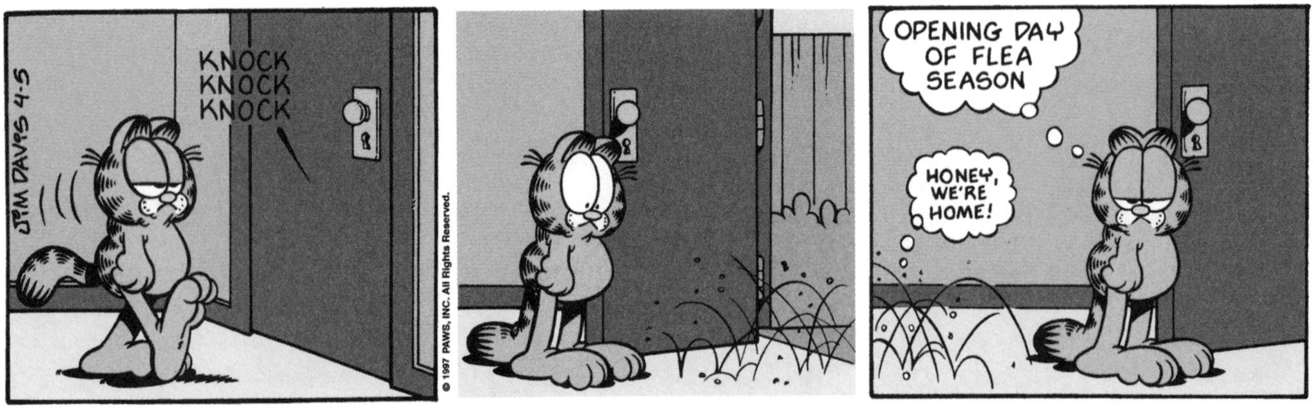
JIM DAVIS 4-5
KNOCK KNOCK KNOCK
OPENING DAY OF FLEA SEASON
HONEY, WE'RE HOME!

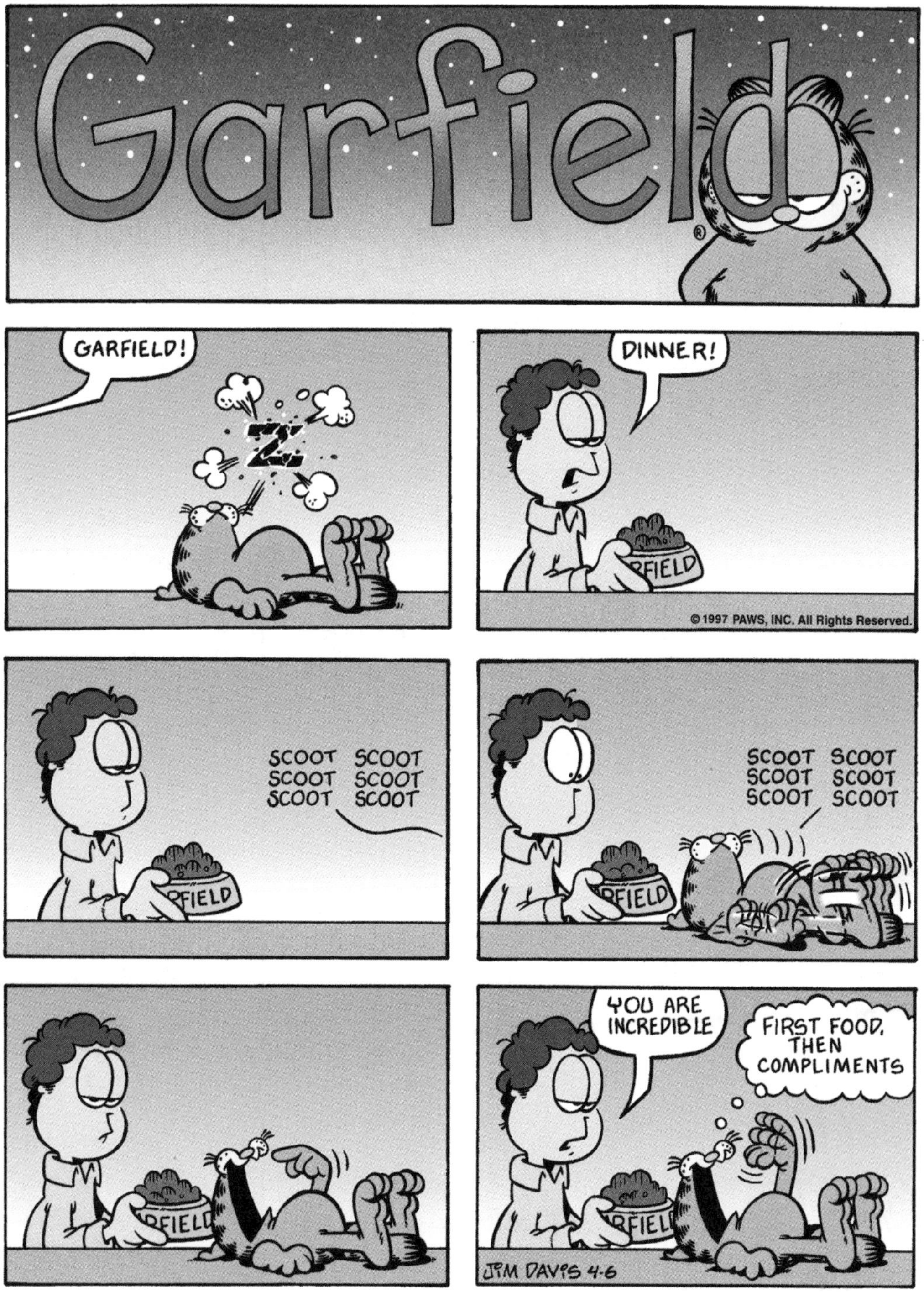
Garfield®
GARFIELD!
Z
DINNER!
FIELD
© 1997 PAWS, INC. All Rights Reserved.
SCOOT SCOOT SCOOT SCOOT SCOOT SCOOT
SCOOT SCOOT SCOOT SCOOT SCOOT SCOOT
YOU ARE INCREDIBLE
FIRST FOOD, THEN COMPLIMENTS
JIM DAVIS 4-6

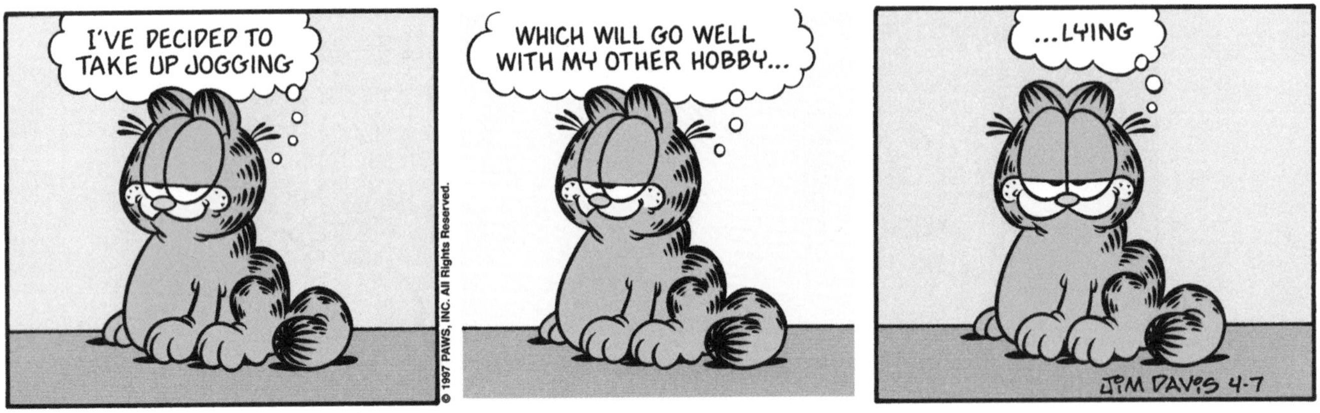
I'VE DECIDED TO TAKE UP JOGGING
WHICH WILL GO WELL WITH MY OTHER HOBBY...
...LYING
© 1997 PAWS, INC. All Rights Reserved.
JIM DAVIS 4-7

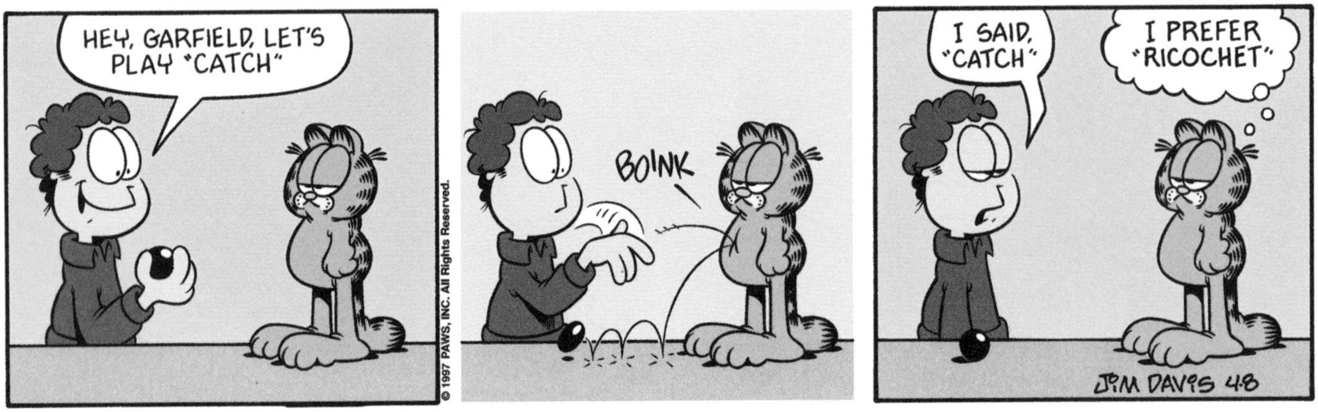
HEY, GARFIELD, LET'S PLAY "CATCH"
BOINK
I SAID, "CATCH"
I PREFER "RICOCHET"
© 1997 PAWS, INC. All Rights Reserved.
JIM DAVIS 4-8

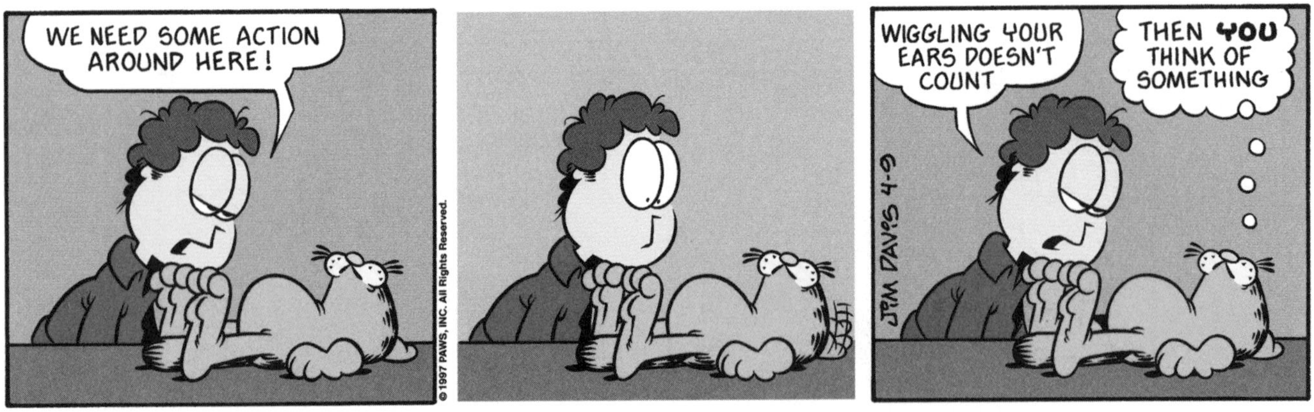
WE NEED SOME ACTION AROUND HERE!
WIGGLING YOUR EARS DOESN'T COUNT
THEN **YOU** THINK OF SOMETHING
© 1997 PAWS, INC. All Rights Reserved.
JIM DAVIS 4-9

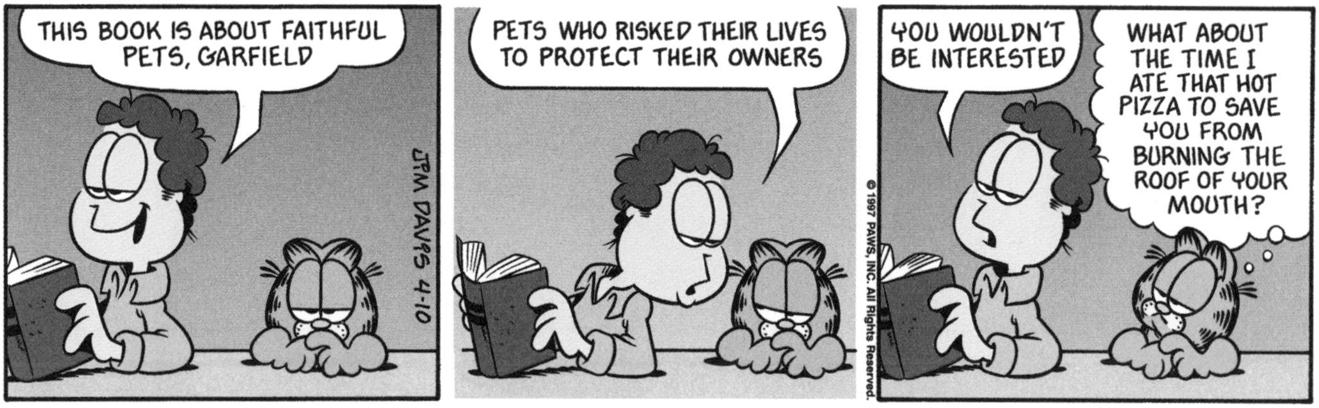
THIS BOOK IS ABOUT FAITHFUL PETS, GARFIELD
JIM DAVIS 4-10
PETS WHO RISKED THEIR LIVES TO PROTECT THEIR OWNERS
© 1997 PAWS, INC. All Rights Reserved.
YOU WOULDN'T BE INTERESTED
WHAT ABOUT THE TIME I ATE THAT HOT PIZZA TO SAVE YOU FROM BURNING THE ROOF OF YOUR MOUTH?

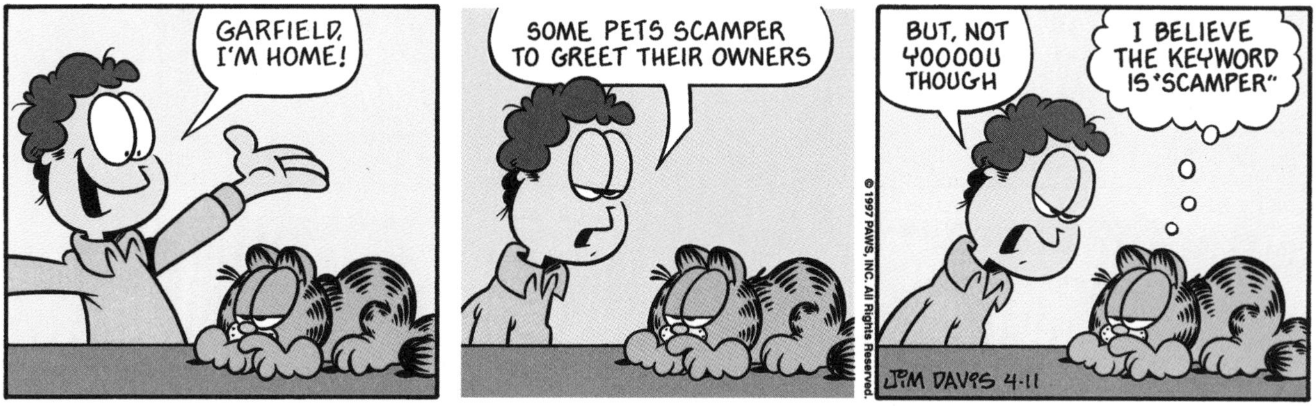
GARFIELD, I'M HOME!
SOME PETS SCAMPER TO GREET THEIR OWNERS
© 1997 PAWS, INC. All Rights Reserved.
BUT, NOT YOOOOU THOUGH
I BELIEVE THE KEYWORD IS "SCAMPER"
JIM DAVIS 4-11

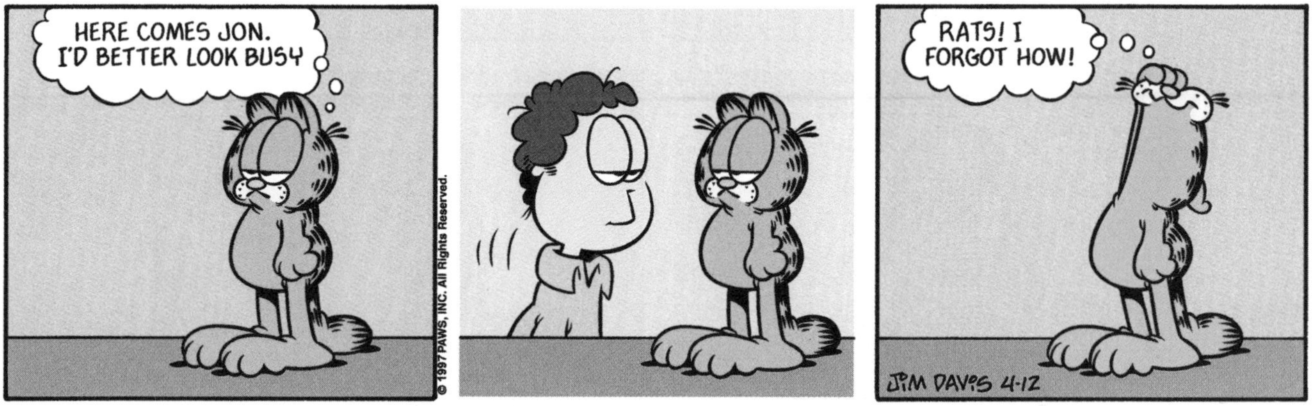
HERE COMES JON. I'D BETTER LOOK BUSY
© 1997 PAWS, INC. All Rights Reserved.
RATS! I FORGOT HOW!
JIM DAVIS 4-12

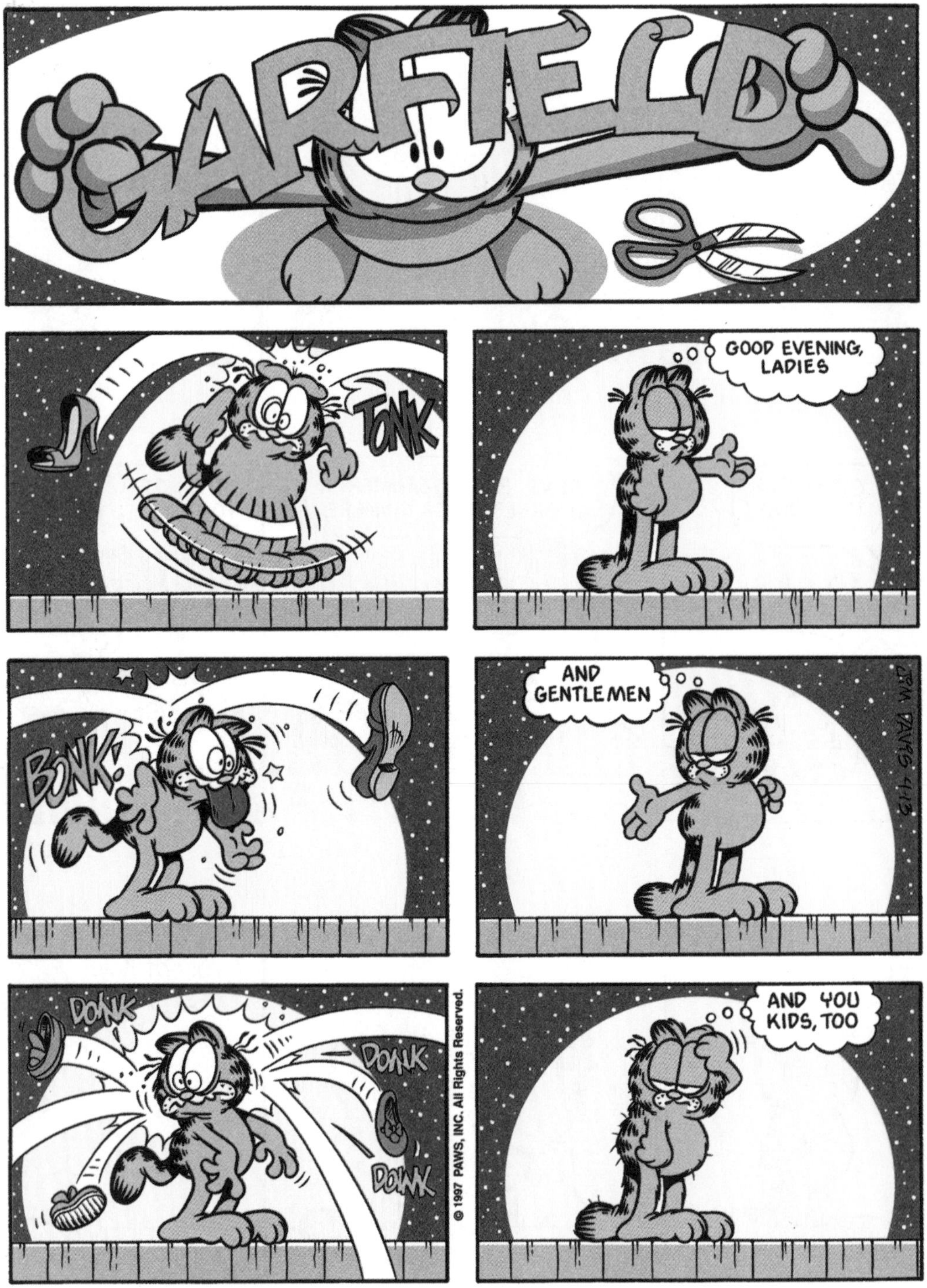
GARFIELD
TONK
GOOD EVENING, LADIES
BONK!
AND GENTLEMEN
JIM DAVIS 4-13
DONK
DONK
DONK
AND YOU KIDS, TOO

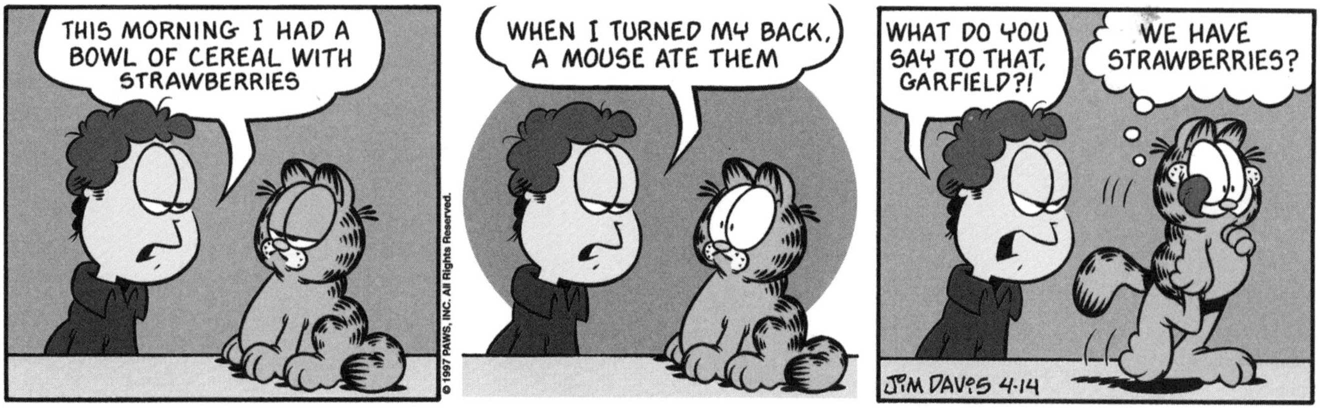
THIS MORNING I HAD A BOWL OF CEREAL WITH STRAWBERRIES
WHEN I TURNED MY BACK, A MOUSE ATE THEM
WHAT DO YOU SAY TO THAT, GARFIELD?!
WE HAVE STRAWBERRIES?
© 1997 PAWS, INC. All Rights Reserved.
JIM DAVIS 4-14

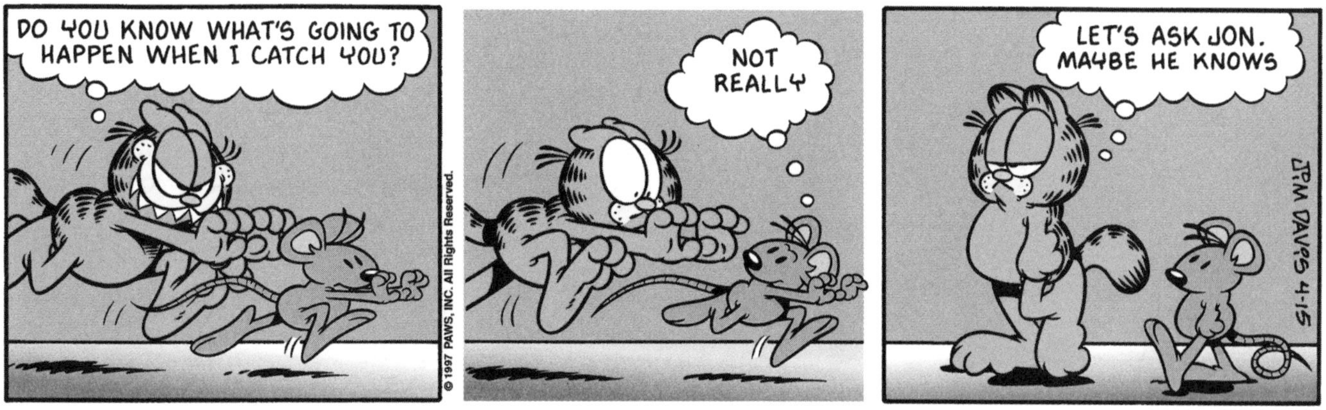
DO YOU KNOW WHAT'S GOING TO HAPPEN WHEN I CATCH YOU?
NOT REALLY
LET'S ASK JON. MAYBE HE KNOWS
© 1997 PAWS, INC. All Rights Reserved.
JIM DAVIS 4-15

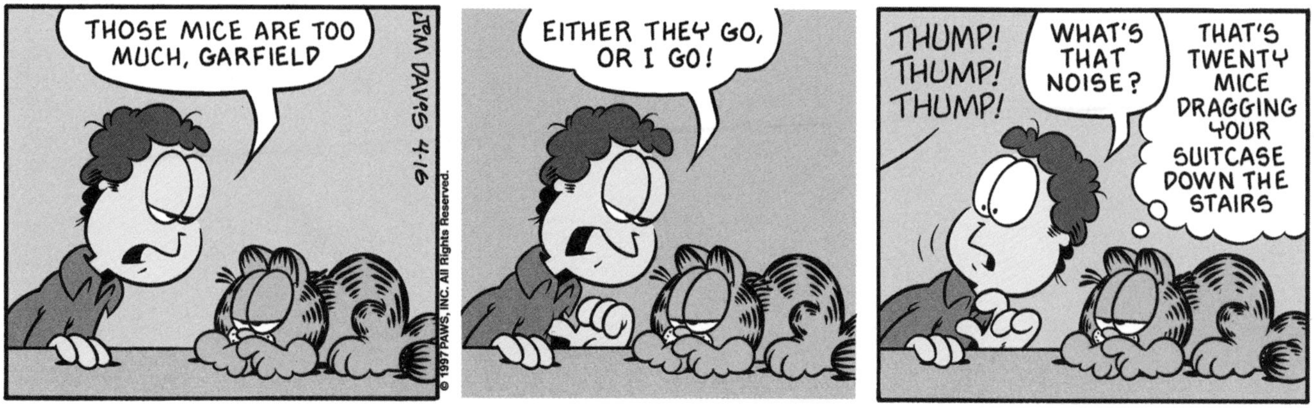
THOSE MICE ARE TOO MUCH, GARFIELD
JIM DAVIS 4-16
© 1997 PAWS, INC. All Rights Reserved.
EITHER THEY GO, OR I GO!
THUMP! THUMP! THUMP!
WHAT'S THAT NOISE?
THAT'S TWENTY MICE DRAGGING YOUR SUITCASE DOWN THE STAIRS

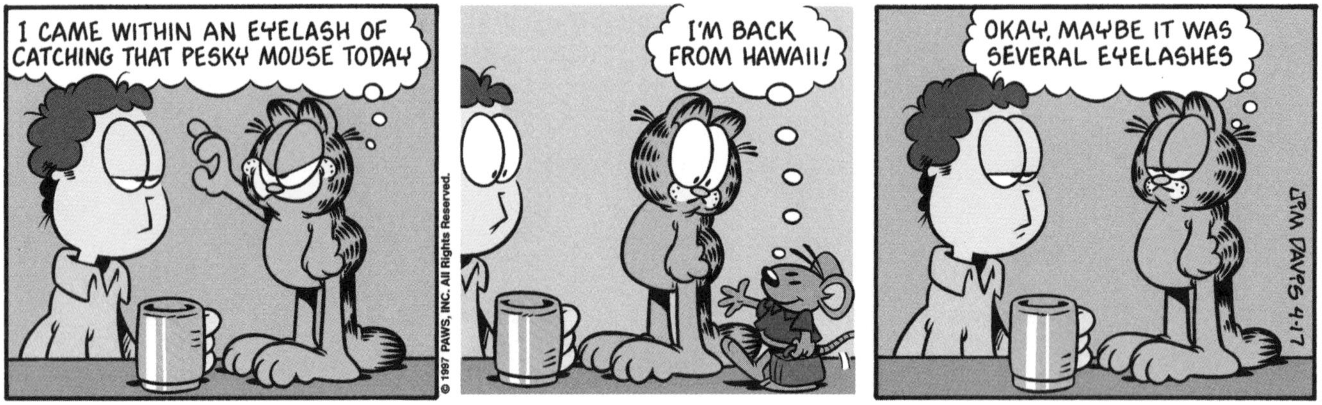
I CAME WITHIN AN EYELASH OF CATCHING THAT PESKY MOUSE TODAY
© 1997 PAWS, INC. All Rights Reserved.
I'M BACK FROM HAWAII!
OKAY, MAYBE IT WAS SEVERAL EYELASHES
JIM DAVIS 4-17

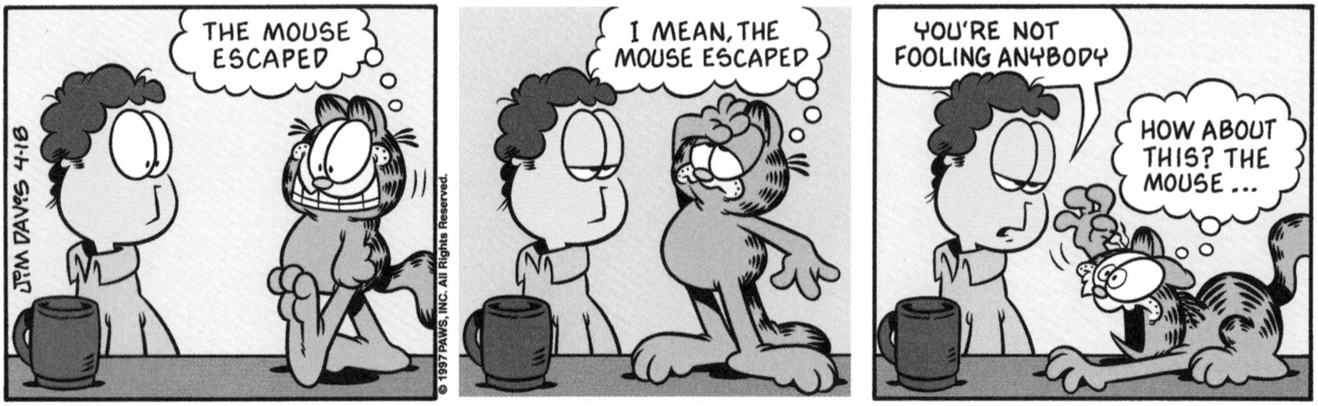
JIM DAVIS 4-18
THE MOUSE ESCAPED
© 1997 PAWS, INC. All Rights Reserved.
I MEAN, THE MOUSE ESCAPED
YOU'RE NOT FOOLING ANYBODY
HOW ABOUT THIS? THE MOUSE ...

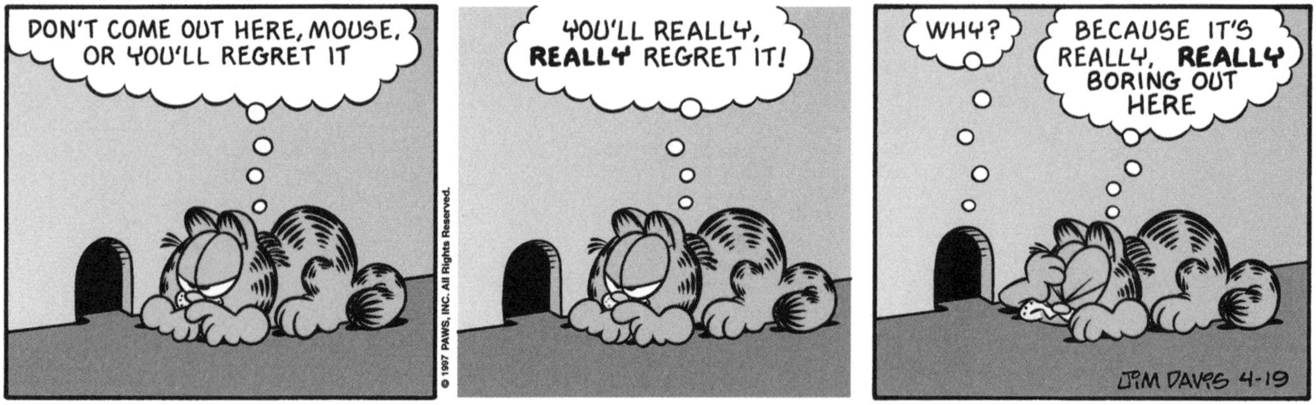
DON'T COME OUT HERE, MOUSE, OR YOU'LL REGRET IT
© 1997 PAWS, INC. All Rights Reserved.
YOU'LL REALLY, **REALLY** REGRET IT!
WHY?
BECAUSE IT'S REALLY, **REALLY** BORING OUT HERE
JIM DAVIS 4-19

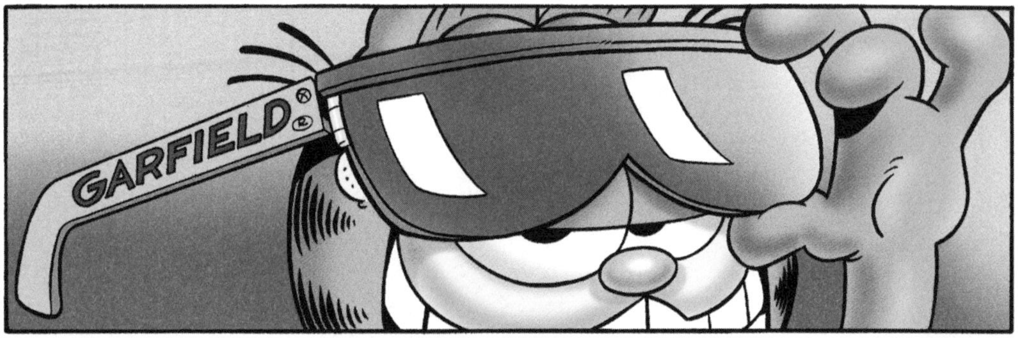
GARFIELD

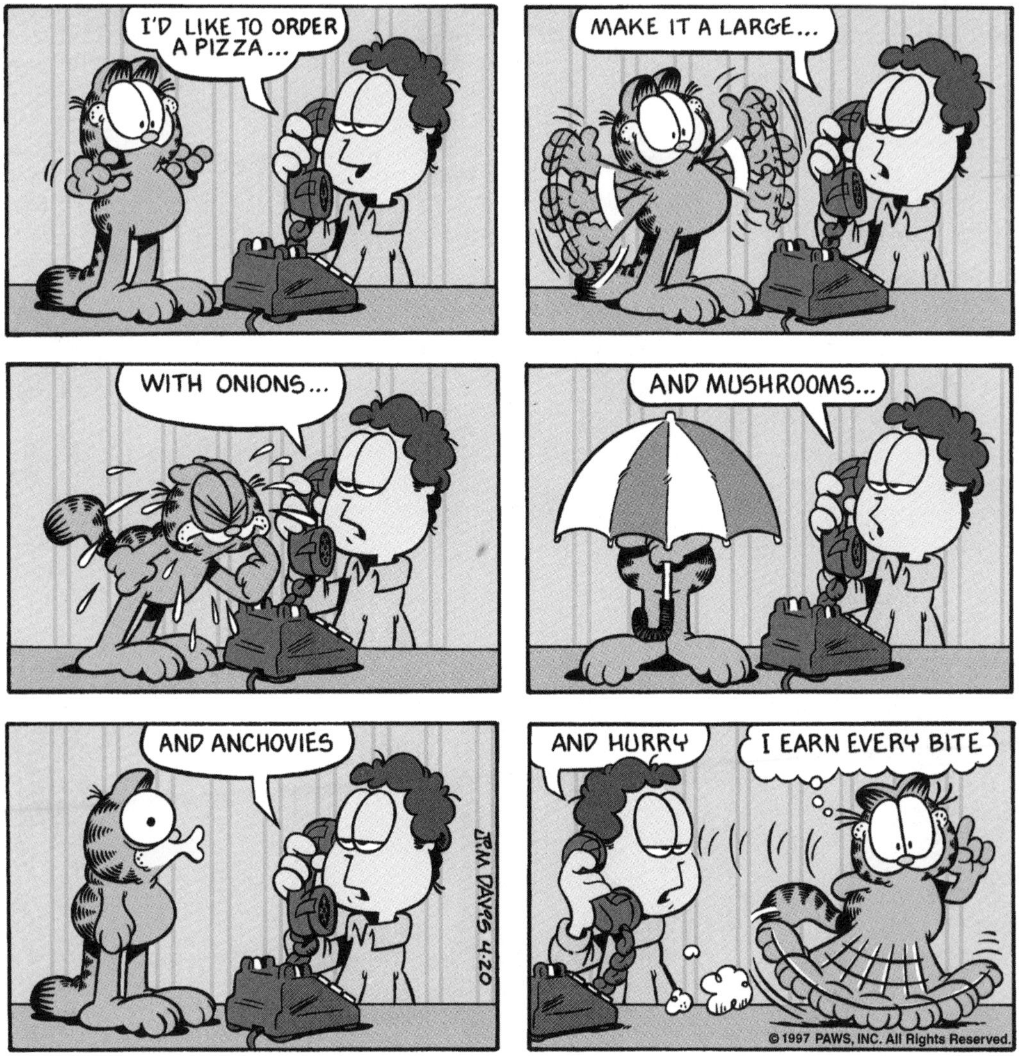
I'D LIKE TO ORDER A PIZZA...
MAKE IT A LARGE...
WITH ONIONS...
AND MUSHROOMS...
AND ANCHOVIES
JIM DAVIS 4-20
AND HURRY
I EARN EVERY BITE

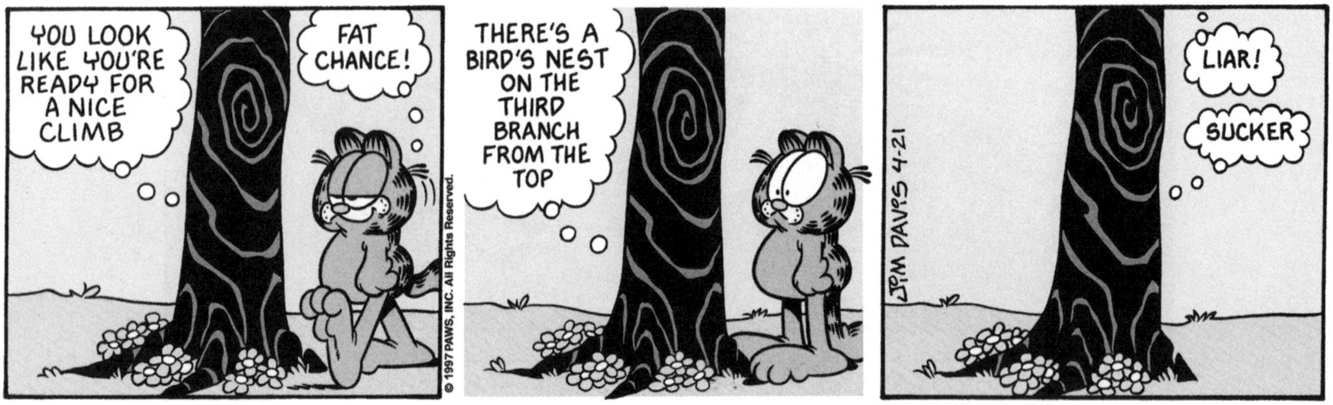
YOU LOOK LIKE YOU'RE READY FOR A NICE CLIMB
FAT CHANCE!
© 1997 PAWS, INC. All Rights Reserved.
THERE'S A BIRD'S NEST ON THE THIRD BRANCH FROM THE TOP
JIM DAVIS 4-21
LIAR!
SUCKER

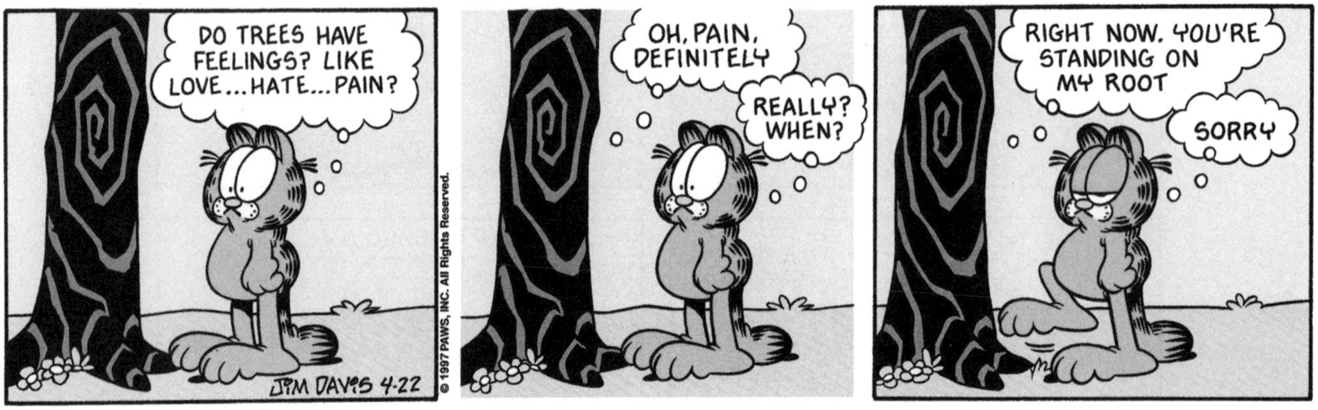
DO TREES HAVE FEELINGS? LIKE LOVE... HATE... PAIN?
JIM DAVIS 4-22
© 1997 PAWS, INC. All Rights Reserved.
OH, PAIN, DEFINITELY
REALLY? WHEN?
RIGHT NOW. YOU'RE STANDING ON MY ROOT
SORRY

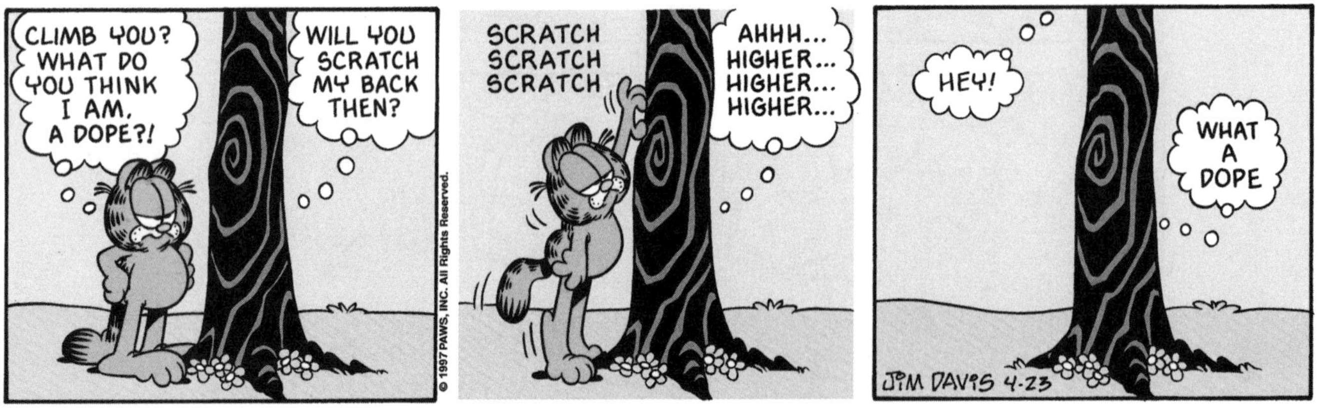
CLIMB YOU? WHAT DO YOU THINK I AM, A DOPE?!
WILL YOU SCRATCH MY BACK THEN?
© 1997 PAWS, INC. All Rights Reserved.
SCRATCH SCRATCH SCRATCH
AHHH... HIGHER... HIGHER... HIGHER...
HEY!
WHAT A DOPE
JIM DAVIS 4-23

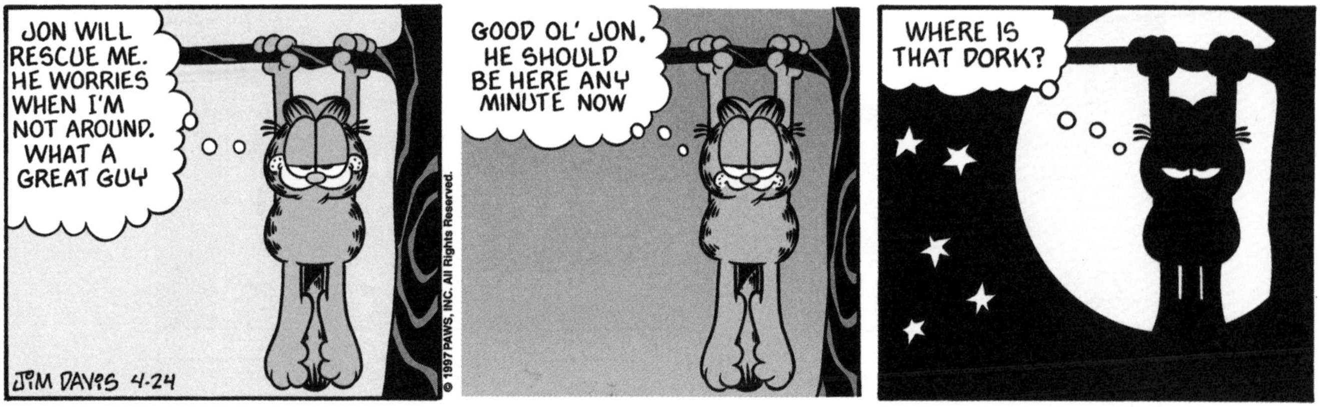
JON WILL RESCUE ME. HE WORRIES WHEN I'M NOT AROUND. WHAT A GREAT GUY
JIM DAVIS 4-24
© 1997 PAWS, INC. All Rights Reserved.
GOOD OL' JON. HE SHOULD BE HERE ANY MINUTE NOW
WHERE IS THAT DORK?

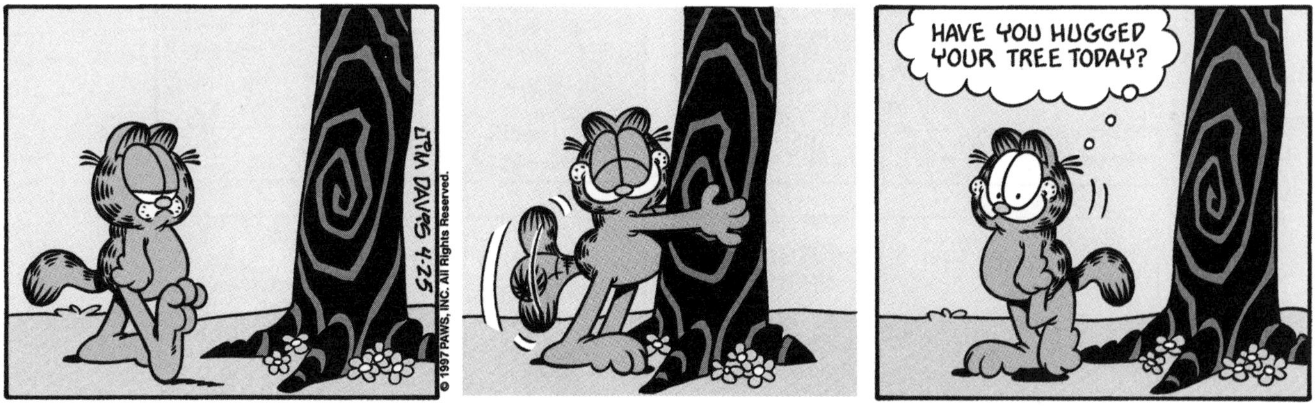
JIM DAVIS 4-25
© 1997 PAWS, INC. All Rights Reserved.
HAVE YOU HUGGED YOUR TREE TODAY?

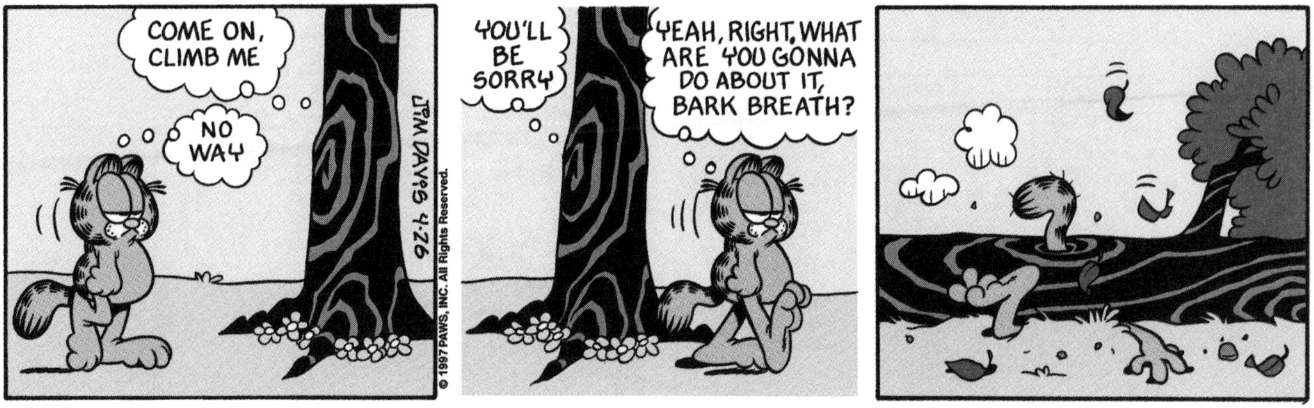
COME ON, CLIMB ME
NO WAY
JIM DAVIS 4-26
© 1997 PAWS, INC. All Rights Reserved.
YOU'LL BE SORRY
YEAH, RIGHT, WHAT ARE YOU GONNA DO ABOUT IT, BARK BREATH?

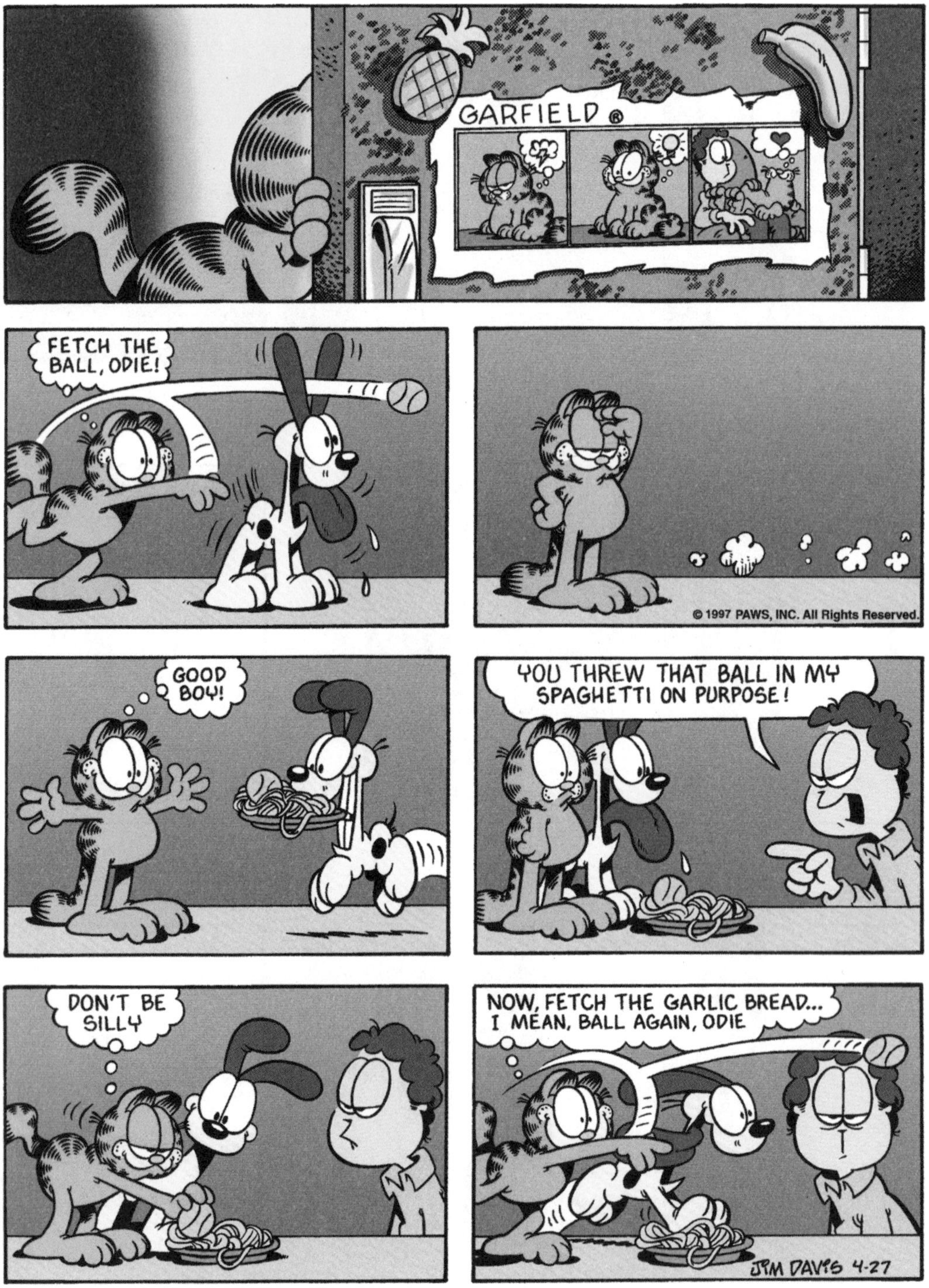
GARFIELD®
FETCH THE BALL, ODIE!
© 1997 PAWS, INC. All Rights Reserved.
GOOD BOY!
YOU THREW THAT BALL IN MY SPAGHETTI ON PURPOSE!
DON'T BE SILLY
NOW, FETCH THE GARLIC BREAD... I MEAN, BALL AGAIN, ODIE
JIM DAVIS 4-27

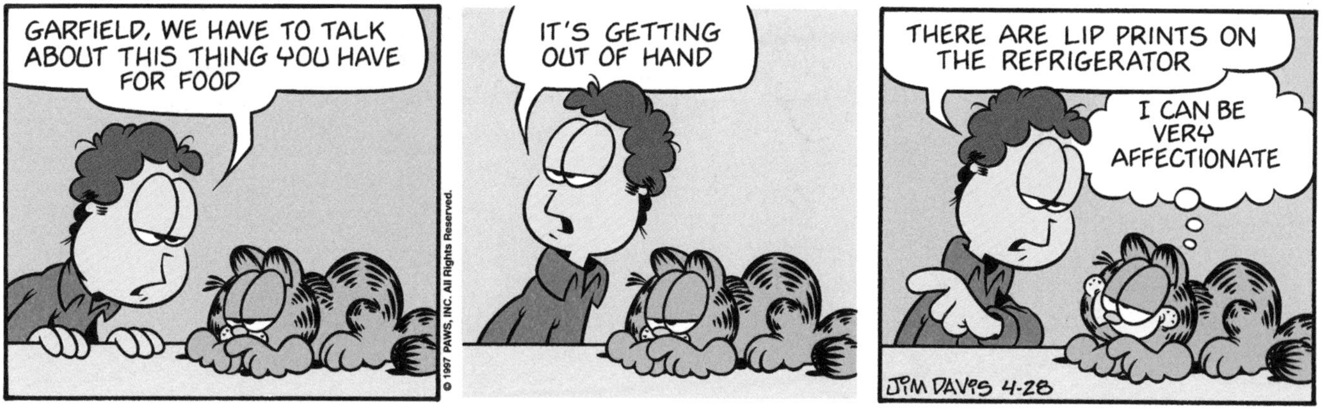
GARFIELD, WE HAVE TO TALK ABOUT THIS THING YOU HAVE FOR FOOD
© 1997 PAWS, INC. All Rights Reserved.
IT'S GETTING OUT OF HAND
THERE ARE LIP PRINTS ON THE REFRIGERATOR
I CAN BE VERY AFFECTIONATE
JIM DAVIS 4-28

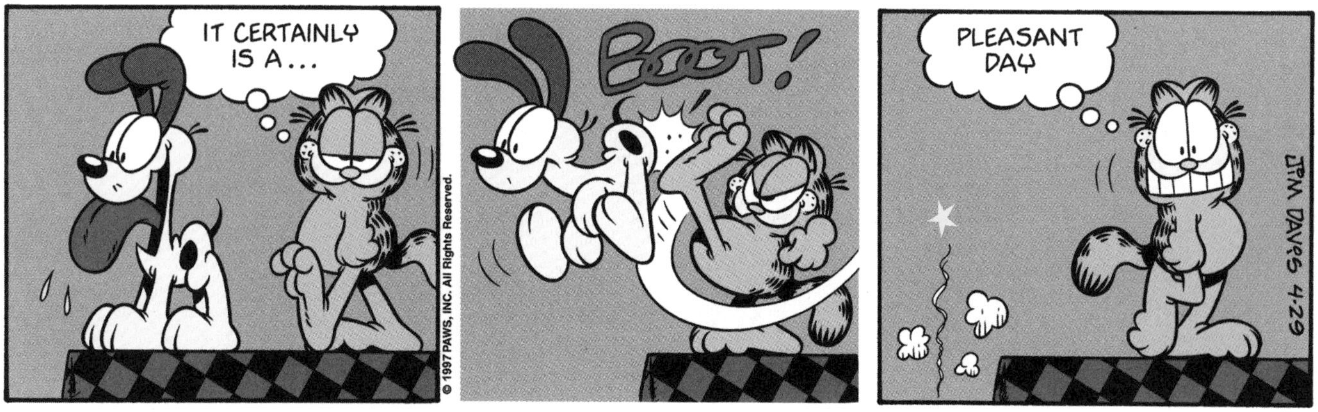
IT CERTAINLY IS A...
© 1997 PAWS, INC. All Rights Reserved.
BOOT!
PLEASANT DAY
JIM DAVIS 4-29

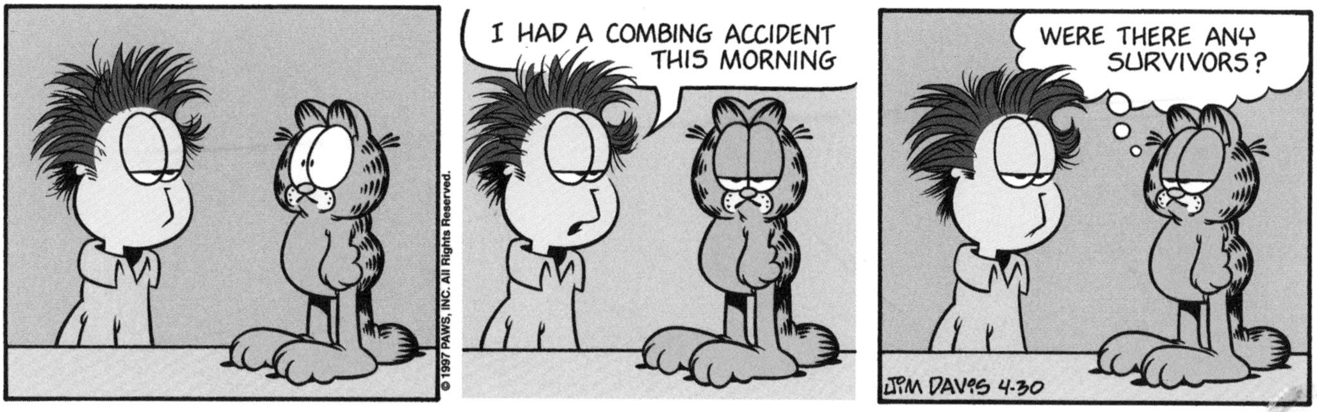
© 1997 PAWS, INC. All Rights Reserved.
I HAD A COMBING ACCIDENT THIS MORNING
WERE THERE ANY SURVIVORS?
JIM DAVIS 4-30

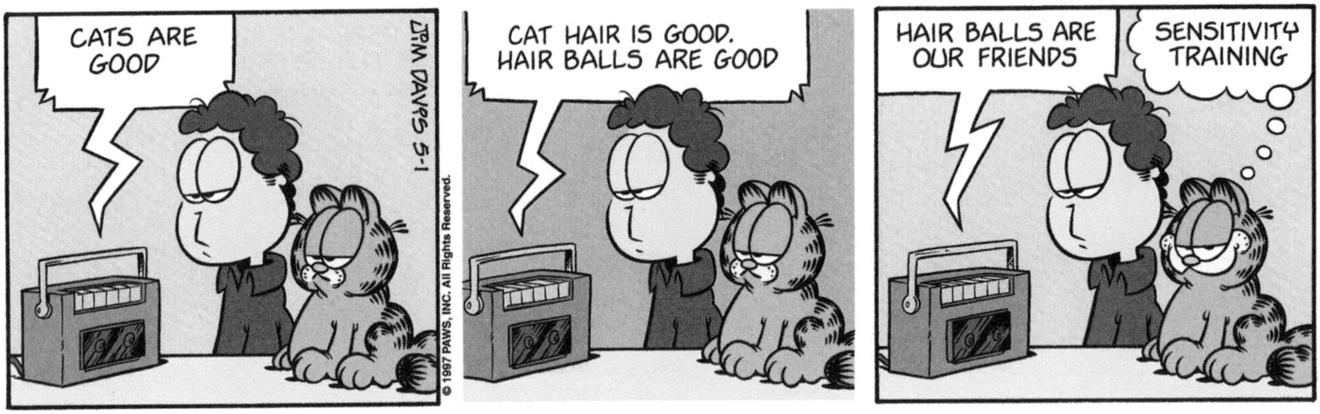
CATS ARE GOOD
CAT HAIR IS GOOD. HAIR BALLS ARE GOOD
HAIR BALLS ARE OUR FRIENDS
SENSITIVITY TRAINING
JIM DAVIS 5-1
© 1997 PAWS, INC. All Rights Reserved.

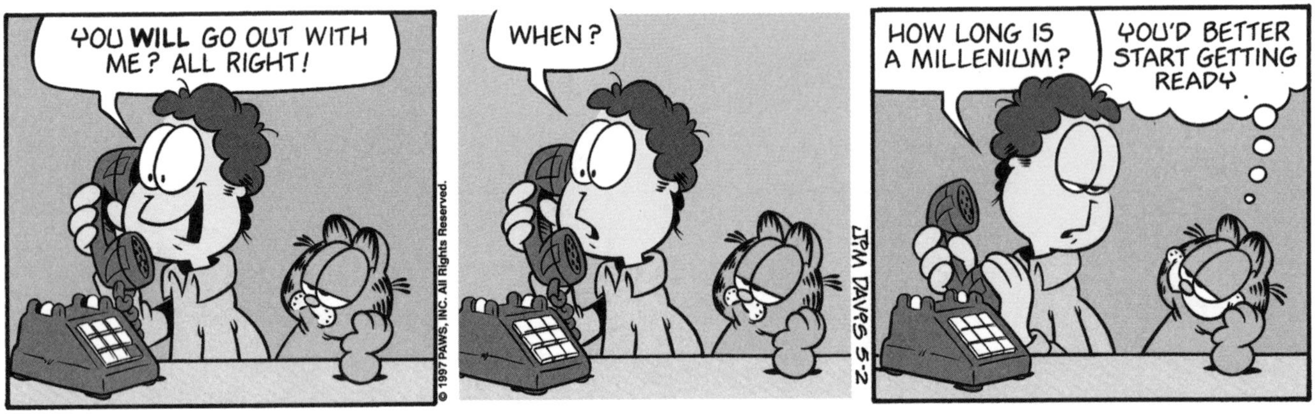
YOU **WILL** GO OUT WITH ME? ALL RIGHT!
WHEN?
HOW LONG IS A MILLENIUM?
YOU'D BETTER START GETTING READY
JIM DAVIS 5-2
© 1997 PAWS, INC. All Rights Reserved.

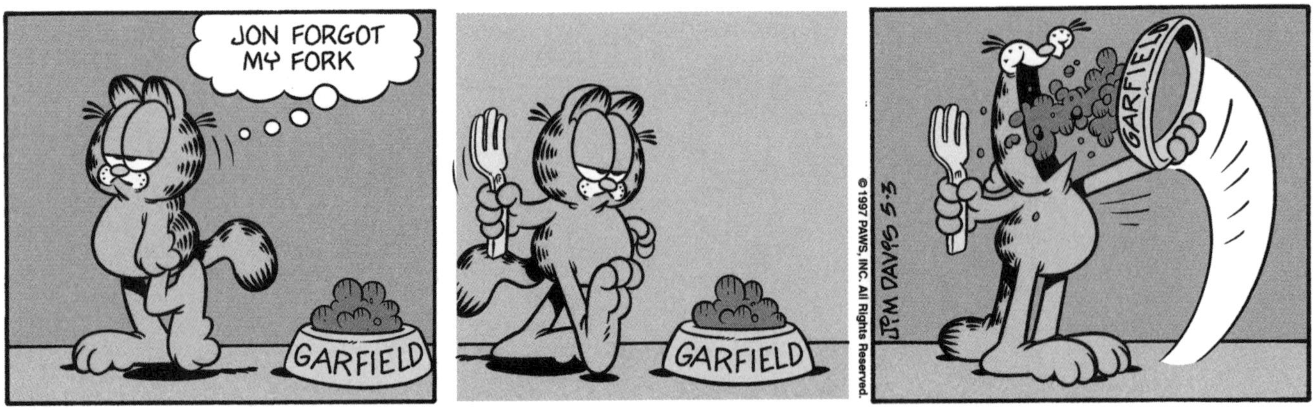
JON FORGOT MY FORK
GARFIELD
GARFIELD
GARFIELD
JIM DAVIS 5-3
© 1997 PAWS, INC. All Rights Reserved.

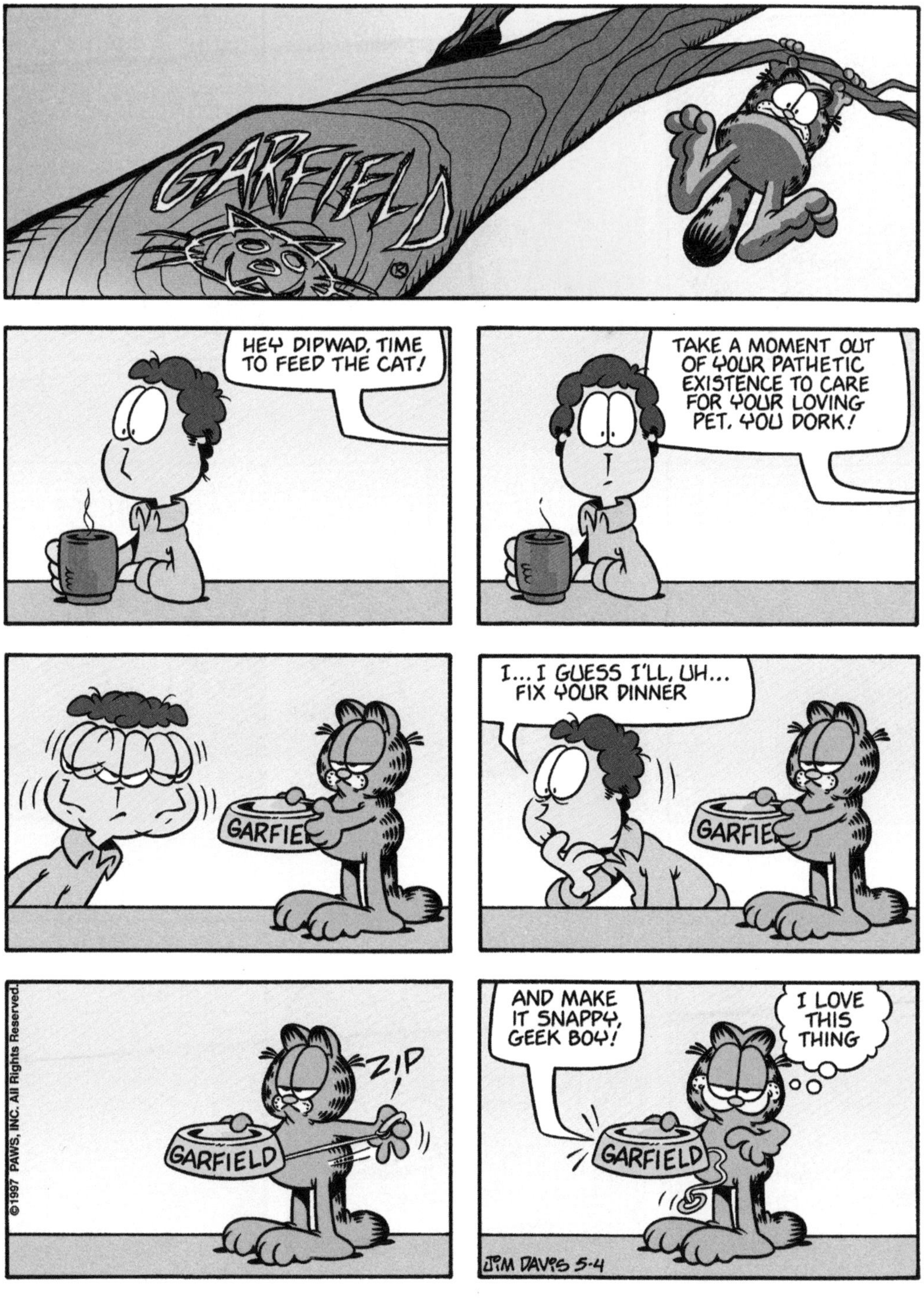
GARFIELD
HEY DIPWAD, TIME TO FEED THE CAT!
TAKE A MOMENT OUT OF YOUR PATHETIC EXISTENCE TO CARE FOR YOUR LOVING PET, YOU DORK!
GARFIE
I... I GUESS I'LL, UH... FIX YOUR DINNER
GARFIE
ZIP
GARFIELD
AND MAKE IT SNAPPY, GEEK BOY!
I LOVE THIS THING
GARFIELD
JIM DAVIS 5-4

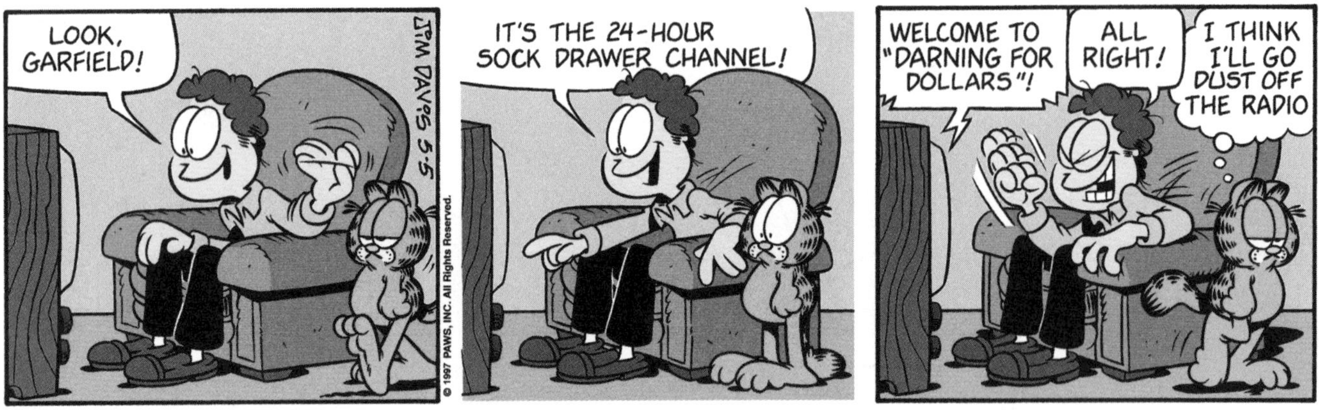
LOOK, GARFIELD!
JIM DAVIS 5-5
© 1997 PAWS, INC. All Rights Reserved.
IT'S THE 24-HOUR SOCK DRAWER CHANNEL!
WELCOME TO "DARNING FOR DOLLARS"!
ALL RIGHT!
I THINK I'LL GO DUST OFF THE RADIO

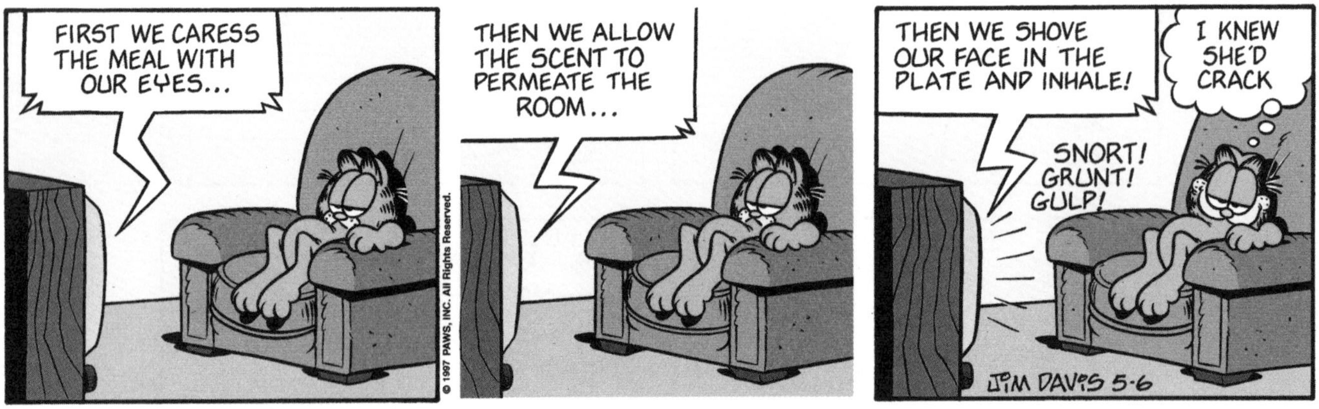
FIRST WE CARESS THE MEAL WITH OUR EYES...
© 1997 PAWS, INC. All Rights Reserved.
THEN WE ALLOW THE SCENT TO PERMEATE THE ROOM...
THEN WE SHOVE OUR FACE IN THE PLATE AND INHALE!
SNORT! GRUNT! GULP!
I KNEW SHE'D CRACK
JIM DAVIS 5-6

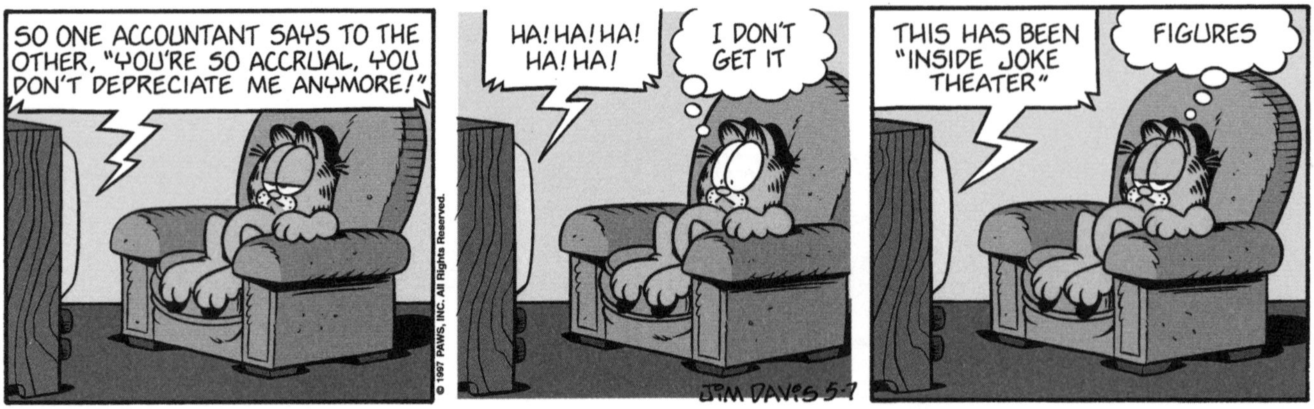
SO ONE ACCOUNTANT SAYS TO THE OTHER, "YOU'RE SO ACCRUAL, YOU DON'T DEPRECIATE ME ANYMORE!"
© 1997 PAWS, INC. All Rights Reserved.
HA! HA! HA! HA! HA!
I DON'T GET IT
JIM DAVIS 5-7
THIS HAS BEEN "INSIDE JOKE THEATER"
FIGURES

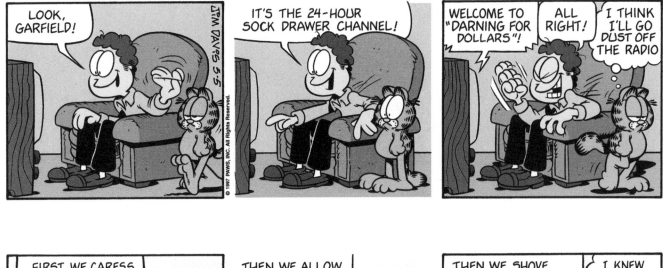

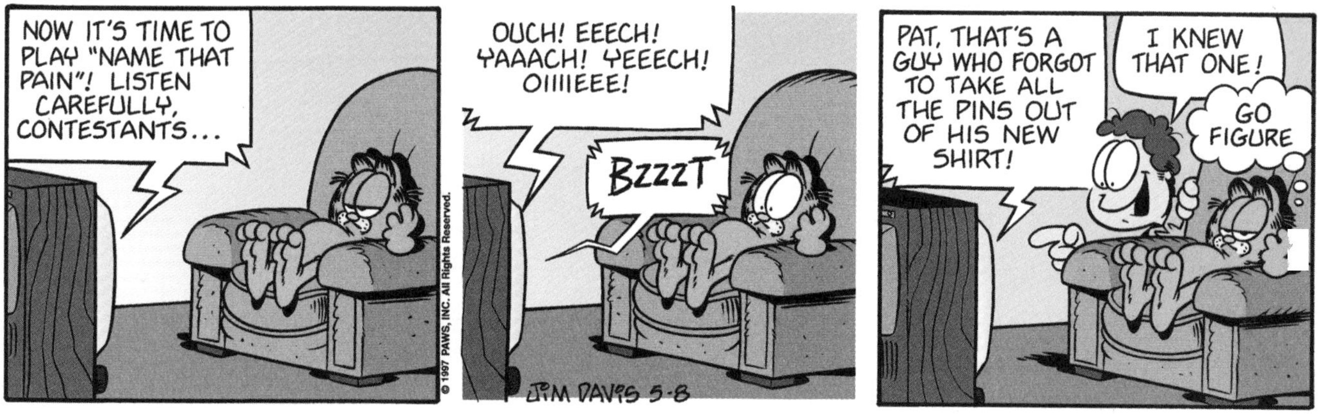
NOW IT'S TIME TO PLAY "NAME THAT PAIN"! LISTEN CAREFULLY, CONTESTANTS...
© 1997 PAWS, INC. All Rights Reserved.
OUCH! EEECH! YAAACH! YEEECH! OIIIIEEE!
BZZZT
JIM DAVIS 5-8
PAT, THAT'S A GUY WHO FORGOT TO TAKE ALL THE PINS OUT OF HIS NEW SHIRT!
I KNEW THAT ONE!
GO FIGURE

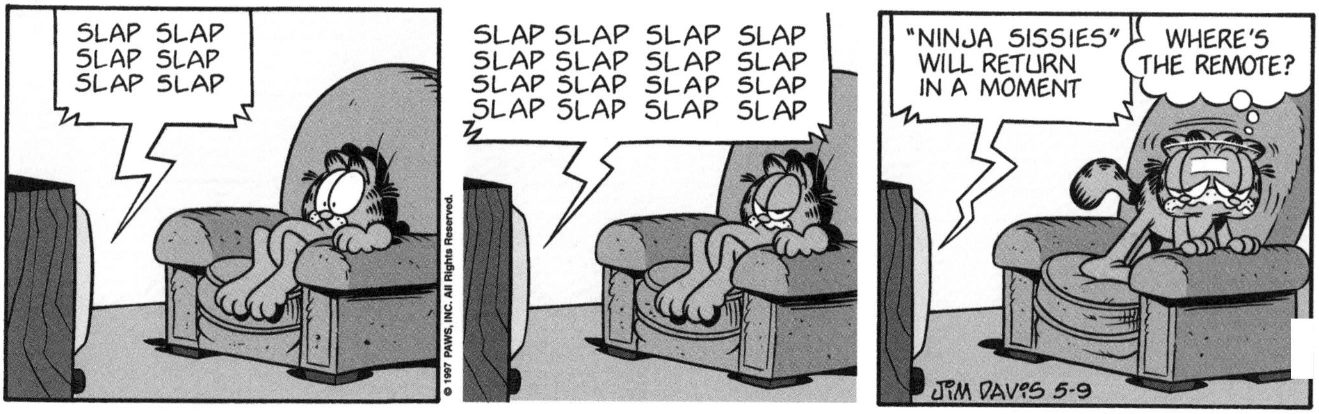
SLAP SLAP SLAP SLAP SLAP SLAP
© 1997 PAWS, INC. All Rights Reserved.
SLAP SLAP SLAP SLAP SLAP SLAP SLAP SLAP SLAP SLAP SLAP SLAP SLAP SLAP SLAP SLAP
"NINJA SISSIES" WILL RETURN IN A MOMENT
WHERE'S THE REMOTE?
JIM DAVIS 5-9

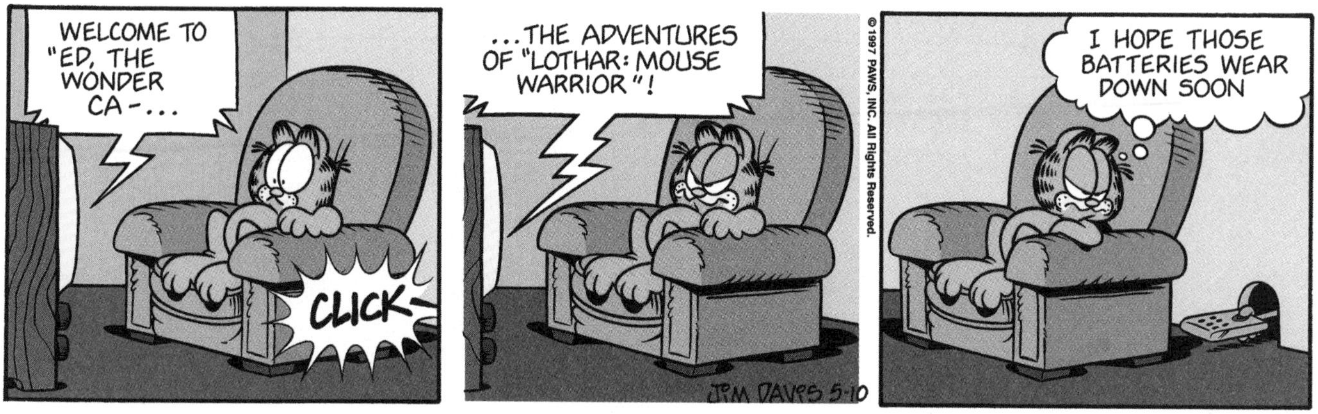
WELCOME TO "ED, THE WONDER CA-...
CLICK
...THE ADVENTURES OF "LOTHAR: MOUSE WARRIOR"!
JIM DAVIS 5-10
© 1997 PAWS, INC. All Rights Reserved.
I HOPE THOSE BATTERIES WEAR DOWN SOON

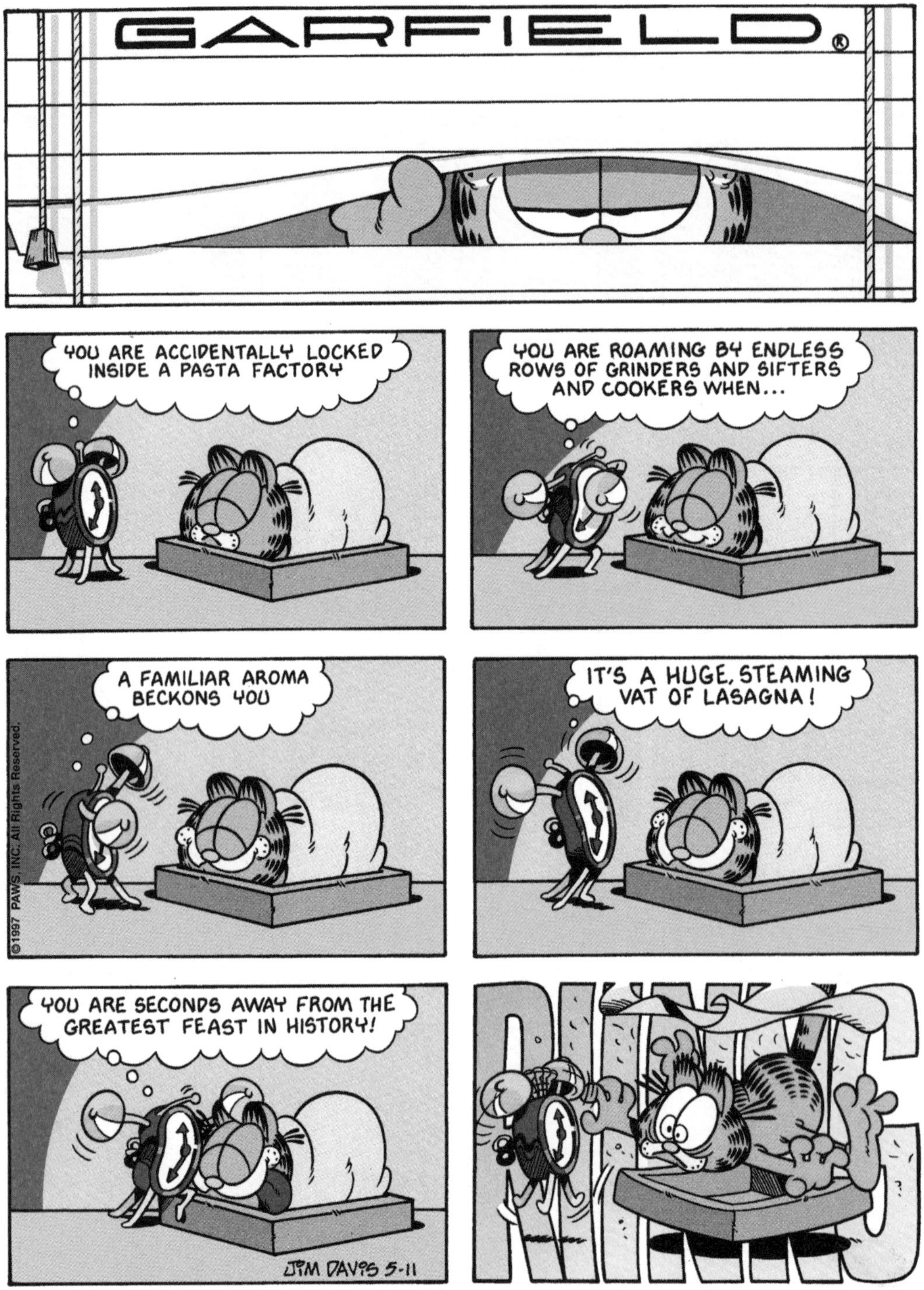
GARFIELD®
YOU ARE ACCIDENTALLY LOCKED INSIDE A PASTA FACTORY
YOU ARE ROAMING BY ENDLESS ROWS OF GRINDERS AND SIFTERS AND COOKERS WHEN...
A FAMILIAR AROMA BECKONS YOU
IT'S A HUGE, STEAMING VAT OF LASAGNA!
©1997 PAWS, INC. All Rights Reserved.
YOU ARE SECONDS AWAY FROM THE GREATEST FEAST IN HISTORY!
JIM DAVIS 5-11

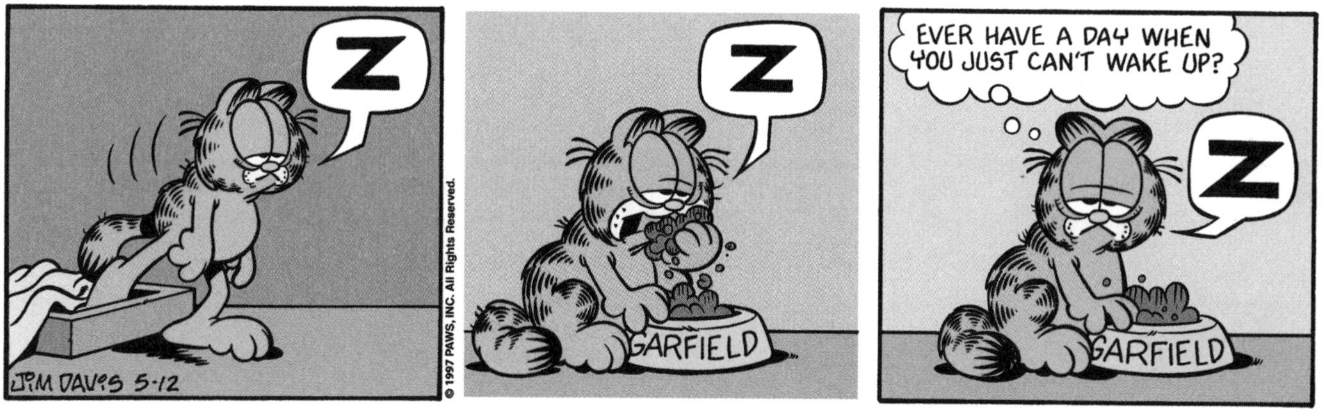
Z
JIM DAVIS 5-12
© 1997 PAWS, INC. All Rights Reserved.
Z
GARFIELD
EVER HAVE A DAY WHEN YOU JUST CAN'T WAKE UP?
Z
GARFIELD

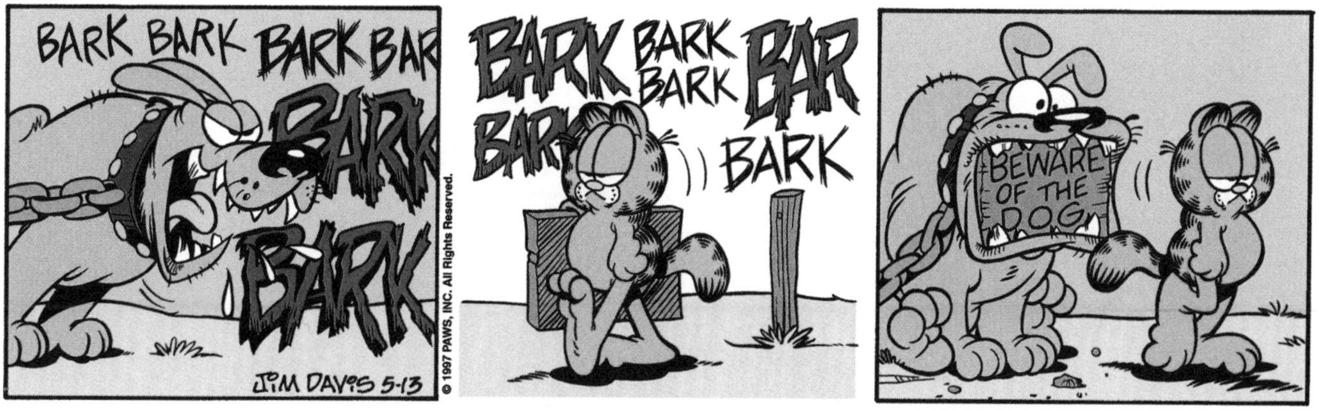
BARK BARK BARK BAR
BARK
BARK
JIM DAVIS 5-13
© 1997 PAWS, INC. All Rights Reserved.
BARK
BARK BARK
BAR
BARK
BARK
BEWARE OF THE DOG

SIGNS YOU'RE GOING TO A BAD VETERINARIAN...

- moonlights as a taxidermist
- keeps excusing himself to set the traps
- can't work a "pooper scooper"
- only licensed to treat insects
- tries to floss a piranha
- was once fired for trying to put Lassie to sleep
- wears a coonskin cap
- performs surgery with a steak knife
- tries to give mouth-to-mouth to your badger

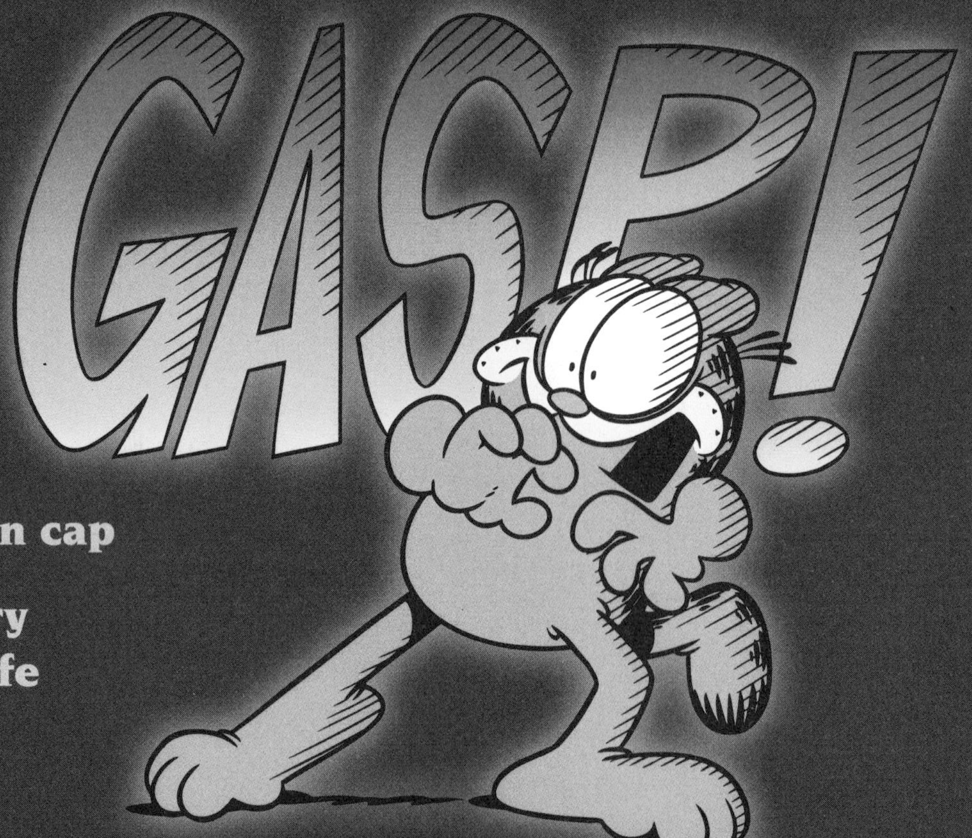
GASP!